35

The Royal Navy and the Slave Trade

RAYMOND HOWELL

ST. MARTIN'S PRESS
New York

© 1987 Raymond Howell
All rights reserved. For information, write:
Scholarly & Reference Division,
St. Martin's Press, Inc., 175 Fifth Avenue, New York, NY 10010
First published in the United States of America in 1987
Printed in Great Britain

Library of Congress Cataloging-in-Publication Data

Howell, Raymond.
    The Royal Navy and the Slave Trade.

    Bibliography: p.
    Includes index.
    1. Great Britain. Royal Navy — History — 19th century.
2. Slavery — Africa, East — History — 19th century.
I. Title.
VA454.H67 1987   326   87-9608
ISBN 0-312-00854-6

Contents

*For My Mother
and in Memory of My Father*

Preface

During the first half of the nineteenth century, abolitionist fervour in Britain brought an end to the British slave trade, legislation against the institution of slavery in British possessions, and finally an attack on the slave trade conducted by other countries. The key instrument in the campaign against the foreign slave trade was the Royal Navy which waged a long conflict against the slavers operating on the West Coast of Africa. This protracted action against slavery, with the associated horrors of the Middle Passage to the Americas, has been investigated by a long line of historians. Of particular interest are the specifically naval studies, including those of Lloyd and Ward, which have dealt with the navy's role off the coast of West Africa. While the trade in slaves from West Africa was finally being checked in the 1860s, however, a significant new battle against slavery was developing on the other side of the continent. Major diplomatic moves combined with 30 years of persistent naval pressure were required before the slave shipments from Zanzibar and other East African ports were stopped. Despite the magnitude of this suppression problem, however, these naval operations have generated less interest among historians.

Many aspects of nineteenth-century naval history are in need of review. Broad strategic and tactical considerations have been skilfully treated in Marder's analysis of naval developments from 1880 to 1905 and Hearnshaw has examined seapower within an Imperial context. Nevertheless, numerous questions remain concerning an era which saw a total transformation of the Royal Navy. During the second half of the nineteenth century, there were fundamental changes including the shift from sail to steam, from wooden vessels to armoured iron ships, and from solid, muzzle-loaded shot to explosive breech-loaded shells. As significant as this revolutionary development in equipment during the later-nineteenth century undoubtedly was, the role of the navy as a tool of government was even more important in the broader historical context. As Hearnshaw has suggested, 'It is not too much to say that the invincible British Navy was the main instrument of British foreign policy during the eventful century.' The first example cited in support of that contention was the navy's role in slave trade suppression. It is obvious that the continuing slave trade suppression campaign was an important one and the general need for additional historical work in nineteenth-century naval studies is even more obviously acute in terms of specific study areas such as the response to the slave trade. As Preston has observed, the principal role of the late-nineteenth century navy was 'an Imperial gendarmerie' and the slave trade campaign offers the best means of studying that role in depth since the one area in which the Imperial gendarmes were assured of continuing action during the last half of the nineteenth century was the slave trade campaign. An officer like William Creswell, later chief architect of the Australian Navy, would seek transfer to the slave trade squadron hoping that the certainty of action in an otherwise routine naval milieu would advance his career. It is also useful to observe general daily operation of a station against the background of technological change. Particularly important is the operation of one arm of the fleet during the late 1870s and early 1880s — a period historians such as Preston and Rodger have called the 'Dark Ages' of the Admiralty in which weakness grew from over-confidence and neglect. Interestingly, Philip Colomb, one of the leading proponents of the 'Blue Water School' of naval thought which attempted to correct the growing weakness, gained his experience of command on the slave trade patrol.

As has been noted, Ward and Lloyd dealt with earlier naval operations off the West African coast but specific studies of the response to the Arab slave trade from East Africa have been limited. Sir William Laird Clowes in his *The Royal Navy: A History*, volume 7 (1903) identified the problem and pointed the way toward needed historical research. In tracing naval developments through the 1880s, he observed that:

> During all these years the slave-trade on the east coast of Africa remained astonishingly active, seeing that steady efforts continued to be made for its repression. Much might be written about the good work done by Her Majesty's ships on the station, and by the boats which were detached from them to cruise for suspicious dhows. Indeed, the subject deserves a book to itself.

That need still had not been met some 50 years later. The one attempt to deal with the naval aspects of East African history is Lloyd's book, *The Navy and the Slave Trade* (1949). The East African portions of the book offer only the briefest overview. A particularly unfortunate aspect to this introduction to the subject is that Professor Lloyd chose to end his study in 1883 which he saw as the effective end date for the naval attack on the East African slave trade. This decision led him to overlook significant developments which occurred after that year and, as a consequence, to largely dismiss the general effectiveness of naval activity. Therefore, the need for the in-depth study suggested by Clowes still remains today and I hope this book will meet that need.

Of course, there are a number of significant studies of the British reaction to the East African slave trade. Notable among them is Sir Reginald Coupland's *The Exploitation of East Africa 1856–1890* (1939) which has become the standard starting point for all researchers. Coupland centred his work on the consul at Zanzibar, Sir John Kirk, and gave little consideration to the role of naval officers or the relative importance of the naval aspects of slave trade suppression activities. A recurring theme which I have found to be of considerable significance is the influence of individual personalities on the slave trade campaign and the inter-action between the men-on-the-spot in East Africa, both consular and naval. By stressing the contribution of the consul, Coupland tended to overlook the influence and importance of the senior naval officers, and I hope that my study will produce a more balanced picture in this respect. Among other books which set the stage for this study are C. S. Nicholls's, *The Swahili Coast* (1971), which provides good background to the development of the East African littoral and its slave trade, and Gerald Graham's *Great Britain in the Indian Ocean* (1967), which presents the naval back-ground to 1850. Suzanne Miers has produced a good overview of the final phases of the campaign and Moses Nwulia has written a book which includes consideration of the generally ignored subject of disposition of Africans liberated by the British cruisers. R. W. Beachey's *The Slave Trade of Eastern Africa* (1976) provides a useful overview of the pattern of slave trading and of the British response not only at Zanzibar but also in Mozambique, Sudan and other areas. Frederick Cooper has recently investigated the nature of plantation slavery in East Africa. All of these books are extremely useful but tend to share with Coupland an inclination to dismiss the navy as a cypher and to minimise the naval side of East African developments. I hope that this book will redress the balance and produce a clearer picture by offering a detailed analysis of the naval aspects of slave trade suppression on the East Coast of Africa. It may also correct certain minor errors concerning naval operations which have been perpetuated in previous studies. Sulivan did not, for example, command the *Star* and McCausland was certainly not investigating the inland slave trade when he was killed.

A particular merit of Beachey's book is that it deals with areas which of necessity have been considered only peripherally in this study. For example, the navy was involved with the southerly aspects of the slave trade from Portuguese territory. That whole question, however, demands detailed research in its own right and is only marginally considered in this study. For most of the period under review, different men and ships, reporting to a different station commander were responsible for naval operations off Mozambique. For similar reasons, the northern slave routes originating in the Sudan, which ultimately attracted naval attention, are considered only as they affected naval actions in the Indian Ocean. The principal purpose of this book is to trace the naval impact on the Arab slave trade from Zanzibari dominions and the political implications of that involvement. The naval contribution to the broader 'Imperial debate' is also considered.

I hope that this work has broken new ground by dealing with naval operations off East Africa in detail and by presenting an analysis of the inter-action of the various Imperial officials on the scene — an inter-action basic to the development of British policy in the region. It is important to consider the Royal Navy as a tool of policy; it is also essential to treat the naval officer as an official influencing policy through his position as an Imperial man-on-the-spot. It is arguable that this role was the most important falling upon Victorian naval officers; I have been quite fortunate in locating material dealing with these matters. The fact that officer service records for the period, located in the Public Record Office, have now been opened, has allowed me to study the backgrounds of naval personnel in more depth than was previously possible. In addition, I have been successful in finding private papers which have been quite helpful. There is, however, one negative note about papers which should be mentioned. The Kirk papers, held by the family, would have been useful in assessing consular-naval inter-action, but I was not allowed access to the documents. While this problem was troublesome, it was not insurmountable since I was able to trace important letters from Kirk in other private collections. The Mackinnon papers at the School of Oriental and African studies have been especially useful on this point.

I have been much more fortunate with other collections held by heirs and would like to express my appreciation to Lady Claude Hamilton, granddaughter of Sir Leopold Heath, who kindly provided me with family documents as well as sharing her personal recollections of Sir Leopold who commanded the East Indies station in the 1860s. Even more significant for the study has been my discovery of the hitherto unknown Sulivan papers which hold a wealth of valuable information concerning one of the major officers to have served on the East Coast. Sulivan served on four ships off East Africa and commanded three of them, including the stationary depot ship at Zanzibar, HMS *London*. Sulivan was one of the most important naval men-on-the-spot who spent more time on the station than any of his contemporaries. I am most grateful to Sulivan's grandson, Major D. L. S. Hodson, who made a special effort to make all of these papers available to me. I am also appreciative of the assistance given by another Sulivan heir, Colonel J. A. Sulivan.

Another collection of personal papers which has been most helpful is in the National Maritime Museum. Sir Edmund Fremantle commanded the East Indies station at the end of my period of study and guided the last major naval thrust against the East African slave trade. His papers provide useful insight into his handling of station routine, his outlook on the slave trade, and his relationship with the consul at Zanzibar.

During the course of this research, I have benefitted from guidance and advice from established historians. I am grateful to Mr D. H. Simpson, librarian of the Royal Commonwealth Society, who provided the first clue which ultimately led to my discovery of the Sulivan papers. My special thanks go to Dr Andrew Porter. The bulk of the research for this book was completed during my doctoral study at the University of London; the book is based on my Ph.D. thesis. Dr Porter was my supervisor at King's College, London, and went out of his way to help at all stages of my research. He was extremely helpful in guiding my work and offered invaluable suggestions for its improvement. I am also grateful to my wife, Jadwiga, for her patience, the endless cups of coffee, and for typing the manuscript. I am grateful to all those who have helped in the development of this book. While they share no responsibility for errors or omissions, their help was crucial in its completion.

1

The First Phase

In the aftermath of the Napoleonic wars, Britain emerged as the dominant power in the Indian Ocean. Throughout the nineteenth century, there was an effort to maintain this unrivalled position by relying in large part on a small number of naval vessels which served as symbols of British interest in the region. While initially regarded as an unimportant backwater, the East Coast of Africa steadily increased in significance through the century until a presence there was seen as an important factor in maintaining the British stance in the Indian Ocean. The reasons for the emergence of an aggressive East African policy were basically three-fold. First, and most significant, were strategic concerns. With France supplanted from the Indian Ocean island stronghold of Mauritius, the East Coast appeared the most likely area for an attempt to re-assert French influence. The attempt to forestall intervention by another European power was a persistent feature of British East African policy. Another consideration was trade, an interest which blended well with broader strategic questions since an active British trading community in East Africa could be a vehicle for maintaining a British presence without the complications and expense of direct government involvement. The third major factor was a steadily growing opposition to the East African slave trade. While initially of secondary concern, by 1860, anti-slavery moves were of great importance since they provided justification for an aggressive naval policy off the coast. It was hoped that this naval activity would not only put down the slave trade, but would also support the other basic British interests by forestalling foreign intervention and by stimulating legitimate commerce.

In strategic terms, the principal British interest in the Indian

1

Ocean was protection of the sea lanes to India. The major threat to control of these sea lanes was France, smarting under the reverses of the Napoleonic wars and seeking to regain lost prestige in the Imperial arena. In the peace settlement of 1814, France lost the strategically significant Isle de France, Mauritius. The French retained the smaller island of Bourbon but recognised that its strategic role was limited since its harbour could not provide adequate shelter during the hurricane season. Thus attempts to establish French influence in other areas which could offer suitable port facilities increased with interest shown in a number of places including Madagascar and the Comoro Islands. A particularly important area was Zanzibar and the coast opposite, a region claimed by the Sultan of Muscat. In 1819, unrest in the southern slave port of Kilwa prompted France to consider military intervention against the Omani overlords from Muscat as a means of gaining the islands of Zanzibar and Pemba. The project was abandoned, however, largely due to the overpowering British military presence in the area. Nevertheless, France continued to view Zanzibari lands with interest although it was decided that diplomacy was a safer approach than direct military intervention. Consequently, there followed a period of diplomatic manoeuvre culminating in a flourish of activity in the 1830s, a period when Anglo–French relations were strained by developments in the Middle East.[1] British policy makers were thus forced to keep a watchful eye on French activities and, as will be seen, when the permanent commitment of ships to a slave trade campaign in East Africa was made in 1860, suspicion of French activity at Zanzibar was an important factor in that decision.

French trading interest in Zanzibar was clearly reflected in trade figures with the island. Throughout the early years of the nineteenth century, France out-traded Britain in the region and, by 1811, had established a trading factory. Much early French trade was channelled through colonies, primarily Bourbon; commercial arrangements for trade between Bourbon and Zanzibar were negotiated in 1822 and 1827. It was not until the 1850s that trade directly with France reached significant proportions but during that decade the volume of activity startled British observers. The value of direct French trade more than doubled from 1856 to the beginning of 1860 when it was estimated at approximately $116,451 per year. In contrast, British traders were initially few in number on the coast although the firm of Newman, Hunt and Christopher appointed Robert Norsworthy as their commercial agent in Zanzibar during the 1830s. Through the 1830s and 1840s, British merchants became increasingly active in the region providing, among other goods, the majority of imported arms. Total transactions were valued at $214,000 by 1846–7. Direct British trade declined during the 1850s, but British Indian traders continued to be active in the region and through them, Britain retained a significant stake in the coastal trade. A long-standing association between the coast and Indian traders, especially from Kutch and Surat, and the importance of Indian cloth as an article of barter aided Indians in taking over many 'middleman' roles in the East African trade. During the 1850s, some 35 Indian vessels per year were regularly engaged in the Zanzibar trade. By the mid-1820s, another factor became significant with increasing United States interest in the trade prospects on the coast. Cheap American cloth, 'merikani', rapidly became a dominant medium of exchange and aggressive Yankee traders soon gained an impressive total of the region's business. By 1838, the value of American sales at Zanzibar was put at $100,000 per year and the total grew to $550,000 by 1856. In 1860 the Americans were taking approximately 31 per cent of Zanzibari exports, Britain, largely through Indian traders, 26 per cent, France 14 per cent and German traders 9 per cent. Throughout, the principal items of export from the East African coast were cloves, copal, coconut oil and ivory, along with the clandestine traffic in slaves.[2] The fear that growing French or American influence might undermine the British position in the region gave strength to attempts to increase Britain's share of the legitimate trade, but, in the end, the aspect of Zanzibar trade which most attracted British governmental attention was the export trade in slaves.

The slaves exported from Zanzibar were drawn from the African interior where slaving parties would buy or steal inland inhabitants and then march them to the coast. Initially, Arab traders confined themselves to the littoral with African middlemen bringing the slaves to the coast. By the 1830s, however, the slavers themselves began mounting caravans which pushed further inland until they reached as far into the interior as Lake Nyasa. Coastal towns such as Kilwa grew to prominence as receiving points for the slaves before they were shipped to the major market in Zanzibar. Slaves marketed in Zanzibar might go to local slave owners for use in the clove plantations of Zanzibar or the nearby island, Pemba, or to European slavers discouraged by the Royal Navy patrols off the coast of West Africa. More common, however, was for slaves to be purchased by northern Arab dhowmen who would then carry them to markets in Arabia, Persia or even India. These northern Arabs used the prevailing winds and currents to come down to Zanzibar between October and April each year and then, when the winds shifted, from April to September, to carry slaves back to the lucrative northern markets. As many as 100 dhows might make the journey in any year. In the early-nineteenth century up to 20,000 slaves per year were sold on the East African coast and while that number fluctuated during the next 50 years, it has been estimated that some 20,000 slaves annually were still passing through the Zanzibar market in the late 1850s.[3] Nevertheless, the British response to the trade was initially limited. During the years when the navy was actively attacking the slave trade on the West Coast of Africa, it maintained a much lower profile off the East Coast and, along with its sister service the Indian Navy, was only minimally involved in anti-slavery activities in East Africa. The reasons for this limited response, despite the active anti-slavery campaign of humanitarian groups in Britain, were two-fold. In the first place there was simply a lack of knowledge about the extent of the traffic which was not fully overcome until the exploration of the interior focused public interest on East Africa in the late 1850s.[4] Even more important as a reason for limited action was the unique position of the Sultan of Muscat. Saiyid Said established himself as sultan in 1806 and then began a long period of consolidating his holdings which included territory on the East Coast of Africa as well as in the Persian Gulf. Through the years, the southern possessions of the sultanate assumed increasing importance and, in 1840, Said proclaimed Zanzibar as the capital of his dominions. From the British point of view, Said was a significant potential ally who was a symbol of stability at least nominally in control of major portions of the East African coast and lands in the Persian Gulf which made him the 'gate-keeper' of the sea lanes to India. The Sultan was a powerful indigenous ruler who was competent but not altogether secure in his position. Britain thus adopted a policy of supporting Said in hopes of thwarting European intervention in the region while maintaining British pre-eminence at the same time. Relatively minor concessions on the question of the slave trade enabled the Sultan to enhance his own security by maintaining a *de facto* alliance with Britain. For his part, the sultan recognised the dominance of British naval strength in the area.[5] It has been suggested that 'without British naval support, Said's projected Imperial structure would have tottered precariously between sand and sea; and he knew it.'[6] The unofficial alliance produced actions ranging from joint operations against the Joasmi pirates leading to the capture of their major city, Ras al Khaima, in 1819 to the intervention of British ships to put down an attempted coup in Muscat in 1832.[7] Through such actions, Britain hoped to secure influence by making the sultan increasingly dependent and thus increasingly pliant in supporting British strategic, trade and anti-slavery policies.

The trend is seen especially clearly in connection with the slave trade despite the fact that Said's usefulness and the importance of the slave trade to his subjects prompted the British government to move cautiously on slavery matters. The sultan's dependence on British naval strength did, however, allow the government to gain some concessions to British anti-slavery sentiments. The first of these was negotiated by Captain Fairfax Moresby, senior officer at Mauritius, in 1822. Provisions of the agreement prohibited sub-jects of the Sultan from engaging in slave trading beyond the limits of the Muscat–Zanzibar dominions. Sale to any Christian was specifically prohibited and dhows found with slaves east of a line extending from 60 miles east of Socotra to Diu Head were to be subject to capture by ships of the Royal Navy.[8] The treaty led to apprehension and opposition within the sultanate but anti-slavery critics in Britain were ill-disposed to accept the limits of the document. The agreement seemed to check any traffic to the Americas or dhow shipments to regions beyond the sultanate such as India, but the main traffic to ports around Muscat was unaffected.

One of those who believed that the Moresby concession had not gone far enough was Captain William FitzWilliam Owen. Owen was an experienced naval commander who had once been entrusted with an abortive plan to burn the French fleet in Boulogne by Nelson himself.[9] Unlike most of the anti-slavery agitators, however, Owen, who had been sent to survey the East Coast of Africa, was in a position to put his views into action. Con-sequently, he decided, on his own initiative, to reverse the gradualist approach which had hitherto been employed in Said's realm. His orders instructed him to employ his two ships, the *Leven* and the *Barracouta*, to survey the coast and rivers in the region as well as to observe the native inhabitants of the coast.[10] It did not take long, however, for the captain to assert his authority and exceed his instructions. On 6 June 1823, he informed the Admiralty that since it was impossible for him to perform the duties with the ships on hand, he had purchased the schooner *Albatross* on his own authority to serve as a tender. He assured his superiors that he would ordinarily have avoided incurring the extra expense but decided to proceed 'considering that this inconveniency ought not to deter me from doing what I know is right'.[11] That phrase could have served as a motto for the remainder of the cruise since Owen repeatedly took independent action to do what he felt needed to be done. The result was that a simple surveying mission took on major political overtones. As one historian has put it, 'he exceeded the scope of his instructions so widely that his surveying expedition was transformed into a political mission'.[12]

The survey was completed and it is of interest for several reasons, not the least being the quality of the charts produced, charts which helped open the coast to new trade initiatives. But the geographical knowledge was purchased dearly as the crews suffered the ravages of tropical diseases. Owen reported 'seriously heavy' losses and petitioned for replacements for his crews as totals in less than a year came to 25 dead on board *Barracouta* and 37 on *Leven*.[13] It is little wonder that the losses were so high as the medical wisdom of the day called for bleeding and large doses of calomel to combat fever. When the remedy failed to work, second and third bleedings were prescribed and Owen, who cursed the 'bloody scene' observed that 'this practice has been most unsuccessful and . . . our surgeons were in my opinion quite as much in the dark as to the nature of the disease as if they had never studied medicine at all'.[14] It is not surprising that from 1822 until 1826, some 200 men died.[15]

As the ships battled with fever and the currents up the coastline, Owen became more and more concerned with matters beyond his survey and the health of his crews; he became increasingly agitated by the state of the slave trade. Describing it as 'diabolical commerce', he decided to attack the trade.[16] The first step was to negotiate treaties with chiefs along the Tembe River in Delagoa Bay in March 1823.[17] Owen's biggest attempted coup, however, involved Mombasa, ostensibly the possession of Saiyid Said. The leaders of the coastal port, in an effort to secure independence from Said, had already sent a delegation to petition the East India Company for protection. The request was refused due to the existing *entente* with the sultan and a reluctance to become involved on the African mainland. Owen, however, who met the delegation in Bombay, was not reluctant at all and citing a lack of instructions, he set out to gain Mombasa as a British base for attacks against 'this infernal traffick' in slaves. Arriving in Muscat, the captain explained his plan to the sultan and suggested that Said should go beyond the Moresby treaty by proclaiming the end of the slave trade within three years. Failure to do so would prompt Owen to offer British protection to Mombasa if it were sought when he arrived at that port. The sultan wisely saw that there was no future in arguing with the captain and assured him that 'he would be happy to see the dominions of England extend from the rising to the setting sun' and would derive great pleasure from a British protectorate at Mombasa. 'I thought I observed symptoms of insincerity', Owen reported in a monument of understatement.[18]

As soon as the captain left Muscat, the sultan immediately protested to the British government against the encroachment into his claimed territory. For Said the difficult question of sovereignty over Mombasa had been a sore point for several years and Owen's arrival on the scene came at a particularly awkward time. The Mazrui clan had long before usurped control of Mombasa and maintained themselves for over 50 years. The initial break resulted from a dynastic clash in Oman where the Mazrui supported a rival to the ultimately successful Al Bu Saidis. In the 1740s, the Mazrui governor of Mombasa refused to accept the authority of the new dynasty, establishing *de facto* independence for the city.[19] Supported by the native Swahilis, the Mazrui maintained the independent city state which at one time claimed large tracts of the coast as well as the island of Pemba. They even attacked Zanzibar itself in 1753 but were turned back by supporters of the sultan. As Said consolidated his holdings after assuring his throne, he bided his time until he felt strong enough to re-establish his claim to Mombasa. Recognising the danger, Abdallah ibn Ahmad al-Mazrui, who had led the faction controlling Mombasa since 1814, twice petitioned Bombay for support. The special relationship with Said caused Britain to refuse to consider the plea and by 1823 the sultan was ready to try to bring the Mombasa rebels to heel. It was at this juncture that, quite inconveniently for Said, Owen appeared on the scene.[20]

In addition, a letter to Mombasa from Bombay had further confused the situation. The letter, written in English, was simply a routine request for permission for the navy to survey the region and buy bullocks there. No one in Mombasa, however, could read the correspondence and they decided it must be instructions for a British captain to set up a protectorate. The Mazrui thus made a red ensign which they hoisted when Said's fleet appeared off the city.[21] As a consequence, when Owen sailed to Mombasa he found a British flag already flying there and promptly extended British protection pending the government's pleasure.[22] The government's pleasure, much to Owen's chagrin and Said's relief, was to repudiate the whole affair and maintain the integrity of the sultan's claimed dominions. However, before the episode ended, a form of naval supervision of Mombasa was maintained for almost two years. Owen made abolition of the slave trade a prerequisite for his protectorate and left Lieutenant John Reitz as commander of a small garrison which included Midshipman George Phillips, a corporal of marines, and three seamen. Before leaving, Owen told the 22-year-old Reitz to try to learn something about the history and topography of the region as well as supervise the city itself. The young commandant tried to follow the instructions and so led an expedition up the Pangani River. On the journey, however, he contracted fever and died leaving Midshipman Phillips in command. Phillips tried to thwart the slave traders and even went so far as seizing a slave dhow with 20 slaves aboard in the harbour despite protests from the residents of Mombasa. A third commander, James Emery, an acting-lieutenant, took command to return the strength of the detachment to two officers. The change was short lived, however, as Phillips died shortly afterwards. By the time the government rejected the Owen protectorate, the residents of Mombasa had become disenchanted with naval meddling in matters like the slave trade, and the garrison along with the liberated slaves on hand were withdrawn by Captain Charles Acland of HMS *Helicon* on 25 July 1826.[23] Said finally regained control of Mombasa in 1827.

The Owen affair was a colourful episode but its practical impact was slight. By repudiating Owen's initiative, the government upheld the existing balance and stressed the significance of Said as a viable indigenous ruler in the strategically important area. The steady use of influence in advancing British policy was seen as more productive than the bellicose forward policy of Owen. This approach was maintained over the following decade with relations between the sultan and Britain not being undermined since Said continued to recognise his dependence on British support. A **significant step in the programme of expanding British influence** in Zanzibar came in 1841 when Atkins Hammerton arrived as the first British consul in the sultan's new capital. Hammerton had been a captain in the Bombay Infantry where he showed considerable skill as an interpreter. There was a slightly anachronistic feature in the control of the new consulate which represented a compromise between London and Bombay. Hammerton was placed in the dual role of consul and political agent reporting both to the Foreign Office in London and to the Secretary to the Government of Bombay. An officer of the East India Company appointed by the Governor of Bombay, he held consular authority from the Crown and was subject to dismissal by either Bombay or London. The appointment was motivated by all three major British policy objectives in the region. One incentive was continuing fear of French activity. French manoeuvres had unsettled both the British government and Said who requested the appointment in 1839. It also reflected increased commercial interest in the area. Norsworthy, the British commercial agent in Zanzibar, had agitated for the appointment of a consul since 1837. He argued that he, not to mention some 2,000 British Indian subjects engaged in mercantile activities in the region, were at a great disadvantage since there was an American consul in the town but no official British representative. Ultimately, the Board of Control took up the request.[24] Of course, the appointment was also a useful tool in slave trade matters. The presence of a permanent consular representative strengthened the existing ties between Said and Britain but also provided the means for exerting pressure on the sultan to take additional action against the slave trade. The continuing pattern of concessions on slave trade matters in return for British support led to an agreement in 1845 usually called the Hammerton Treaty. The document, signed on 2 October 1845 to become effective in 1847, prohibited the export of slaves from any part of Africa into Said's possessions in the Persian Gulf. An enforcement clause gave the ships of the Royal Navy, as well as vessels of the Indian Navy, the right to seize and confiscate vessels belonging to Said's subjects found carrying slaves except within his African territories between Lamu in the north and Kilwa in the south.[25]

On paper the treaty was a major blow against the slavers but in practice its impact was minimised by the situation on the coast. There were three major elements of British influence in Said's realm — the treaty structure, the consular establishment and the navy. As has been seen, the treaty structure, based on the

Moresby concession as extended in 1839 and the new Hammerton Treaty, rendered the northern dhow commerce illegal and provided the basis for naval enforcement. In addition to provisions for right to search given to the navy in these documents, a host of existing agreements with other European powers extended the right to inspect vessels at sea to include ships of some 30 other nations. Significantly, however, after 1845 such agreement with France lapsed.[26] Adjudication within this structure was by Vice-Admiralty courts with the most important during the early years being located at the Cape. Another key factor in the British presence was of course the consul who, as the British representative permanently on the scene, was charged with guarding British interests while securing adherence to the treaties. In the early years, the consul generally acted in his role as political agent of the East India Company. In fact, Hammerton did not know that he was consul when he took up the Zanzibar post and was surprised to discover the fact on a visit to Bombay in mid-1842. In either capacity, however, Hammerton was instructed to maintain British interests while exerting pressure for reduction of the slave trade. It was hoped that his presence would assure British influence with Said and, despite Hammerton's high-handed approach to his task and his drinking habits which startled some observers, he did manage to achieve and maintain the desired dominant position with the sultan.[27] This influence had strengthened the treaty structure with the agreement of 1845 and continued consular pressure was directed at assuring Zanzibari adherence to the document. Nevertheless, there can be little doubt that both the consul's influence and the enforcement of treaty provisions rested heavily on the symbol of British military might in the region — the navy. Operating in the early years under the direction of the commander-in-chief of the Cape of Good Hope Station, ships served as graphic representations of the British military presence in the region. The navy was the key element both in enforcing treaties and in supporting the consul. This continued to be the case despite later attempts to reduce the naval role and strengthen the other elements. From 1844, the Cape Station extended to 26°W and 15°54'S in the Atlantic Ocean and in the Indian Ocean, north to the equator for as far as 66°E where it dropped to 10°S as far as 75°E where it plunged south to the Antarctic circle. In 1845, the commander at the Cape had nine vessels to cover this vast region and was primarily charged with protecting the Cape itself, and thus the sea lanes to India.[28] Nevertheless, he also had responsibilities for shoring up all three British interests in East Africa. In the first place, the navy was expected to enforce the treaty provisions for the limitation of the slave trade. The only effective enforcement clauses in the various treaties relied on naval ships, documents such as the Hammerton Treaty would have been totally ineffective without naval prosecution of violators. At the same time, however, the navy was also charged with protecting legitimate trade and trade routes. As will be seen, the navy was at times accused of interfering with legitimate dhow commerce, but it was still seen as protecting legal trade by British authorities. Of course an even more obvious role was providing a political presence and a visible manifestation of British power which propped up the sultan and helped counter the French at the same time. A related aspect of this political activity was supporting the consul — a role which also helped entrench British influence with Said while checking similar efforts by the French.

It must be emphasised, however, that this structure was plagued with problems. One difficult area concerned the sultan whose increased dependence on Britain tended to reduce his authority and undermine the loyalty of his subjects. Even a treaty as limited as the Moresby concession was granted only over opposition within the sultanate and Said's position was made more difficult as a result. Nevertheless, Said was skilful and powerful enough to maintain a fairly secure position. The chronic dependence of the sultan on British arms was very obviously increased on his death in 1856. When Saiyid Said died his realm was divided to form a sultanate of Muscat and a sultanate of Zanzibar. Saiyid Majid, who succeeded to the Zanzibar throne, was less imposing than his father. In addition, as will be seen, British naval support was required to stabilise his regime when his younger brother, Barghash, led a revolt in Zanzibar. Intervention by the navy increased British prestige but at the same time underlined the dependence of the sultan on British support.

Furthermore, there were other problems inherent within the East Coast structure. Although the anti-slave trade treaties were dependent on naval enforcement, the navy was unable to make any appreciable headway against the trade in the decade or so following the Hammerton Treaty. The problem was too few ships to enforce the document. As has been seen, the Cape Station was extensive and the number of ships allocated to the command was small. Between 1845 and 1860, station strength fluctuated between a low of four ships and a high of eleven; the average number was nine. Of course, the problem of ship allocation must be seen within the context of naval strategic planning. There were eight major naval stations with vessels operating away from home waters, The Cape was the smallest in terms of ship strength, reflecting relative geographical size as well as strategic emphasis. Following closely in terms of ships were the stations centred on the west and south-east coasts of the Americas. The West Coast of Africa command, separated from the Cape in 1840, and the Baltic fleet followed with between 12 and 17 vessels. The East Indies command frequently consisted of 20 ships or more during the 1850s but the numbers were required since that station included Australian waters until 1859 and China until 1864. The North America and West Indies Station also enjoyed some priority in ship allocation with numbers averaging around 20 vessels. By far the most significant of the foreign stations was the Mediterranean which had over 70 ships as a routine fleet strength. The relative importance of the Mediterranean reflects the naval emphasis which explains the low numbers of ships available for slave trade purposes. As Marder has pointed out, the principal purpose of British naval strength was protection of commerce and food supplies while countering potential European rivals. With a series of 'invasion scares' coupled with fears of the naval threat posed by France and Russia alternatively, the major concentration of the fleet was in home and European waters. In the 1860s, the point was made repeatedly that naval construction and ship assignments should concentrate on meeting potential European threats. For example, E. J. Reed, chief constructor for the Admiralty, stressed the value of ships 'to fight in fleets'. The problem, in his view, was not the ships 'which operate in distant seas . . . of which . . . we have a larger number in proportion than of ships to fight fleet actions, while the reverse is the case both with France and Russia'. With this role having first priority, foreign stations had to share out the remaining vessels for the various far-flung Imperial commitments which by this time spanned the entire globe.[29]

The Admiralty, charged with responsibility for distributing the limited assets set aside for Imperial commitments, received persistent requests for more vessels from each station commander. Pleas from the Cape were echoed by each commander with non-European responsibilities. As a result, requests from the Cape, the smallest of the petitioners, generally went unheeded. In mid-1846, for example, Rear-Admiral J. R. Dacres, commanding at the Cape, informed the Admiralty that at best he could attach only two vessels to slave trade suppression and at times no ships at all were available.[30] Difficult as the situation was, it was little changed ten years later when Rear-Admiral Sir Frederick Grey voiced the same complaint — that a shortage of ships made any attempt at slave trade suppression in the region largely impossible.[31] The situation was so bad that Grey had little information on the trade, let alone ships to stop it. He advised the Admiralty that 'the materials for a report on the present state of the slave trade on this coast are so scanty that I can scarcely venture to make one'.[32] A related problem increasing the navy's difficulties was the condition of the ships themselves. As well as being few in number, they were in many cases well past their periods of peak effectiveness. Not only did stations like the Mediterranean have the majority of vessels available, they also had the newer and more formidable ships which were naturally assigned where they would be best positioned in case of conflict with another European power. Older, smaller vessels found their way to more remote stations like the Cape or East Indies where the debilitating tropical climate speeded their deterioration. The result of all these factors was that operations on the East Coast of Africa were always the responsibility of an over-extended station commander who lacked adequate resources. The commander could only dispatch a captain or commander to patrol the region, enforce the slave trade treaties, and support the consul as well as possible. These captains in turn attempted to 'show the flag' in harbours such as Zanzibar while at the same time making as much progress in slave trade suppression as possible. The only way they could hope to accomplish this task was by dispatching the ship's boats to cruise independently in an effort to expand the patrolling effectiveness of the squadron. The open boat work was debilitating and dangerous but it was unavoidable given the lack of cruising ships available. As will be seen, the shortage of ships was a continuing theme in the naval history of the region and the difficulties of boat cruising was a recurring problem.

A significant, and related, underlying problem was the Admiralty's inability to influence major policy decisions by the government. As Bartlett has argued, although the First Lord was a cabinet minister, the post usually did not attract political leaders of the highest prominence and naval requirements were frequently subservient to the desires of the Foreign Office and the Treasury. It was frequently the case that the Admiralty struggled to maintain what were regarded as the lowest possible station strengths.

Furthermore, the relative weakness of the Admiralty in dealing with the Foreign Office and Treasury was exacerbated by the situation within the Admiralty itself, especially in areas such as slave trade suppression. The concept of the Board of Admiralty was one factor. Each member of the Board, which included the First Lord, the four Naval Lords, the Civil Lord, and the First and Second Secretaries, had clearly defined responsibilities. Even after reforms initiated by Hugh Childers in 1869, compartmentalisation remained an important factor. While the system worked reasonably well in terms of broad naval strategy, specific Imperial commitments could be submerged in the system and what Murray described as 'delicate questions as to individual and collective responsibility' could emerge. For most of the latter half of the nineteenth century, slave trade was under the general cognisance of the Legal Branch of the Admiralty. The branch dealt with matters ranging from courts of inquiry and courts martial through general discipline in the fleet and Queen's Regulations to blockades, prizes, etc. While the department was well enough equipped to deal with matters of adjudication, it was not able to control other aspects of policy intimately bound up in slave trade suppression. For example, matters dealing with protection of trade, distribution of ships, suppression of piracy and colonial defence were the responsibility of the Military Branch. Officering and manning the fleet was the area of yet another department — the Naval Branch. For a coherent slave trade policy to emerge, information and minutes had to be assessed from all three departments. As a result, most important decisions concerning the slave trade were taken by W. G. Romaine or by Vernon Lushington who succeeded him as the Second or Permanent Secretary. Difficulty arose from the fact that the Second Secretary's office was the nerve centre of the Admiralty through which all papers for the Board passed. While Romaine and Lushington manfully attempted to devise a coherent slave trade policy, matters associated with the East Coast of Africa were simply one minor aspect in an intensely hectic range of business. An immediate result of this situation was that there was never a tight rein kept on East Coast commanders from London. The situation in the Admiralty, however, contrasted sharply with that in the Foreign Office and the Treasury. The Foreign Office had a well-established slave trade department charged with dealing with suppression as a primary task. The department was headed for much of the period of this study by W. H. Wylde, an administrator of vision and ability.

The Treasury, too, had a special advisor to deal with matters arising from the slave trade. For over 20 years the post was held by H. C. Rothery. Wylde and Rothery were friends who shared a legalistic approach to slave trade suppression. Both were committed to the extinction of the trade but they were insistent that international law and a sense of fair dealing must be maintained. This attitude frequently conflicted with the pragmatic and more aggressive stance of naval officers who were more concerned with the practical problems of slave trade enforcement than legal precision. The result was that a consistent and coherent slave trade policy emerged from the Foreign Office and the Treasury which was at times at variance with naval attitudes. Given the junior relationship of the Admiralty and the lack of a slave trade advisor of the standing of Wylde and Rothery, the Admiralty was at a constant disadvantage when differences arose. The other ministry involved most directly in slave trade matters was the India Office. But the India Office was unable to maintain a consistent position due to a basic difference of opinion between the Government of Bombay and the Government of India. The former tended to advance a forward policy which was generally resisted by the latter with the result that the India Office was less effective in influencing policy than might otherwise have been the case. In general terms, policy decisions concerning suppression of the East African slave trade were made by the Foreign Office in concert with the Treasury. The Admiralty was a junior partner forced to struggle to enforce these decisions as well as possible.[33]

In practice, responsibility for enforcement was inevitably delegated to the senior officer on the coast. Given the problems from the station commander's point of view and the necessarily loose rein from London resulting from the situation within the Admiralty, the effectiveness of naval operations depended almost entirely on the energy and commitment of the senior officers in the slave trade patrol. Significant questions of positioning of detached boats, general cruising strategy for the ships, and port visits to Zanzibar were generally taken neither by overworked clerks in the Admiralty nor even by the commander-in-chief hundreds of miles from the scene, but by the captain who was the navy's 'man-on-the-spot'. This role is crucial in the development of British policy in the region. Far removed from lines of communication, many officials in far-flung regions were forced into a role more sensitive than simple executor of established government policy. Questions requiring immediate action necessitated quick decisions without the possibility of prior consultation with London, Bombay or the Cape. Both the senior naval officer on the East Coast and the consul at Zanzibar were men-on-the-spot in their own right and this fact gives rise to yet another problem inherent within the East Coast system. The overlapping structure of East African operations continually brought the captains and the consul into potential conflict. The consul was charged with maintaining British influence in the sultanate while gaining slave trade concessions through careful diplomacy. A forward naval policy might alienate the sultan and undermine his efforts, yet given the shortages faced by the squadron, aggressive prosecution offered the navy's only hope for success. In addition, a lack of clear instructions aggravated the situation. Communication with Zanzibar was erratic and the consul's instructions were vague. The senior naval officer was purposely given wide discretion by the station commander and his specific slave trade guidance was largely inapplicable because it had been drawn up for the West Coast trade. Strong-willed and semi-independent men with overlapping jurisdiction sometimes realised the potential for conflict; confrontation between captains and consul will be seen to be another recurring theme in this study.

A key date in the development of British policy in East Africa is 1860. Intervention during the Barghash rebellion in the previous year helped open the door to a new assertion of British influence in the region. Saiyid Thuwaini, Majid's elder brother, became Sultan of Muscat upon the death of Saiyid Said. In March 1859, he sent a maritime expedition to conquer Zanzibar, but his vessels were turned back by a ship of the Indian Navy, the *Punjaub*, and additional British vessels moved into Zanzibar itself.[34] In the aftermath of the abortive attempt by Thuwaini to seize Zanzibar, a younger brother, Saiyid Barghash, led a rebellion of his own, motivated at least in part by French encouragement. Barghash was emboldened by being advanced as a protégé of the French government by the consul, Ladislas Cochet, and by Commodore Flueriot de Langle, the senior French naval officer in the region. On 14 October 1859, the situation deteriorated enough for Majid to seek assistance from the new British consul, Captain C. P. Rigby. The consul turned to two British ships in harbour, the Royal Navy's *Lynx* under Lieutenant Henry Berkely and the *Assaye* of the Indian Navy commanded by Commander G. N. Adams. Seven officers, headed by Berkely, agreed to accompany the sultan's forces in an attempt to rout Barghash and his followers. The sultan's forces, strengthened by navy guns, moved quickly to the rebel camp where their foes fell back into a fortified building. When the rebels opened fire, however, the sultan's army retreated in confusion beyond the range of their guns. Incensed by the turn the fighting had taken, the naval officers, accompanied by three Turkish gunners, advanced on their own, dragging a cannon to within about 50 yards of the building. They opened fire while finding that their main danger was not from the rebels but from the sultan's forces who were firing from such a great distance that their shells were falling on the officers' position. Despite the shelling from their allies, they managed to shoot down the main gate, then moved a second cannon into position and destroyed another gate. The sultan's forces were not, however, prepared to storm the position and as darkness fell with no sign of progress, the officers returned to their ships in disgust.[35]

Finding his own forces impotent, the sultan asked Rigby for more substantial assistance. As a result, on the next day 70 seamen were transferred from the *Assaye* to the *Lynx* and that vessel sailed as near as possible to the rebel stronghold. Berkely then led some 100 seamen and marines to the scene of the earlier battle only to find that the building had been abandoned. Blowing up the structure, they returned to Zanzibar where Barghash had fled to a house in the town. A detachment of seamen from the *Assaye* led by Lieutenant H. C. Carey was sent to surround the house and Barghash surrendered in return for safe passage from Zanzibar.[36] The action met with praise at home and *The Times* lauded the naval forces 'to whose assistance the sultan handsomely acknowledged himself indebted for the security of his throne and dominions'.[37] A well-pleased Rigby suggested that Majid 'is fully sensible that it is chiefly owing to the prompt assistance afforded him by the British ships of war that this island and town have been saved from anarchy and ruin'.[38]

While Rigby was somewhat over-enthusiastic, the action did stress the importance of the navy while at the same time underlining the increased dependence of the sultan. Moreover, exploration in the interior was producing an increased awareness of East African problems during the later years of the 1850s. Livingstone's first trans-African journey had been completed and the Zambezi expedition was underway. Burton and Speke had been to Lake Tanganyika and, in 1860, Speke and Grant were to set off into the interior again. A major impetus to anti-slavery sentiment in Britain was provided by the accounts which the explorers brought back. Gruesome scenes from the slave caravan's transit to the coast were vividly described by Livingstone. Nor were the descriptions exaggerations in their author's eyes.

> When endeavouring to give some account of the slave trade of East Africa, it was necessary to keep far within the truth, in order not to be thought guilty of exaggeration; but in sober seriousness the subject does not admit of exaggeration. To overdraw its evils is a simple impossibility.[39]

Burton, while not as inclined toward emotion as Livingstone, was also instructive. In a book published in 1860, Burton wrote that 'the traffic practically annihilates every better feeling of human nature'. He dismissed some of the generalisations about the damages of the trade but still concluded that 'the practice of slavery in East Africa, besides demoralising and brutalising the race, leads to results which effectually bar increase of population and progress towards civilisation'. Burton provided an argument for naval intervention but warned that such action alone would not be sufficient. 'A "sentimental squadron", like the West African, could easily, by means of steam, prevent any regular exportation to the Asiatic continent,' he wrote but believed that 'these measures would deal only with effects, leaving the causes in full vigour'.[40] The accounts of Livingstone, Burton and Speke helped capture public imagination and focus it on the African interior while ensuring that the ravages of the slave trade became obvious in the process.

In addition, there was increased agitation for a permanent naval presence and more active naval prosecution by the British representatives in the region. The slaves transported north had already attracted the attention of British officials. In late 1858, for example, Captain Felix Jones, political resident in the Persian Gulf, complained to Bombay that the Indian Navy's *Punjaub* had failed to stop a slaver which passed under her bows off Bushire. The *Punjaub*'s captain had misunderstood his position within the treaty structure, believing himself prohibited from interfering with slavers in harbours or roadsteads. The political resident, however, insisted that he should have intervened. Jones suggested 'that such open disregard of slavers and their acts must lend to the augmentation of a traffic which it was the object of our treaties to eradicate.'[41] The argument was accepted and attempts were made to clarify existing station orders accordingly.[42] Moreover, the next year an even more forceful argument for naval pressure against the trade was voiced by Brigadier W. M. Coghlan, commissioner for the affairs of Muscat and Zanzibar. Coghlan, who was political resident at Aden, had been appointed to arbitrate in the accession controversy between Majid and Thuwaini and included in his report a detailed analysis of affairs in both sultanates.[43] Writing from Aden, Coghlan urged the strengthening of the Cape of Good Hope squadron to counter 'a yearly average export of no less than 30,000 slaves from the African territories dependent on Zanzibar'. Relying on accounts by explorers and missionaries as well as the consul at Zanzibar, Coghlan painted a grim picture of poorly provisioned dhows packed with slaves suffering from lack of food or water when the vessel became becalmed by contrary winds. Describing conditions along the coastline, he suggested that 'districts which a few years ago were populous and productive are now entirely destitute of inhabitants'.[44]

Coghlan's main source of information concerning conditions on the coast opposite Zanzibar was Rigby, the British consul and political agent. During 1860 when Coghlan was urging naval intervention, Rigby was calling for the same thing in a series of reports from Zanzibar. Rigby, who was at times given to enthusiastic overstatement, still seems to have been a careful and interested observer of the slave trade. Putting the number of slaves imported to the island at the lower total of about 19,000, he suggested that while the price for adult slaves in Zanzibar ranged from £2 to £7 their resale value in Arabia or Persia could be as high as £20. Attacking the slave dealers as 'vile unfeeling wretches' totally lacking compassion for the slaves, he claimed a high mortality rate from the trade. 'This miserable traffic is fast depopulating vast tracts of fertile country,' he wrote.[45] Rigby's contentions were frequently repeated. One year later, for example, he reported that the slave trade was increasing and was being carried on in a more organised fashion by traders forcing their way further into the interior.[46]

Such reports had the desired effect of awakening the government to the existence of the problem although the magnitude of its suppression was not immediately apparent. The fact the government was slow to grasp the extent of activity necessary to check the trade is reflected in the attitude of Wylde. As the Foreign Office's senior clerk in the slave trade department, he was to play a continuing and significant role in the affairs of East Africa for years to come. In a memo relating to the Zanzibar slave trade, Wylde confidently looked forward to an early end to the problem

and hopefully predicted 'that means may be found to suppress it
. . . within a few years'.[47] The Prime Minister himself was
shocked by reports of major slave trading on the East Coast just as
the long contested West African trade was going into decline. The
ageing Lord Palmerston, who had guided the suppression of the
Atlantic slave trade, had some difficulty in grasping the nature of
its Indian Ocean counterpart. 'Where do all these slaves go to?' he
questioned incredulously. Thinking in terms of the Atlantic trade
he seemed bewildered by the fact that the figure of 30,000 slaves
exceeded the total number thought to be landed in Cuba. Could
some be going to Brazil, he wondered.[48]

Even if the reports coming from Zanzibar and Aden were reluctantly accepted, they did leave little doubt that there was a slave
trade on the East Coast which would have to be dealt with. The
anti-slavery sentiment which had prodded the government to keep
cruisers on the West Coast for so many years could hardly overlook a trade of such magnitude in the east. Stemming from the
long agitation of the anti-slavery societies as well as Palmerston's
own convictions, there was within the government a conviction
that suppression of the slave trade was, in itself, a desirable object
of policy. It has been suggested that there was an 'assumption of
the "official mind" that action against the slave trade was a good
and proper function of policy.'[49] While other factors changed, this
attitude remained constant. It should be noted, however, that the
motives for increased naval activity still clearly reflected the basic
tenets of British policy. During this period there was renewed
suspicion of French activity in the region; cruisers on anti-slave
trade patrols could serve the useful additional purpose of keeping
an eye on the French in and around Zanzibar while serving as a
visible symbol of British military might. Fear of French activity
had been heightened since the Barghash rebellion. The banish-
ment of the rebel prince did not stifle French interest in Zanzibar.
Increased naval activity was directed by de Langle who was given
the grandiose title, Commandant of French Naval Forces on the
East Coast of Africa. Activity on the coast led to fears in Whitehall
that France might consider outright seizure of Zanzibar itself.
Issues closer to home also intensified British concern over naval
activities of the France of Napoleon III. The invasion scare of
1859–60 gave rise to Palmerston's fear that 'steam has bridged the
channel'. The era which brought the fortifications dubbed
'Palmerston's follies', also stimulated efforts to check possible
French expansion into areas of British paramountcy such as the

Indian Ocean.[50] Even after 1862, when the two countries signed a declaration binding themselves to respect the neutrality of Zanzibar and Muscat, there was continuing suspicion of France — suspicion intensified by the continuing naval rivalry between the two nations.[51] It was thus a dual function which was reflected in a detailed request from the Foreign Office to the Admiralty in February of 1860. The traffic in slaves was so great that a British cruiser was constantly needed near Zanzibar the communication stressed. In addition, reports of French activity required that the government should be supplied with information. As a result, the Admiralty was to provide for the permanent presence of a British ship 'in the neighbourhood of Zanzibar and for keeping HM's Government informed of what is passing there'.[52] In response, the Admiralty tried to clarify the responsibilities of the commander-in-chief in these East African duties. After discussions with the Foreign Office, draft instructions for East Coast operations were drawn up. In general terms, these instructions were taken from existing West African directives with the principal modification being a warning to exercise caution and discretion in any situation involving France. A particularly important point was that freedom of action on the coast was necessary and that questions of specific actions 'should be left to the discretion and judgement of the Commander in Chief'.[53] This policy decision taken in the Admiralty, largely because it was organisationally unable to exercise tight control, and reinforced by Foreign Office approval, provided ground rules which would generally remain in effect throughout the anti-slave trade campaign on the East Coast — maximum local discretion and loose control by the Admiralty.

On the East Coast, the navy enjoyed limited support for interference with the northern slave dhows since, while the sultan wanted to protect the traffic carried on by his own subjects, he was ready enough to see some control over the intrusive northern elements which undermined his authority. Rigby described the scene when the northern dhows arrived in Zanzibar as being like a city with a hostile army camped nearby. Asserting that people were afraid to venture out of their houses after dark, he reported that widespread instances of kidnapping of both slaves and children of the townspeople had prompted the residents who could afford it to send their children and younger slaves into the interior until the Suri season was over.[54]

The situation in 1861 reached crisis proportions as the **northerners not only stole from local residents, but also threatened**

Europeans in Zanzibar as well. The United States consulate bore the brunt of the hostilities; four servants of the consul were attacked and wounded while the consul himself was locked in by the Suris who blockaded the consulate all day. In the meantime, other northern dhowmen swarmed through the town brandishing swords and calling for the blood of a white man. The sultan was powerless to deal with the invaders, and responded to the rampaging slavers by barricading himself on the top floor of his palace and hoping they would go away.[55] As the situation deteriorated, the steam sloop *Lyra* commanded by Commander R. B. Oldfield, arrived in harbour. On finding that several of the northern dhows had just left with an estimated 2,000 slaves, Oldfield immediately moved north to intercept the slaving flotilla. On 22 March, a whaleboat from the *Lyra* engaged in a running battle leading to the capture of one of the northern slavers with 99 slaves on board. After capturing three more of the dhows with about 150 slaves, Oldfield returned to Zanzibar to try to stabilise the situation there.[56]

When the ship reached harbour on 31 March, Oldfield found that the northerners were still on the rampage and Rigby requested that the captain remain in harbour to protect British subjects. With the ship in harbour as a deterrent, Oldfield detached all of his boats to try to cut off any shipments of slaves. The boat blockade soon produced results as another Suri dhow, with 95 slaves on board, was captured. The success was, however, followed by a major reverse the next day. On 4 April, two whalers commanded by Gunner George Magee closed on a dhow with a number of slaves on board. Five members of the whaler crew managed to board the dhow only to be repulsed in a wild fight on deck. Some 20 dhowmen were reported killed; three British seamen suffered sabre wounds and to make matters worse, one of the navy boats was sunk during the fray.[57]

Feeling that matters could not be allowed to deteriorate further and capitalising on the compliance of the sultan during the confusion, Oldfield and Rigby worked together to assert British power as the arbiter of the situation. The captain and consul wrested an agreement from the sultan that the northerners should be given a grace period of three days in which they could load legal cargoes and depart from the port. No slaves could be shipped during the period and all departing dhows were to be subject to search by the *Lyra*'s boats. Any northern dhows in harbour after the grace period would be burned as pirates. The dhowmen, however, were unconvinced and on the afternoon of the proclamation attacked Oldfield himself. The captain was in his gig visiting the guard boats stationed outside the harbour when two large dhows slipped their moorings and attacked his boat. In the battle which followed, Oldfield managed to come alongside and board one of the dhows while keeping the second under fire. The first dhow was captured; two of its crewmen were killed and two others wounded. The second managed to escape but not before at least two of its crew had been killed by naval fire. The gig, despite having been hit by six shots, escaped with only one crewman slightly injured.[58]

This victory by the gig over the two large dhows frightened many of the northerners but a few of the more daring of the dhow-men were still determined to ship slaves. That evening, they sent a number of men up the coast about seven miles from the town where they began wildly firing into the sea. From the harbour it sounded as if one of the picket boats were under attack, and all the guard boats set off to render assistance. The ruse gave eleven Suri dhows just enough time to slip from the harbour with slaves on board. An incensed Rigby then insisted that Majid enforce his proclamation. The sultan finally agreed that 'they are all thieves and rogues and will not obey my orders to quit the harbour, and therefore the captain of the steamer may seize and destroy all the vessels'.[59] Thus armed with the sultan's blessing, Oldfield and Rigby went round the harbour by boat the next morning warning every northern dhow that they had until 2.00 p.m. to leave or they would be destroyed. Most of the dhowmen chose discretion and left immediately but the lure of slave profits was too much for a few of the remaining northerners. That afternoon, three dhows tried to load slaves up a nearby creek but were seized and burned by the *Lyra*'s boats. Two more dhows failed to leave the anchorage by the deadline and they too were burned to completely clear the harbour of northern dhows.[60]

Despite the escape of some of the dhows, the action was seen as a major triumph for Oldfield who personally supervised the whole operation despite the fact that he was recovering from a severe attack of fever. In all, 16 dhows from the northern fleet were destroyed and approximately 250 slaves, including an Arab girl from one of the leading Zanzibar families, were rescued. In addition, Oldfield felt that he had probably prevented the shipment of another 1,500 slaves. Rigby was ecstatic and over-optimistically asserted that the action of attacking the northerners had 'broken the spirit of these pirates'. Commending Oldfield and his crew, he suggested that by attacking the dhowmen and clearing the harbour, they had become the terrors of all the slave dealers on the coast. Rigby could not conceal his delight when he reported that 'the *Lyra* is spoken of everywhere along the coast as "El Sheitan" (the devil)'.[61]

One key to the success which was achieved was the cooperation between Rigby and Oldfield and the harbour conflict of 1861 was only one of several cases where Rigby relied on Oldfield for assistance. In August of the previous year, the consul had received information that a slaver was operating nearby. Rigby turned to Oldfield who quickly captured an American clipper-rigged ship completely equipped for the slave trade. When the *Lyra* towed the slaver into Zanzibar it created a sensation since it was the first time a clipper had actually been captured and brought into the harbour.[62] The seizure strengthened Rigby's hand as did the slightly later capture of another clipper at Lamu. This slaver, the *Formosa Estrella*, was part of the slaving network of Buena Ventura Mass, a slave trader Rigby had been trying to thwart for months. Again it was Oldfield that the consul looked to for assistance. The *Lyra* found the clipper and forced it to Lamu where it was captured by the sultan's officer there.[63] Throughout the early 1860s, Oldfield proved a constant thorn in the side of the Zanzibar slave traders. He relinquished command of the *Lyra* in August 1861 but did not leave the slave trade campaign. Instead, he transferred to the *Ariel* and commanded that ship for over a year off the East African coast. During his full tour on the coast, Oldfield consistently maintained good relations with the consul and was even named godfather of the consul's daughter.[64] In view of future developments at Zanzibar, Oldfield's ability to get on with the consul was not the least of his many accomplishments. The amicable tone which marked the relationship between Oldfield and Rigby did not apply to relations between the consul and some of the other officers on the station.

Even more important, however, was the fact that Oldfield was able to make his ship's presence felt by the slave traders. It is important to remember the limitations imposed on the Cape Station. During the period from 1858 to 1862, ships on station varied in number from a high of eight to a low of four. Even when the station books carried eight vessels, however, the total included the stationary coal depot at the Cape, the flagship and a tender to the flagship. Consequently, the commitment to the slave trade campaign frequently consisted of only one vessel and never

exceeded three.[65] Thus, if the navy were to make any impact in
suppressing the slave trade, protecting British strategic interests or
guarding trade routes, the ships that were sent to the east coast of
Africa had to be as effective as possible. Oldfield showed a way —
aggressive prosecution of the slavers at the point of debarkation
and maximum use of detached boats — which offered hope of
reducing the traffic in slaves with the slender resources available.
Given the government's decision to mount a continuing naval
attack on the traffic and the limitation of ships available for that
service, Oldfield's approach set the pattern for the squadron in the
early years of its attack on the Arab slave trade.

Notes

1. Graham, Gerald S., *Great Britain in the Indian Ocean* (Oxford, 1967),
pp. 1–23 and 73–109; and Nicholls, G. S., *The Swahili Coast* (London,
1971), pp. 96, 134–8 and 154–6. Graham provides an excellent analysis
of British activity in the area during the first half of the nineteenth century
and Nicholls gives good detailed background on the East African littoral.

2. Nicholls, pp. 74–96 and 324–75; Graham, pp. 203–8; Coupland,
R., *The Exploitation of East Africa, 1856–1890* (London, 1939, reprinted
1968), pp. 76–81; and Bennett, Norman, R., 'Americans in Zanzibar
1825–1845', *Essex Institute Historical Collections*, XCV, 1959, pp. 239–62.
For a detailed analysis of the economic development of the region, see
Sheriff, Abdul, 'The Rise of a Commercial Empire: An Aspect of the
Economic History of Zanzibar, 1770–1873', Ph.D., London, 1971.

3. For a general assessment of the early state of the trade, see Nicholls,
pp. 202–7. See also below, page 28, fn 46.

4. See pages 17–18.

5. Jackson Haight, Mabel, *European Powers and South-East Africa*
(London, 1967, first published 1942), p. 109.

6. Graham, p. 169.

7. For details of the actions resulting from the British cooperation with
the sultan see Belgrave, Sir Charles, *The Pirate Coast* (London, 1966),
pp. 33–7,135–42 and 147–9; Graham, pp. 248–51; Low, Charles R.,
History of the Indian Navy (London, 1877), vol. II, pp. 330–1; Kelly, J. B.,
Britain and the Persian Gulf (Oxford, 1968), pp. 141–66; and Nicholls,
pp. 116 and 145–6. Low's work was also serialised in the *United Services
Magazine* in 1877. Kelly's book is encyclopaedic concerning activities in the
Persian Gulf.

8. Details of negotiation, specific aspects of the treaty and general background are in Graham, pp. 196–210 and Kelly, pp. 411–51. The
Moresby Treaty was reconfirmed in negotiations between Said and
Captain Robert Cogan in May 1839. The government had hoped that
slave trade provisions could be extended but, in the end, the only
significant modifications were extension of right of search to ships of the

Indian Navy and tightening of boundaries so that Pussien became the most northerly legal terminus for the slave dhows.

9. COO/3/C Nelson to Lieutenant Owen, 2 October 1801.

10. ADM 1/2269 Captain Owen to Acting-Lieutenant Charles Browne, 10 May 1823.

11. Ibid., Captain Owen to Admiralty (J. Croker) number 30, 6 June 1823.

12. Jackson Haight, p. 176.

13. ADD 33837, f. 20 'Description of the Coast of Africa & c., *Leven* and *Barracouta*' Captain Owen; and ADM 1/2269 Captain Owen to Admiralty (J. Croker) number 25, 14 April 1823; and Owen, William F., *Narrative of Voyages to Explore the Shores of Africa, Arabia, and Madagascar* (London, 1833), vol. I, p. 151.

14. ADM 1/2269, Captain Owen to Admiralty (J. Croker) 12 May 1823.

15. COO/3A summary of service, William FitzWilliam Owen.

16. ADM 1/2269, Captain Owen to Admiralty (J. Croker) number 58, 9 October 1823; and COO/3A. Several documents appearing in ADM 1/2289 are repeated in COO/3A.

17. ADM 1/2269, certificate left with King Kapell and His Chiefs by their request Captain Owen, 9 March 1823; and Duffy, J. E. *Portuguese Africa* (Cambridge, Mass., 1959), pp. 205 – 6.

18. ADM 1/2269, Captain Owen to Admiralty (J. Croker) 8 March 1824; Gray, Sir John, *History of Zanzibar* (London, 1962), pp. 116 – 22; and Nicholls, pp. 139 – 40.

19. Nicholls, pp. 48 – 9.

20. Gray, Sir John, *The British in Mombasa 1824 – 1826* (London, 1957), pp. 16 – 18; Freeman-Grenville, G. S. P., 'The Coast, 1498 – 1840', chapter V in *History of East Africa* ed. by Roland Oliver and Gervase Mathew, (Oxford, 1963), vol. I, pp. 158 – 60; Nicholls, pp. 48 – 9; Berg, F. J., 'The Swahili Community of Mombasa, 1500 – 1900', in *Journal of African History*, ix, I, (1968), p. 56. Sir John Gray's book, volume I of the *Transactions of the Kenya History Society*, provides a useful synthesis of available information concerning the Owen protectorate.

21. Gray, pp. 21 – 2.

22. ADM 1/2269, Captain Owen to Admiralty (J. Croker) 8 March 1824.

23. Gray, pp. 59 – 68, 103, and 161 – 5; and Graham, pp. 194 – 6; and ADM 52/3940, Lieutenant Emery's journal.

24. Nicholls, pp. 165 – 71; and Jackson Haight, pp. 250 – 3.

25. For a copy of the treaty, see ADM 123/23, pp. 45 – 9, enclosure in Hammerton to Rear-Admiral Dacres, 9 April 1846.

26. Treaties in force with other European nations resulted from the attack on the West African slave trade. Lists of nations with which such arrangements existed can be found in the various editions of the *Instructions for the Guidance of Officers employed in Suppression of the Slave Trade.* These instructions were much maligned on the grounds that they, like the treaties, were designed for West African operations.

27. Nicholls, pp. 174 – 80.

28. ADM8/126, List Books, Cape of Good Hope Station; and Lloyd,

Christopher, *The Navy and the Slave Trade* (London, 1949, reprinted in 1968), pp. 285 – 6.

29. ADM 8/126 – 139, List Books, 1845 – 1860; Graham, 455 – 9; Lloyd, 279 – 84; Marder, Arthur J., *British Naval Policy 1880 – 1905* (London, 1941), pp. 66 – 85; and ADM 1/6138, Report and notes, E. J. Reed, submitted 3 February 1869.

30. ADM 123/170, pp. 104 – 5, Rear-Admiral Dacres to Admiralty, number 118, 6 July 1846.

31. ADM 50/283, Journal of Rear-Admiral Grey, 23 May to 31 December 1857, various entries.

32. Bartlett, C. J., *Great Britain and Sea Power 1815 – 1870* (Oxford, 1963), pp. 1 – 35 and 129 – 72; Sainty, J. C., *Admiralty Officials 1660 – 1870* (London, 1975), especially pages 1 – 17; Vesey Hamilton, Admiral Sir R., *Naval Administration* (London, 1896), pp. 20 – 40 and 55 – 62; and Murray, Sir O., 'The Admiralty', in *Mariner's Mirror*, 23, 1937, pp. 1 – 35.

33. ADM 123/179, Rear-Admiral Grey to Admiralty, extract of copy, number 9, 11 February 1858.

34. FO 84/1100, pp. 108 – 24, Commander Oldfield, to Rear-Admiral Grey, 8 July 1859; and Low, p. 332.

35. FO 54/17, Lieutenant Berkely to Rear-Admiral Grey, 10 January 1860. Rigby took up the appointment in 1858; Hammerton had died in July 1857.

36. Ibid., Rigby to Rear-Admiral Grey, 20 October 1859; and Low, vol. II, pp. 333 – 5. For Coupland's account of the episode see Coupland, pp. 23 – 6.

37. *The Times*, 9 January 1860.

38. FO 54/17, Rigby to Lieutenant Berkely 20 October 1859, misdated as 1860.

39. Livingstone, David, *Last Journals* (Edinburgh, 1874), vol. II, p. 212.

40. Burton, Richard, *Lake Regions of Africa* (London, 1860), vol. I, p. 99, and vol. II, pp. 368 and 377.

41. R/15/1/17, Jones to Secretary to the Government, Bombay, number 404, 17 November 1858.

42. Ibid., Secretary to the Government, Bombay to Jones, 15 January 1859. The disestablishment of the Indian Navy in 1863 eliminated that service from the developing naval attack on the slave trade.

43. For the impact of the 'Canning Award' growing out of the arbitration on later developments in the region, see pages, 60 – 1.

44. FO 84/1120, pp. 215 – 42 and ADM 123/178, Coghlan to Secretary to the Government, Bombay, number 14 (secret), 1 November 1860.

45. FO 54/17; Rigby to Principal Secretary of State for India, number 3, 1 May 1860. This correspondence also appears in P.P. (Accounts and Papers, 31) 1861, vol. LXIV. Much routine correspondence on the slave trade was printed in the Parliamentary Papers, but for simplicity's sake these printed versions will not be cited below. As with much of the consular material copies of this report were sent both to London and to Bombay. The letter can also be found in L/P&S/9/37. In an effort to streamline citation below, Foreign Office copies will be cited.

46. FO 84/1146, pp. 282–91 and ADM 123/178, Rigby to Secretary to the Government, Bombay, number 23, 14 May 1861. The question of the total numbers of slaves involved in the East African trade is an interesting but difficult one. Even before Curtin's work on the census of the West African trade, there had been some efforts at revision of the numerical estimates for the east. The only reliable statistical information available consists of returns from the Zanzibar Custom House which were regularly sent to London in the consular reports. For the additional numbers smuggled north, estimates from observers on the scene, especially the British consul, must be used since no records existed for the clandestine traffic. It seems clear that export figures from Zanzibar as high as Coghlan's 30,000 were highly exaggerated and at least one historian (see Sheriff, below) argues that both consular and naval officials were consciously exaggerating numbers as an exercise in self-justification. Nevertheless, the indication from Custom House returns and local observers is that actual annual figures at this time were approximately 20,000 per annum imported into the Zanzibar slave markets with about half that number being shipped to the northern markets. For a discussion of the question, see Nicholls, pp. 202–7. Two interesting unpublished theses are useful in this connection: Sheriff, Abdul, 'The Rise of a Commercial Empire: An Aspect of the Economic History of Zanzibar 1770–1873'; Ph.D., London, April 1971; and Glyn-Jones, Eleanor, 'Britain and the End of Slavery in East Africa', B. Litt., Oxford, Dec. 1956. Also of some interest is Bennett, Norman, 'The East African Slave Trade', chapter XIII, in *Emerging Themes of African History* ed. by T. O. Ranger (London, 1968), pp. 141–6.

47. FO 54/18, memo, W. H. Wylde, 22 January 1861. For an interesting brief account of the organisation of the Foreign Office during this period see Jones, Ray, *The Nineteenth Century Foreign Office* (London, 1972).

48. FO 84/1146, memo, Palmerston, 12 February 1861. Palmerston had, of course, long been a key figure in slave trade suppression and his policy toward East Africa was not always marked by confusion. For the best analysis available see Gavin, R. J., 'Palmerston's Policy Towards East and West Africa 1830–1865', Ph.D., Cambridge, 1959.

49. Anstey, Roger T., 'Capitalism and Slavery: a Critique', in *Economic History Review*, series 2, 21, 1968, p. 320. For the best account of the influence of the anti-slavery societies at this time, see Temperley, Howard, *British Anti-Slavery 1833–1870* (London, 1972).

50. ADM 123/178, Coghlan to Secretary to the Government, Bombay, 10 December 1860, see also PRO 30 22/116, Earl Russell to Sir Henry Bulwer, 16 July 1859; Coupland, p. 21; and Marder, p. 67.

51. Fears over a large French storehouse, purportedly planned as a hospital for seamen, was the immediate reason for the declaration. See Kelly, pp. 550–1; and Coupland, pp. 34–6.

52. ADM 123/178, Foreign Office (Wodehouse) to Admiralty, 2 February 1860.

53. ADM 1/5745, Admiralty to Foreign Office, 9 March 1860; and Foreign Office to Admiralty, 21 March 1860.

54. ADM 123/24, Rigby to Secretary to the Government, Bombay, 28 March 1860. At times, the scope of the northern markets extended even to

India. See Banji, D. R., *Slavery in British India* (Bombay. 1939), pp. 73–6 and 298–9.

55. ADM 123/178, Rigby to Rear-Admiral Walker, 9 April 1861.

56. L/P&S/5/506, Rigby to Secretary to the Government, Bombay, number 19, 18 April 1861; and ADM 123/178, Commander Oldfield to Captain Crawford, number 3, 23 March 1861.

57. L/P&S/5/506, ibid., ADM 123/178, Oldfield to Crawford, 5 April 1861.

58. L/P&S/5/506, ibid., ADM 123/178, Commander Oldfield to Rigby, 10 April 1861.

59. Ibid., and Kelly pp. 616–8.

60. Ibid.

61. L/P&S/5/506, ibid., and ADM 123/178, Rigby to Rear-Admiral Walker, 9 April 1861; and ADM 123/179, Commander Oldfield, regular report, 30 June 1861.

62. L/P&S/9/37, Rigby to Secretary of State for India, number 5, 28 August 1860.

63. L/P&S/5/506, Rigby to Secretary to the Government, Bombay, numbers 44 and 79, 27 August and 26 November 1860. The forward policy met with approval, see Resolution of the Honourable Board, 25 February 1861.

64. Russell, C. E. (Rigby's daughter), *General Rigby, Zanzibar and the Slave Trade* (London, 1935), p. 91n.

65. ADM 125/139, List Books, Cape of Good Hope Station, 1845–1860.

2

The Boat Patrols

By the beginning of 1862, at least two points were already clear concerning the naval response to the slave trade from Zanzibar. One was that only aggressive action by the captains commanding cruisers would result in significant inroads against the trade. Second, and perhaps equally important, was that the necessity for forceful action by naval commanders produced an atmosphere in which conflict might develop with the consul at Zanzibar and the resulting tension could weaken the structure of British control in the region. The man-on-the-spot found that questions requiring immediate action demanded quick decisions without time for prior consultation with London or Bombay and a lack of clarity in treaties and general instructions made matters worse. In the early 1860s, the consul at Zanzibar was clearly a man-on-the-spot with wide responsibility and authority. As Wylde lamented, 'I should be very glad if any means could be found of communicating regularly with our Agent at Zanzibar'. He explained that the government depended on native vessels sailing to Aden for dispatches from Zanzibar and the system was erratic at best. As Wylde put it:

> It has happened more than once that we have received intelligence of a late date from our consul at Zanzibar which required acting upon, but which it was hardly possible to act upon in consequence of the previous dispatches not having been received.[1]

Inevitably the isolated consul had wide scope for independent action which forced him to use his initiative. Just as clearly, however, the senior navy officer on the East Coast of Africa was a man-on-the-spot in his own right and the fact is crucial in the historical development of the region. Responsible at times for several ships and at least for the operation of his own ship and a host of detached boats, the navy commander was also far from other links in his chain of command. He was forced to take independent decisions without any possibility of consultation with his station commander or the Admiralty. Issues which could produce months of consultation between the Foreign Office, Bombay authorities, the Admiralty and the Law Officers, were regularly faced and settled quickly by the men-on-the-spot. For example, a particularly sensitive area was justification for boarding a vessel to verify its nationality. The question was especially difficult if the vessel was flying a French or American flag. The Law Officers counselled the Foreign Office that visitation should only be made if there were a strong presumption that colours were being misused. In the Admiralty's view, the obvious question was upon what the presumption was to be based. As Clerk Thomas Wolley minuted, under the Law Officers' interpretation the boarding officer 'would in reality be required to be previously in possession of all the information which it is the express object of the visitation to obtain'.[2] While the problem was being debated in London, however, it was being faced and aggressively met by boarding officers on the coast. When boardings produced local complaint, the consul found himself directly involved and obliged to adopt the legalistic Foreign Office response to any criticism. As a consequence, the situation was rife with potential problems. The structure of East Coast operations, relying on the consul and senior navy officer on the scene, placed frequently strong-willed men face-to-face with overlapping jurisdiction. Nor did the structure provide any clearly defined precedence to simplify the situation. The consul saw himself as the representative of government and principal instrument of policy in the region while the senior navy officer was equally adamant that he was solely responsible for the operation of his ship, and the other vessels under his command, in enforcing the slave trade treaties. In a real sense both were right and only strong government control could separate their spheres of responsibilities — and that control was not forthcoming. Of course, similar goals frequently produced concerted action and complementary personalities sometimes brought about a rapport such as that between Oldfield and Rigby. Conflicting personalities on the other hand, sometimes brought about open hostility which could have serious repercussions for the attack on the slave trade.[3]

It was certainly hostility which typified relations between Rigby and the second major cruiser captain on the station during the early 1860s. Captain Richard Crawford commanded the *Sidon*, a powerful paddle steamer classed as a fifth-rate man-of-war. Crawford outranked Oldfield and was at times senior officer on the East Coast of Africa, directly responsible to the commander-in-chief at the Cape. It is safe to say that he felt his seniority when dealing with Rigby, who while holding the civil post of consul also held an army rank inferior to a navy captain. Rigby was not willing to play a subordinate role and became convinced that Crawford's attitude was an intolerable affront to his dignity. Nor did the issue stop at Zanzibar. Rigby summarised complaints about Crawford in reports which led to government investigation and an additional confrontation between the two in London. These complaints were in a sense the tip of the iceberg since the personality conflict between the men had been festering for months with Crawford asserting his military seniority and Rigby responding with wounded dignity.

The consul's charges which were investigated first by the Foreign Office and then by the Admiralty centred on the capture of a dhow, the *Bechair*, by the *Sidon* and a visit to the sultan by Crawford. On the question of the dhow, nationality and the problem of colours was the major issue. Rigby accused his rival of having seized a vessel which was flying the Turkish flag and then illegally destroying it. He then suggested that Crawford had lied to him by reporting the vessel to have been under the Zanzibar flag and had then compounded the offence by releasing the crew in town against the consul's specific request. As if that weren't enough, Rigby went on to report that the captain had visited the sultan in an 'irregular manner' without informing the consul prior to the visit, had accepted gifts from the sultan contrary to Admiralty orders, and had sent an insulting verbal message to the consul. The accusations were considered serious enough to prompt investigation and plans were made to set up a court of inquiry. However, Crawford counter-attacked by accusing Rigby of defamation and demanding that the issue be pursued by a court martial to remove the stain from his character. By the time of the court, early 1862, both Crawford and Rigby were in England and in February the Foreign Office ordered Rigby to go to Portsmouth 'to substantiate the charges brought by you against Captain Crawford'.[4]

The court martial was held on board *Victory* in Portsmouth harbour from 24 to 26 February 1862 with Rear-Admiral George Grey as president. The court provided a forum for invective as the two men-on-the-spot challenged one another's use of the freedom which distance, lack of communication, and the structure of East Coast organisation had allowed them to exercise at Zanzibar. Rigby reiterated the charges which he had made against Crawford. For his part, Crawford denied all the charges and launched an attack on Rigby. He accused Rigby of having spared no pains 'to rake up into one huge heap' all the gossip which could have tarnished his character. Asserting that he had always given any consul the respect due, Crawford then turned the tables by suggesting that with the sole exception of Rigby he had always received in return 'the respect which is due to an officer senior in rank to themselves'.[5] The captain was naturally supported by officers and men from the *Sidon*. After the verbal bombast both men's reputations depended on the verdict of the court and neither was completely satisfied by the results. Rigby's most serious accusations were rejected out of hand. Dismissed were the charges of illegally seizing a vessel under the Turkish flag and of falsely reporting that the vessel had been a Zanzibar dhow. Also rejected was Rigby's personal point of honour — that Crawford had sent him an insulting message. The court found that Arab crewmen had been landed in opposition to the consul's request 'but not in such number as to cause danger or disturbance'. Crawford was found to have visited the sultan in an irregular manner but was at least partially exonerated by the court's observation that the captain had considered the visit a private one. If Crawford won on points, however, Rigby did manage partially to carry one charge which kept the captain from receiving a clear vote of confidence. It was found that he had in fact accepted gifts from the sultan contrary to recently issued Admiralty orders. While the court ruled that the gifts 'were of inconsiderable value' it did mildly criticise the captain in passing. On this point, Crawford was 'reprimanded and admonished to be more discreet in future'.[6]

While the results were not what either might have wished, the verdict was certainly more unwelcome to Rigby than to Crawford. The impact of the result for Rigby was underlined by the review of the proceedings by the Law Officers. They suggested that Crawford 'did not wilfully disregard any representations made to him at the time, either by Lieutenant-Colonel Rigby or by any other person, to which it was his duty under the circumstances, to pay attention.' In addressing the specific points of conflict between the two, the Law Officers concluded that the court martial 'exonerates Captain Crawford, upon all material points, from the charges made against him'.[7] Rigby felt especially upset by the results. In his report to Earl Russell, the Foreign Secretary, he complained that there were obviously no witnesses in England from the dhow and that he was villified by being the only witness for the prosecution. The position 'has been a source of great anxiety and annoyance to me, returning to this country in ill health after an absence of many years,' he complained while trusting that Russell would exonerate him from having had any feeling in the case 'save that of public duty'.[8] Nor did the episode fail to rankle with the passage of time. Some ten years later, in testimony before a select committee on the slave trade, latent antipathy for Crawford and his ship crept into Rigby's testimony. 'There was the *Sidon*, an old tub, that any dhow on the coast could beat,' he recalled.[9]

On the surface the conflict between Rigby and Crawford would appear to be a ludicrous footnote to the navy's East African operations. In the end, neither could fully claim victory and the impact of the row on anti-slave trade policy was practically nil. Rigby and Crawford had shown that they could not get along and little else. In the broader sense, however, this conflict in the early 1860s set the tone for a series of mini wars between the consul and the senior navy officials which continued to flare up periodically. The semi-independent consul, in exercising his man-on-the-spot prerogatives, would frequently come into conflict with the similarly placed navy officer trying to exercise the same sort of prerogatives in the same domain.

It did not take long for a new rift to develop. Rigby's replacement at Zanzibar was Colonel R. L. Playfair, appointed in 1863, who was quick to take the navy to task. In an early report, while lauding Commander William Chapman who had succeeded Old-field in command of the *Ariel*, he cited 'a series of arbitrary acts' by cruisers against legal traders which he claimed to have generated 'a feeling of the most bitter animosity against the English'.[10] While the specific attacks against Crawford had been investigated, such general accusations provoked a strong response from the Admiralty. In correspondence with the Foreign Office, W. G. Romaine insisted that Russell must be aware of the difficulties facing the naval officers and suggested that the situation on the East Coast would be better met if the consul began supporting

naval personnel instead of making 'reports to his superiors calculated to convey a most erroneous and unfavourable impression of
their conduct'.[11] Coming as it did on the heels of the Crawford-
Rigby affair, this Admiralty criticism found the Foreign Office
unwilling to become involved in any further squabbles between
captains and consuls. 'Lord Russell did not give entire credence to
the statements contained in that officer's report,' the Admiralty
was assured.[12]

Political criticisms from the Foreign Office posed a problem for
naval operations. Another arose from friction with the Treasury.
The system of tonnage bounties of £4-4s-0d or of £1-10s-0d
coupled with £5 slave bounties was not insignificant to crewmen of
the anti-slavery cruisers.[13] A source of difficulty arose from the fact
that the shapes of the dhows, odd by European standards,
prompted the Treasury consistently to reject measurements and
down-grade bounty claims. The treasury adopted the policy of
routinely deducting 10 per cent on any bounty claim from the East
Coast.[14] Treasury records show, for example, that a 70-ton dhow
claimed by *Ariel* in 1865 was computed on the basis of 63 tons
instead. Four days later a second capture by that ship, put at 45
tons by the captors, was computed at 41 tons by the Treasury.[15]
Navy officers repeatedly argued that the rules for measurement,
like their other instructions, had been written for the West African
slave trade with its European vessels and had no application to the
dhows of the East Coast at all. Their complaints failed to bring
changes and just as consular-naval conflicts became standard bill
of fare, difficulties with the Treasury also characterised the anti-
slave trade campaign for years to come. As will be seen, the issue
continued to re-emerge and a feeling of mistrust on the question
among navymen produced somewhat unsavoury counter measures
by some of them.

In general, however, Treasury procedures and even the conflicts
between captains and the consul seemed remote indeed to the men
charged with the day by day execution of the slave trade patrol.
Far more pressing problems for the officers and men on the station
were wind, weather and tired ships coupled with a determined
opposition. While Rigby's recollections of the *Sidon* reflected
residual hard feeling for her captain, there was certainly an
element of truth in the assertion that the ships charged with slave
trade duties had passed their period of peak efficiency. A case in
point was the *Gorgon*, a paddle wheel steam sloop which came to
the station under Commander Bedford Pim and remained off the

coast under Commander John Wilson. The clerk of the ship, W. Cope Devereux, wrote an account of the vessel's activities in which he recorded some of her shortcomings. For example, he described the *Gorgon* fighting the strong current off the coast in which, 'at noon we find ourselves retrograding, actually 100 miles farther from our port'.[16] In her favour, although slow the *Gorgon* was at least available. When the *Wasp* was disabled in a grounding incident in 1861 and had to be escorted to Bombay for repairs, Rear-Admiral Baldwin Walker, commander-in-chief at the Cape, was forced to turn to the Admiralty for help. 'I beg to observe that the squadron on the East Coast of Africa is reduced to three ships,' he wrote and then pointed out that two of those had already been ordered home.[17] At the end of Walker's tenure in 1864, the Admiralty merged the Cape with the East Indies command in hopes of improving the situation.[18] However, the problem of a shortage of ships, which generally fluctuated between seven and twelve vessels for the vast combined station, remained intense. During the first year of the new plan, Rear-Admiral George St Vincent King had overall command of the station but delegated slave trade matters to the senior officer at the Cape, Commodore Cockburn. The entire strength of the station, which extended now from the eastern edge of the Indian Ocean all the way to the Cape of Good Hope, was nine vessels. The total included three small sloops and two even smaller gun vessels as well as the stationary depot ship at the Cape. During the next year, the station was effectively divided into two separate commands once more with Commodore Charles Hillyar taking over the East Indies portion of the station. Since the respective strengths showed the East Indies station with seven ships while the Cape had only three, Hillyar took over responsibility for the slave trade campaign and operations off Zanzibar continued to be the concern of the East Indies station from this time.[19] This juggling of responsibility failed to produce any increase in ships available for the East Coast of Africa and the shortage of vessels continued to plague operations off Zanzibar.

Because there were so few ships available and the length of coastline to be patrolled was immense, the navy was forced to continue dispatching the ship's boats to patrol for dhows. For 30 years, the navy's technique off the coast was to send a handful of men away in small, usually open, boats to confront the slave traders. As one incredulous junior officer wrote, 'To use ships' boats for open sea work as if they were ships is a practice surely never heard of in any other Navy, one that must be experienced to be realized.'[20] A gunner with considerable boat cruising experience lamented the discomfort of the exposure associated with up to six weeks in a detached boat and stressed that 'the danger also of cruising in so small a boat touches the maximum.'[21] A typical action found boats from the *Gorgon* detached when the gig crew saw several dhows on the horizon. As the wind fell off, the men resorted to oars and after pulling for three hours overhauled one of the suspected slavers. The crew of the becalmed dhow appeared friendly until the gig closed to within about a boat length whereupon they suddenly opened fire. The gig crew hauled off and began to exchange fire before withdrawing to seek assistance. Fortunately a second boat from the ship was not far away and it too was pressed into the fray. The second was one of the *Gorgon*'s larger boats which was equipped with a small paddle wheel engine. As the small steamer closed on the dhow, however, it was found to have another common characteristic with the mother ship — lack of speed. A sudden increase in the wind quickly put the offending dhow out of range. The boats' only hope then was to cut off a second dhow which had fallen somewhat further behind. Giving up on their engine, the men made sail and finally resorted to the oars in managing to come alongside the dhow. The gig crew then boarded and captured the dhow while the larger boat stood off and covered their actions. In the end, it had been a dangerous day-long chase to capture an empty dhow.[22]

The dangers of boat cruising went beyond such occasional volleys of musket fire from a dhow trying to evade capture. Storms took their toll as did the strain of constant patrolling. The log of the *Ariel*, for example, shows that in January 1863 her pinnace, which had been detached to seek slavers, was sunk in a gale. The coxswain, James Whittington, was drowned. Nevertheless, the boat patrols continued and on 16 April, when two gigs returned after a patrol on which they had boarded nine dhows only to find that all were legal traders, one of the boats was so leaky that the carpenter's mate could not repair it.[23] While the weather conditions preyed on the boats, they also had their effect on the men. Most commanders tried hard to maintain the health of their crews. For example, Lieutenant J. G. McHardy commanding the *Penguin* carefully prescribed routine in his standing orders to officers on detached boat service. Every man was to be seen to take a dose of quinine every day, he stressed. Daily washing was required, as was tea both morning and evening since McHardy subscribed to the theory that 'it is most essential to the health of Englishmen that they should have a warm beverage morning and evening'.[24] Despite such precautions, the climate and the routine combined to deplete crews. A typical month in 1863 found the *Ariel* with an average of a dozen on the sick list out of a total complement of 90.[25] That was an improvement over the *Lyra* two years before when in a similar month that 100-man ship averaged 20 on the sick list every day and at times had the list soar to over one-third unfit for duty.[26] The situation was obviously a far from happy one as was stressed by Commodore Frederick Montressor in 1865. Citing conflicts with well-manned and armed dhows as well as the debilitating weather conditions, he advised the Admiralty that 'if it were possible to avoid it, officers and seamen should not be exposed to such fearful odds as they have been'.[27] Such warnings notwithstanding, global requirements meant it was impossible to improve the odds and the system continued largely unchanged.

The worst single disaster in the early years of independent boat cruising came in late October 1862. Lieutenant McHardy of the *Penguin* dispatched his boats to cruise the coast north of Zanzibar. When two of the boats which had been cruising together failed to rendezvous, the *Penguin* steamed north hoping to locate them. On the way the ship met the *Semiramis* with Consul Playfair onboard. Rumours of a massacre on the Somali coast had filtered into Aden and the ship had been sent to investigate the report after taking the consul on board. Both ships proceeded to the scene, a village called Broeda, where bloodstained articles of naval clothing confirmed the loss of both boats with all hands. It seems likely that a dispute about payment for water and fresh provisions caused the Somalis to attack and kill the seamen. One thing is clear and that is that the young officer in charge of the two vessels, Sub-Lieutenant John Fountaine, was inexperienced; he had been commissioned less than a year before. Nevertheless, he had been dispatched to an unknown coast with two boats under his command and 16 men had died as a result.[28]

On confirming the loss of the crews, Playfair and the naval officers agreed that retribution was necessary. As Playfair explained in his report of the incident, prompt action was required so that when people on the coast heard of the massacre they would hear of the retaliatory stroke at the same time. Playfair asserted his man-on-the-spot position. 'There is no time for reference to any superior authority, the example must be made now if at all while the tragedy is yet in men's minds,' he contended. Nor was there any opposition from the naval authorities who agreed that swift and severe action was required. Several houses were burned. They then imposed a series of demands on the local chieftain. He was forced to apologise publicly for the act, surrender all arms on hand, and most important, execute those guilty of the killings in sight of the two ships. Failure to comply, he was warned, would result in the complete destruction of the town. Faced with no real choice in the matter, the chieftain adhered as far as he could. He told Playfair that it was only possible to deliver eight of the 15 men he said were involved. He would execute more if necessary but warned that they would be people who had not been involved in the attack. A compromise was accepted as a temporary expedient. The eight, including a chief elder of a clan, were decapitated on the beach and the Somali leader was given 30 days after which the ships would return and a dozen more would have to be executed. The twelve demanded seemed a minimal number to McHardy who reasoned that 'to believe that fifteen Englishmen armed as these boats crew were could have ever been murdered by anything like an equal number of Somalis is out of the question'.[29] Nevertheless it is likely that the second wave of victims were simply people deemed expedient to meet the arbitrary total demanded. Nor was the fact lost on the more dispassionate observers in the squadron. Typical of these was Devereux who wrote that the *Penguin* had finally filled her maw and went on to suggest, 'fifteen more Somalis have been given up to appease her; their heads have been struck off, and justice cries "enough!" ' Arguing that the first eight executed should have been sufficient for the sake of example, he continued that the last group was comprised of poor friendless wretches 'wholly innocent of the horrid crime for which they have suffered'.[30]

Clearly the response to the massacre of the *Penguin*'s boat crews seemed unnecessarily harsh even to some naval observers. It should be remembered, however, that the demands of boat cruising sometimes prompted such sharp reactions — reactions which would have appalled Victorian sensibilities had they been common knowledge. Jokingly discussing the activities of the boats of the *Gorgon* under the boatswain, Devereux suggested, 'The boatswain was indeed suppressing the slave trade with a vengeance, blazing away grape and canister on the slightest provocation; burning and sinking, killing and wounding, illegally capturing, and such unboatswain-like conduct.'[31] There was enough truth in the description to bring cautions from London against 'any arbitrary acts on the part of Commanders of British cruisers'.[32] One charge which particularly concerned the Foreign Office was that of looting on board detained dhows. While the official navy position was that there was none, Devereux reported that it was common practice which he feared could lead to dire consequences. He suggested that as an officer was dealing with the mechanics of a capture, more than a few of his men would slip below to pounce on anything of value they could find. Nor was the looting particularly surprising. 'Having undergone all the dangers and vicissitudes of boat-work, he (the seaman) thinks he should be allowed to keep all loot, whether money or jewelry, &c., collected during the cruise — honestly or dishonestly,' Devereux explained. As a consequence routine searches by the ship's police became a regular ritual on the return of the boats. The clerk reported that 'Jack rolls forward with his arms full of spoil, growling like a great bear.'[33] Nor were the judicial procedures associated with capture likely to correct any discrepancies. During the early years of the patrol, there was no vice-admiralty court in Zanzibar and adjudication of captures generally waited until the vessel returned to the Cape. According to Devereux the judges there were content not to ask 'impertinent questions' and routinely condemned the long lists of captures. Not only that, he found the lawyers at the Cape most accomplished in reversing the Treasury's tendency of paying smaller bounties by their ability to 'transform the most trifling deeds into acts of humanity, and the slave-coffin dhows into huge ships'.[34] A reconstruction of the court helps underline some of the less legalistic aspects of the slave-trade adjudications:

> The best act of the farce was the swearing in of the 'Gorgons', those furies of the Mozambique, whose ideal dress is made up of red worsted caps, huge belts, and larger buckles, high-topped boots and murderous pistols, and with ferocious countenance, not at all like the meek little fellows here assembled. We are all at a stand-still for the Sacred Book — the learned lawyer looks on complacently — our proctor has failed to discover one; but at last, with a very grave face says, 'Ah! here is a "Nautical Bible"' (which really was a Walker's Dictionary), on which we were all sworn accordingly.[35]

Even if the naval crews sometimes seemed more than slightly piratical, it must be remembered that their foes on the African coast were known for amorality in pursuit of a trade cruel by definition. Poorly provisioned and overcrowded dhows, unable to tack and totally dependent on the prevailing winds and currents, were death traps for thousands of the native inhabitants of the African interior. Slaves arriving on the short voyage to Zanzibar were frequently reported to be in the final stages of starvation on landing.[36] The dhow masters or *nakodas* frequently had little regard for their cargoes and conditions on the dhows were appalling. Rigby reported an 1861 capture by the *Lyra* in which a dhow with 105 female slaves was boarded not far from the harbour of Zanzibar. The stench was said to be so great that every man who boarded the vessel was straightaway taken violently ill. The surgeon ordered the immediate destruction of the dhow and the consul suggested that 'had this vessel not been captured in all probability not one slave would have survived the voyage to Arabia.'[37] The problems were not confined to the seaborne traffic. It was suggested that if one in three slaves survived the overland route to the coast, a caravan would be financially successful; some-times slavers failed to stay within that margin.[38] Of course, the slave traffickers frequently did not hesitate to attack boat crews in defence of their profits. The sailor's violent, and at times unscrupulous, tactics can be seen as a natural outgrowth of a confrontation with a violent and always unscrupulous traffic.

The difficulties on the station led to a series of experiments including attempts to establish local contacts so that native informers could help to determine dhow movements. One of the most successful innovations was borrowed from the old West Coast squadron. Ships in the west had profitably employed the native African seamen of the Kru coast and late in 1861 Rear-Admiral Walker approached the Admiralty to allow him to use 'Kroomen' on the Cape Station.[39] The idea received rapid approval and in January of the following year, authorisation was received for large ships to carry ten native seamen plus a head Krooman and a second head Krooman while the smaller ships were allowed six with two supervisors. From that time 'vessels ordered to the Cape of Good Hope will in future touch at Sierra Leone for the purpose of procuring Kroomen.'[40] Walker informed the fleet of the approval in his General Memo 24 of 1862[41] which must have caused a few raised eyebrows among the captains in the squadron. Kroomen had already been in service on the station without the blessing of London. In fact, 56 of the black seamen were serving on the station at the end of 1861 including a dozen on Oldfield's

Lyra.[42] The next year, with the Kroomen then authorised, there were immediate moves to exceed the allowance on the ships carrying them. The *Gorgon* had 15 but seemed conservative next to the flagship which boasted a total of 51. By 1863 every ship on the station carried Kroomen who numbered nearly 100 on the East Coast.[43] The quickness to capitalise on this source of manpower reflects the usefulness of the Kroomen; there was even consideration given to employing vessels officered as well as manned by these native African seamen during the early 1860s.[44] As will be seen, the service of the Kroomen earned them the continuing admiration of naval commanders on the East Coast.

Despite such experiments, however, the trade continued to thrive with the slavers pushing deep into the interior. Commander W. S. deKantzow found that examination of slaves taken off captured dhows always revealed variations on the same story. Local warfare in the interior was followed by forays of Arab traders who purchased the prisoners and marched them to the coast at Kilwa. They were then transported to Zanzibar where they were bought by the northern dhowmen.[45] Depositions taken from slaves captured by the flagship show the nature of the trade with its associated destruction of families; a 9-year-old girl named Chonsiko told the navy's interpreter that her whole family had been captured while they were fleeing from a local conflict. She was with her mother for as far as Zanzibar, but her mother had been sold and taken north some time before. She had already been owned by three different masters before being sold to the dhowmen. Another girl, named Amienha, had been stolen from her parents the year before. The 16-year-old had been married to another slave at Zanzibar but their owner had sold her while retaining her husband. The corruption of family bonds was underlined by the story of Ballideh who told how she and her two sisters had been sold to the slavers by their own brother.[46]

Given the problems confronting the naval squadron, it is not surprising that they were unable to stop the slavers. In fact, there is evidence that the trade might have increased during the early 1860s. Bounty payments rocketed between 1860 and 1865. Total slave trade expenditure estimates for 1860–1 amounted to £37,000. The next year it was necessary to increase the total to £50,000 and an 100 per cent increase in tonnage bounties within three years led to an outlay of £86,000 by 1863–4.[47] Estimates from the coast also indicated that within five years from 1862, exports from the southern slave markets increased. H. A. Churchill, who became consul in 1865, was so shaken by the extent of the trade that he actually welcomed hostilities by the warrior Maviti tribe, a Ngoni group, near the major slave port of Kilwa. The Maviti presence would be a blessing 'if it could only last, for it would effectually put a stop to the exportation of slaves from that place.' Churchill estimated that the exports from Kilwa during the 1862–3 season had been some 18,500 slaves while by 1866–7 the figure had risen to over 22,000. He also suggested that the slaves 'are so poorly fed on the way that they can scarcely carry their own weight when they reach Kilwa'.[48] In June of 1866, Livingstone complained to the Earl of Clarendon that 'Zanzibar is now, about the only spot in the world where from one to three hundred slaves are daily exposed for sale in the open market'. According to Livingstone, a British man-of-war should always be in the harbour of Zanzibar during the visitations of the northern Arabs. Citing conversations with navy officers, he argued that a depot should be established to receive captured slaves and thus allow the cruisers to remain on station for longer periods of time.[49]

In response to the obviously thriving trade the navy's procedure remained unchanged — a handful of ships dispatching boats to seek the slave dhows. At times the seamen were lucky. In May 1867 the *Penguin*, now commanded by Lieutenant E. Garforth, chased and boarded a large northern dhow which was found to be loaded with 216 slaves, mostly children.[50] Easy captures of packed dhows, however, were not the norm and even when the navy was fortunate enough to find a full dhow the results were sometimes disastrous. A typical manoeuvre of the dhow *nakodas* when they felt threatened was to sacrifice the dhow and usually a portion of the slaves by running aground. The theory was that this would protect them from capture while still allowing them to march the surviving slaves north overland. On 26 April 1866, the *Penguin* set out after a dhow and fired several shots in an effort to make the crew come to. When the dhow failed to lower its sail, Garforth felt certain that she was a slaver and ceased firing for the sake of the slaves onboard. However, he managed to close with the dhow which then made for the rocks through a heavy surf. By the time the ship's boat could be lowered to follow, the Arab crew had fled but the pounding surf made any attempt by the slavers to salvage the human cargo too dangerous. To their horror, the boat crew found that they, too, could not reach the dhow which was rapidly filling with water drowning the slaves. The boat officer decided that he could not risk coming in close to the dhow but several of the crewmen of the cutter recklessly dived in and swam through the surf to the dhow. In a remarkable display of courage, the sailors managed to bring 28 of the slaves back to the boat. But the dhow appeared to have had more then 200 slaves on board and most died in the pounding waves.[51]

Such losses had a demoralising effect on the cruiser force. So did the condition of its ships. Captain N. B. Bedingfeld, senior officer on the East Coast in 1866, stressed the problem of overworked ships. His own vessel, the *Wasp*, had weakened the squadron by running aground five years before. She had been repaired at Bombay and was still on the station. What was most disconcerting was that by the time Bedingfeld took command, she was in better condition than any other available cruiser. 'With three crippled vessels the *Wasp* being now the most efficient of the three I fear but little can be done to check the immense and I hear increasing trade in slaves', Bedingfeld lamented.[52] In the Foreign Office, Wylde felt that the ships had done good work off the coast despite their condition but recognised that if the slave trade was to be stopped more effective ships and a more organised system of operations would be required.[53] As obvious as that need was, broader strategic questions conspired to cause the exact reverse to happen. From three crippled ships the squadron soon went to no ships at all. Naval support of Sir Robert Napier's Abyssinian expedition of 1868 required all available vessels and the squadron was for all practical purposes withdrawn for the year. As the new commodore of the East Indies Station, Sir Leopold Heath, explained, the incursion into Abyssinia made it impossible for him to do anything significant about the trade during the peak season of 1868.[54]

By the time that the Abyssinian campaign interrupted steady prosecution of the slave trade, certain problems were painfully obvious. The lack of ships continued to make it impossible to stop the trade. In fact, the cruisers and their boats had only managed to make a dent in the trade which is hardly surprising given the difficulties involved and the lack of available resources. Treaty provisions caused additional difficulties since many slavers were able to carry their cargoes in compliance with the laws of Zanzibar. There was clearly no way to prove that a dhow putting out from Kilwa was not bound legally for Zanzibar rather than illegally for Arabia. As a result, suppression tended to be concentrated at Zanzibar where northward traffic could be monitored. Even then, equipment clauses, sometimes of questionable applicability, had to be employed in many cases and numbers of dhows were taken empty.

As a result, from 1860 until mid-1867, 166 dhows were captured but only slightly over 3,000 slaves were liberated. While the number is not altogether insignificant, it is obvious that the total represents a minute percentage of the numbers being exported from Zanzibar. If the navy had made inroads, it had hardly struck a crippling blow to the slave traffic. In assessing its impact, it is interesting to compare the effectiveness of individual ships assigned to the slave trade campaign. Typical was the *Gorgon* which during the period took 25 dhows with 121 slaves on board. After taking command of the *Ariel*, Chapman was credited with 14 slave dhows and 80 slaves and Crawford in the *Sidon* captured 23 dhows with cargoes of 264 slaves. Some ships were lucky enough to stop one of the northern traders with a dhow full of people bound for sale in the Arabian markets. A notable example was in December 1863 when Commander C. T. Jago's steam sloop *Rapid* captured a dhow packed with 198 slaves. Even more important than capture totals, however, was the fact that individual cruiser captains stamped their personalities on the campaign and in some cases significantly influenced the development of policy in the region. The period under review starts and ends with two such captains. There is no question which of the early slave trade captains had the greatest impact on the trade. Oldfield's decisive action against the Suri dhows in Zanzibar harbour was mirrored in a whole series of actions on a smaller scale. Oldfield energetically prosecuted the slavers in both the ships he commanded. From mid-1858 when he made his first capture in the *Lyra* to October 1862 when he was relieved of command of the *Ariel*, Oldfield was credited with capturing 63 dhows with 358 slaves on board.[55] Unlike many of his contemporaries, Oldfield did not return to the East Coast of Africa. Leaving on promotion to captain, he went on to serve on four more ships but was taken ill on board the *Indus* in 1876 and died shortly thereafter.[56] But before leaving the squadron, Oldfield gave the naval force a measure of credibility. Actions such as the ultimatum to the Suri slavers followed by quick and decisive enforcement produced the navy's largest single blow against the trade. In addition, his ability to maintain cordial relations with the consul, while pursuing an active policy against dhows of the northern Arabs and of subjects of the sultan of Zanzibar as well, helped Oldfield to capture far more slavers that any of his contemporaries. The prestige of Oldfield and the widespread reputation of the 'devil sloop' *Lyra* enhanced British slave trade activities, and entrenched the British strategic pre-eminence in the sultanate.

Since assignments to the coast usually lasted for three years, there was a steady turn over of commanding officers on the station. New arrivals in 1866 included Captain Thomas Pasley in command of the *Highflyer*, a 21-gun steamer classed as a sixth-rate ship of the line. Active cruising combined with the inevitable reliance on his ship's boats, allowed Pasley to run up impressive capture totals which rivalled even Oldfield's. He took 19 dhows along with nearly 500 liberated slaves. Pasley also forcibly underlined the navy's growing political influence in the region, as well as the old problem of increasing dependence of the sultan, by dabbling in the domestic politics of the sultanate. In the summer of 1866, Majid's sister, Saida Salme, became pregnant by a German merchant, Heinrich Reute. The couple planned to leave Zanzibar but were prevented when the sultan learned of the situation. Given the accepted Muslim sanctions against liaison with a Christian, the unfortunate princess was left in real danger. It was at this stage that Pasley intervened on his own initiative. Without consultation with any authority, British or Zanzibari, he whisked the princess off in the *Highflyer*. The affair created a local sensation at the time and proved an embarrassment some 20 years later when Salme, by then a German subject, was brought back to Zanzibar as a trump card during the German incursion into East Africa.[57]

By the time that the Abyssinian campaign allowed a review of naval policy, several points were clear. Among the most obvious was that the number of ships assigned to the station could not begin to maintain an adequate watch on well over 2,000 miles of coastline. The navy's expedient of dispatching boats was only partially successful and had been proved to be a system fraught with difficulties and dangers. There was also a clear tendency for beleaguered seamen manning the widely dispersed boats to reject legal niceties in their conflicts with the dhowmen. Probably the most important lesson from the early phase of the campaign was that the personalities of the British representatives on the scene were decisive, as strong-willed men-on-the-spot continued to dominate the region. The Crawford-Rigby episode detracted from the vigorous prosecution of the slave trade campaign. Oldfield's activity, however, gave the naval force a measure of credibility and Pasley used the independent action open to the navy to confirm that naval officers were more than cyphers. Given the legal, geographical and tactical difficulties involved, such aggressive individual leadership offered the naval squadron's only hope for inroads against the slave trade. In the aftermath of the Abyssinian interlude, there was no shortage of strong-willed and aggressive naval commanders. Moreover, their effectiveness was increased as the rapid technological developments in naval construction which were revolutionising the Royal Navy became more apparent in the Indian Ocean with the arrival of a new group of ships on the station.

Notes

1. FO 54/18 memo, W. H. Wylde, 15 August 1861.
2. ADM 1/5745, minute, Thomas Wolley, on Foreign Office to Admiralty, 28 April 1860.
3. It should be noted that consular-naval conflicts were not limited to East Africa. Devolved responsibility produced friction in a number of Imperial settings. For an example of West African inter-action at about this time, see ADM 1/5745, Foreign Office to Admiralty, correspondence concerning Old Calabar, packet dated 19 April 1860. For general information, ibid., Foreign Office to Admiralty, 15 December 1860.
4. FO 84/1146, pp. 249–54, Rigby to Sir Charles Wood, number 4, 14 May 1861; and FO 84/ 1179, pp. 304–7, Foreign Office (draft) to Rigby, 19 February 1862.
5. ADM 1/5808, Crawford, statement to court martial, 26 February 1862.
6. Ibid., verdict of court martial.
7. FO 83/2360, Law Officers (William Atherton and Roundell Palmer) to Earl Russell, 22 August 1862. Crawford was also excused costs and damages, see ADM 1/5904, Treasury (F. Peel) to Admiralty, 5 November 1862.
8. FO 54/19, Rigby to Earl Russell, 10 March 1862.
9. P.P., Reports From Committees, 6, 1871, XII, Rigby's testimony, p. 44.
10. FO 84/1204, pp. 340–6, Playfair to Secretary to the Government, Bombay, number 11/19, 23 May 1863.
11. FO 84/1228, pp. 9–12, Admiralty (Romaine) to Foreign Office (Layard) 4 April 1864.
12. FO 84/1226, pp. 77–8, Foreign Office (draft) to Admiralty, 13 April 1864.
13. For general information on the working of the slave bounty system and associated problems, especially from the Treasury point of view, see Rothery's testimony, Select Committee, P.P. 1871, vol. XII. For a brief general discussion of payment of bounties and the evolution of the system, see Lloyd, pp. 79–88. On the East Coast, the effective bounty was generally 30 shillings per ton. When few slaves were taken with a capture, the navy would opt for the £4-4s-0d. award which was a holdover from the West Coast with its equipment clauses and applied to fully equipped, but empty, slavers. For detailed consideration see also below pp. 65–6,

105–6 and 164–5.

14. ADM 1/5904, Treasury (F. Peel) to Admiralty, No. 15315 5/11, 11 November 1864.

15. T5/4, pp. 534–5, Treasury (Hamilton) to Messrs. Chard, numbers 5179 3/4 and 5290 6/4. 6 April 1865 and 10 April 1865. For methods of measurement under the Merchant Shipping Acts, see Dowdeswell, George, *The Merchant Shipping Acts* (London, 1856), especially pages 248–56.

16. Devereux, W. C., *A Cruise in the Gorgon* (London, 1869, reprinted with introduction by D. H. Simpson, 1968), p. 126.

17. ADM 123/178, Rear-Admiral Walker to Secretary of Admiralty number 16, 20 May 1861.

18. ADM 123/180, Admiralty (Paget) to Rear-Admiral Walker, 18 February 1864.

19. ADM 8/139–145, List Books, Cape of Good Hope and East Indies Stations.

20. Creswell, Admiral Sir William, *Close to the Wind* (London, 1965), p. 145.

21. Holman, Thomas, *Life in the Royal Navy* (London, 1892) pp. 124–5. Some excerpts from Holman's book are included in Baynham, Henry, *Before the Mast* (London, 1971).

22. FO 84/1228, pp. 16–20, extracts from Mr R. Jones, Journal of Proceedings, March 1863.

23. ADM 53/8067, log of HMS *Ariel*, 28 January 1863 and 16 April 1863.

24. ADM 123/178, Lieutenant McHardy, standing orders.

25. ADM 53/8067, log of HMS *Ariel*, May 1863.

26. ADM 53/7044, log of HMS *Lyra*, April 1861.

27. ADM 127/10, Commodore Montressor to Secretary of Admiralty, number 66, 6 November 1865.

28. ADM 123/178, Lieutenant McHardy to Captain Adams, 27 October 1862, information from Mahmood Balecory given before R. Playfair, 27 October 1862; and ADM 196/15, p. 38, service record, John Fountaine.

29. FO 84/1204, pp. 306–319, Playfair to Acting-Political Resident Aden, 1 November 1862; and ADM 123/178, Lieutenant McHardy to Rear-Admiral Walker, 13 November 1863.

30. Devereux, p. 367.

31. Ibid., pp. 388–9.

32. FO 84/1224, pp. 153–63, Foreign Office (draft) to Playfair, number 2, 14 March 1864.

33. Devereux, pp. 128–9.

34. Ibid., p. 268.

35. Ibid., pp. 268–9.

36. FO 84/1120, pp. 215–42 and ADM 123/178, Coghlan to Secretary to the Government, Bombay, number 14 (secret) 1 November 1860. It should be noted in passing that while the dhows could not tack, they could wear round, a more difficult way of going on the tack. See Hourani, George, *Arab Seafaring in the Indian Ocean in Ancient and Early Medieval Times* (Princeton, 1951), p. 109.

37. ADM 123/178, Rigby to Secretary to the Government, Bombay, 14 May 1861, and P.P. Reports From Committees, 6, 1871, XII, Rigby testimony, p. 44. The story is one of those most often cited in discussions of the East African slave trade.

38. FO 84/1120 pp. 215–42; and ADM 123/178, Coghlan to Secretary to the Government, Bombay, 1 November 1860.

39. ADM 123/48, Rear-Admiral Walker to Secretary to Admiralty, number 197, 20 December 1861. For a general account of the Kru seamen see Brooks, George, *The Kru Mariner in the Nineteenth Century* (Newark, Delaware, 1972).

40. Ibid., Admiralty (Romaine) to Rear-Admiral Walker, number M 39, 30 January 1862.

41. ADM 50/289, journal of Rear-Admiral Walker.

42. ADM 8/140, List Books, Cape of Good Hope Station.

43. ADM 8/141 and ADM 8/142, List Books, Cape of Good Hope Station.

44. PRO 30 22/24, pp. 105–6, Secretary of Admiralty to Earl Russell, private, 13 September 1861. See also, ADM 1/5768, Notes on the African Slave Trade, Captain A. E. Wilmot.

45. ADM 127/40 and FO 84/1311, pp. 11–16, Commander deKantzow to Commodore Heath, 9 June 1869.

46. FO 84/1328, pp. 136–40. Extracts from depositions made by some slaves captured by HMS *Forte*, 18 May 1869.

47. P.P. (Accounts and Papers), number 6, 1861, vol. XXXIX, 131–V, p. 17; number 7, 1862, vol. XXXV, 112–V, p. 19; number 9, 1863, vol. XXXVII, 55–V, p. 18; and number 8, 1864, vol. XXXIX, 103–V, p. 15. For the general naval estimates for 1860, see ADM 1/5746, Treasury to Admiralty, 4 February 1860.

48. FO 84/1292, pp. 101–6, Churchill to Secretary to Government, Bombay, number 14/46, 4 March 1868.

49. FO 84/1265, pp. 458–65, Livingstone to Earl of Clarendon, 11 June 1866; and p. 467, Livingstone to Clarendon, enclosure, number 1, 20 August 1866.

50. FO 84/1282, Lieutenant Garforth to Admiralty, 20 May 1867. (Portions of FO 84/1282 have been re-bound into FO 83/2361.)

51. FO 84/1267, pp. 357–8, Lieutenant Garforth to Admiralty, 29 April 1866.

52. FO 84/1268, pp. 86–7, Captain Bedingfeld to Commodore Hillyar, extracts, 20 April 1866.

53. Ibid., pp. 81–2, memo W. H. Wylde, 23 July 1866.

54. PRO 30 29/258, tab 10, Commodore Heath to Admiralty, 7 April 1868 (printed copy). Heath's account of his Crimean service, *Letters from the Black Sea during the Crimean War* (London, 1897) is of interest for the commodore's background and prior service. Heath's first ship was the *Melville* and while on board, Midshipman Heath went boat cruising in the Indian Ocean. See Heath Family Records, *Records of the Heath Family 1744–1913*, Sir Leopold's personal sketch of his past written at Anstie Grange, 13 August 1885. The Heath family also hold an album of photographs from the Abyssinian campaign.

55. Compilations of totals for captured dhows and released slaves are

drawn from station records found in ADM 123/178 and from High Court of Admiralty documents, HCA 35/80 and HCA 35/81.

56. ADM 196/16, p. 170, service record, R. B. Oldfield.

57. FO 84/1292, pp. 141–3, Churchill to Lord Stanley, number 20/127, 9 July 1868; Ruete, Emily (the spelling of the name had been changed), *Memoirs of an Arabian Princess* (New York, 1888) and Coupland, pp. 45–8, 336–8, and 437–9.

3

The Spider's Web

Naval historians have described the period from mid-century to about 1872 as the first in a series of development periods which radically transformed the Victorian navy. Design changes saw not only the refinements of steam propulsion but also application of lessons learned in the Crimean War resulting in such innovations as armour and rifling. Among ship types employing these new concepts were a series of steam sloops launched in 1866; design features included wooden, ram-bowed hulls. These paved the way for the later and even more efficient composite, ram-bow corvettes with timber and iron cross beamed construction. In addition to the experimental hull design, the sloops carried new armament consisting of two swivel, 7-inch, 6½-ton guns. Of the four vessels of the genre to see extended active service, all had distinguished periods on the East African slave trade campaign. The sloops included the *Dryad*, the *Nymphe*, the *Vestal* and a ship to have a particularly long and effective East Coast service — the Welsh-built *Daphne* which was launched from Pembroke in October 1866.[1] Small, manoeuvrable and swift, the ships were thought to be ideally suited for the slave trade service and there was a desire to test their design in the active patrolling which could best be gained in the slave trade campaign. Assignment of these vessels did not indicate a new priority for East African operations. The relative importance of the station remained secondary to European and other Imperial considerations. Nevertheless, the ships were sent to the slave trade campaign because they were too small for fleet action and because the Admiralty was keen to see how they would stand up to strenuous, active patrolling. Even more important than the ships themselves, however, were the men who brought them to the station — Commodore Heath was fortunate to have a group of young captains eager to pursue a forward policy. There was deKantzow in the smaller gun vessel *Star*, Commander E. S. Meara in the *Nymphe*, Commander Philip Colomb with the *Dryad*, and Commander G. L. Sulivan in command of the *Daphne*.

Sulivan was especially significant among the new station captains. He had already gained a reputation for bravery. As a midshipman he was commended for diving from a ship under full sail to rescue a seaman who had fallen overboard. Later service as a lieutenant in the Crimean War was highlighted by four successive days of dangerous diving to recover much-needed stores from the wrecked gunboat *Jasper*. Most significant, however, was the fact that Sulivan served in four ships off the coast of East Africa and was to spend more time on the station than any of his contemporaries. He first came to the region as a midshipman in the *Castor* in 1849, when he served as a boat officer in an attack on Arab forts at Angoxa. He returned 15 years later in command of the *Pantaloon*; the *Daphne* was his third ship on the station.[2]

Among other new captains was Colomb who had spent over a year at the Admiralty before taking over the *Dryad*. He had already made a major contribution to the field of signalling and the system of sending morse code by flashing lights came to be known as 'Colomb's Flashing Signals'. Attached to a number of committees, he had a hand in revising the navy's signal code before coming to the East Indies Station and later worked on lighting British ships and promulgating revised signal books. Colomb's most significant contribution to naval defence was made after he left active service to take a post as lecturer at the Royal Naval College at Greenwich. While there, he wrote several books including *Naval Warfare* (1891) which established him as a leading spokesman of the 'Blue Water School' which supported a naval-centred defence policy for Britain.[3] Both Sulivan and Colomb are of particular interest to students of the slave trade patrol because they recounted their experience in books about their activities off East Africa. The slave trade blockade was to be the final active service for both deKantzow and Meara. They retired as captains at the end of their East Coast tours.[4]

The key figure in post-Abyssinian operations was, however, Heath himself. He took a personal interest in the slave trade and had clear views on how to end the traffic. Before the Abyssinian campaign, he had already decided that the Foreign Office should designate one port of export in Zanzibar dominions with a gradual diminution of slaving for six years after which the trade would cease. While the trade lasted, it should be a monopoly of the sultan's government allowed only in vessels carrying some sort of distinctive marking like a specially painted sail.[5] Not only did he suggest such proposals to the government, Heath also lobbied for his changes in a series of private interviews with the sultan. Such action was a usurpation of the consul's authority and, as will be seen, caused hostility in the Foreign Office. Heath was also concerned with disposition of slaves freed by the cruisers and tried to prod the Foreign Office into a more systematic approach to their care.[6] His most important initiative, however, was to take direct charge of the slave trade campaign rather than delegating it to a senior officer on the coast. Moreover, acting strictly on his own authority, he decided to employ his new ships and captains in a new approach to combating the slavers. As has been explained, the northern slave trade was dependent on prevailing winds and currents. *Nakodas* were loath to attempt open sea navigation and the monsoon, or prevailing trade wind, was well suited for coasting from Arabia to Zanzibar from October to April when the northeast wind and sea were blowing. When the monsoon shifted from April to September, they could make the return journey. Previously, the navy's approach had been to try to stop the slavers near the port of debarkation for slaves — Zanzibar. But Heath decided that 1869 would be different. Hoping to seize the initiative by reversing the strategy, he threw five ships, all his available resources, into the anti-slave squadron and deployed them on the Arabian coast when the dhows should be returning north. Sir Leopold hoped that 'under the new plan the traders remain in perfect ignorance of the intended movements of the cruisers which was not always the case under the old one'.[7] Colomb described the new approach as a spider's web spread all along the northern coastline of the Arabian sea.[8] When the signal was given to part company, the ships fanned out into carefully designated cruising zones. Colomb's *Dryad* held the position off the point of Ras al Hadd. Sulivan in the *Daphne* took the region off Maculla. Heath's flagship *Forte* worked the coastline between Sulivan and Colomb while deKantzow's *Star* patrolled between Socotra and Cape Guardafui and Meara's *Nymphe* cruised from Ras Hafun to Cape Durnford.[9]

Colomb thought that the area allotted to his ship was almost perfect. Dhows coming up the coast were channelled into the cape called Ras Madraka and a peak some 300 to 400 feet high hid a good anchorage behind it. Not only that, the peak served as an observation point and allowed Colomb to employ his theories for signals. The pinnace and cutter were dispatched to a hidden anchorage off a nearby island while lookouts were posted on the peak and the island. The lookouts would signal to the ship hidden behind the cliff, the ship would hoist a signal to the boats and the boats would then pounce on passing dhows. If the boats met resistance which required assistance, a fired rocket would bring the ship itself into the fray. According to Colomb the plan worked perfectly. On the first attempt, eight bewildered dhow crews surrendered to the boats. In fact, the great difficulty was not in stopping the dhows but in finding sufficient evidence of slaving to justify their condemnation. For the *Dryad* there were no clear cut instances of slaving; none of the dhows were packed with large numbers of slaves. Nevertheless, navy officers were convinced that any legal trader would carry a few slaves if the opportunity presented itself and try to pass them off as members of the crew or passengers if the dhow were detained. Colomb's captures fell into this category so long and difficult interrogations through the ship's interpreter were necessary before a handful of the captured dhows were condemned as slavers. Most cases could not be proved and after initial elation at the ease of capturing passing dhows Colomb was reduced to summarising the actions as 'incessant boardings of dhows; constant and prolonged examinations generally resulting in aquittal'.[10]

Nevertheless, the combined activities of the cruisers did achieve results. The squadron forming the spider's web boarded over 400 dhows and managed to find sufficient evidence to condemn 32 of those as slavers. An even more significant total was that 1,117 slaves were liberated.[11]

Many of these slaves were captured at considerable risk to the navymen involved. The individual heroics of the *Penguin's* boat crew in rescuing the slaves trapped in the beached dhow some three years earlier were frequently repeated with only minor changes in the circumstances. For example, Sulivan's *Daphne* pursued a dhow which, true to form, was run aground to avoid capture. As the dhow broke up in the surf, Sulivan sent a boat to try to rescue the slaves taking command himself. As the boat approached the dhow it entered heavy breakers which struck it repeatedly, washing over it from stem to stern. When the boat came through into calmer waters, Sulivan despaired of ever being able to get out rowing against the sea. 'I never saw worse looking breakers,' he later recalled. To compound his discomfort, the dhow was virtually empty as some of the slaves had already drowned and even more had been taken off and away by the dhow's crew. When the sailors searched the wreckage they could find only seven children aged about five to eight who were too weak to escape. Some were even unable to stand after having been stowed in a doubled up position for the duration of the cruise. Gathering the seven into the boat, the crew contemplated casting off when approximately 20 Somali tribesmen approached brandishing spears and flintlocks. A shot temporarily discouraged the potential attackers but left Sulivan with an unpalatable choice. He could make a camp for the night on an isolated and apparently hostile beach or could try to pass through the crashing breakers in his small open boat. Suddenly a slight lull in the sea made his decision for him. 'It was now or never: the crew gave way with a will, and we succeeded in crossing,' Sulivan recalled. One heavy breaker swept over the boat but luckily failed to wash out any of the children who had been stowed as carefully as possible in the bottom of the boat. Again, it was a dangerous mission to rescue a handful of the original cargo of a dhow.[12]

One of the more remarkable aspects of such situations was the slavers' ability to induce the slaves to flee from the seamen who were trying to rescue them. They were able to do the same when a dhow was boarded at sea. Boarding parties found slaves being carried to the northern markets posing as crewmen and asserting that they were indeed regular members of the dhow's crew. Sulivan described such slaves who pretended to be busy at various parts of ship's routine which they obviously knew nothing about. They were described as 'hauling taut ropes that ought to be let go, and letting go ropes that ought to be held taut' as well as 'accomplishing wonders in unstowing some cargo'. Apparently the ploy was the same in either case. Whenever the strange steam ships approached, the slaves who had no idea what the newcomers had in mind, were told by their captors that the billowing smoke was a cooking fire intended for them. It was 'the usual Arab story that — "white men eat black man if he get him" '.[13]

Nor had the dhowmen lost their proclivity for hostile response if they felt they had a chance against the boat crews. In early April 1869, for example, the *Nymphe* put into Zanzibar where Commander Meara was told that a dhow was about to embark a cargo of slaves. He sent two cutters under Acting-Lieutenant Norman Clark to intercept the slaver. At first the capture seemed quick and easy. The dhow was found secured to shore by a stern line and when the dhow's crew saw the boats approaching, they jumped overboard with the exception of the *nakoda* who was futilely trying to cut through the stern line when the boats arrived. The dhow was full of slaves, so Clark, who had boarded, ordered the boats to take it in tow. Suddenly a volley of musket fire from the shore raked the boats. The firing continued and Clark, who had a bullet pass through his hat, was stabbed in the leg as the *nakoda* escaped. Fortunately the fire from shore was intermittent and allowed one of the cutters to take the dhow in tow while the other boat went ahead with the wounded. A total of 136 slaves were taken but one able seaman, William Mitchell, was killed and Sub-Lieutenant Thomas Hodgson was so seriously wounded that he was invalided out of the service.[14]

Such violence carried over to the slaves as well. When the *Daphne*'s cutter captured a dhow with 156 slaves on board many were found to be in the final stages of starvation and dysentery. One woman was brought out of the dhow with a month-old infant in her arms. The baby's forehead was crushed and when she was asked how the injury had happened she explained to the ship's interpreter that as the boat came alongside the baby began to cry. One of the dhowmen, fearing that the sailors would hear the cries, picked up a stone and crushed the child's head.[16]

Escalation of violence by the slavers invariably produced a parallel escalation by the navy. Similarly, the situation which cast the captain in the role of judge, jury and executioner led to widespread local criticism of the commanders. A leading source of complaint was Saiyid Majid. When captured dhows belonged to subjects of the sultan, he complained to London that 'things are turned upside down . . . (they) continued to burn our subjects' vessels — seizing them without any cause, and without due proof'.[16] It is not hard to find the reason for Majid's hostility. The slave trade was a major contributor to his custom house and was a base of the Zanzibar economy. Not only that, the navy had struck personally close to the sultan. DeKantzow's *Star* captured and destroyed a large group of dhows, one of which unluckily belonged to Majid's sister. To make a bad situation worse, the same dhow had been captured by the *Daphne* several days before and Sulivan released it because he didn't feel the evidence sufficient to convict it.[17] An irate Majid complained to Churchill that 'suspicion is not a sufficient reason to justify capture, nor is it befitting a powerful government to condemn on mere suspicion'.[18]

The argument was not an unreasonable one and the complaints, in part supported by the consul, caused concern in the Foreign Office. Wylde went so far as to suggest that it was rare indeed for a native vessel to be brought to a port of adjudication; most were destroyed on the spot. 'However much we may be interested in suppressing the slave trade on the East Coast we have no right to be unjust in carrying out our policy,' he argued.[19] There can be no doubt that the aggressive naval posture which Heath had instigated and the resulting objections of the sultan supported by the consul forced the government to re-examine its slave trade suppression policy on the East Coast. There were, of course, British moves to improve the treaty structure on the coast before Heath spun his spider's web. In fact as early as 1861, Russell directed Rigby to negotiate a new treaty with the sultan which would prohibit carrying slaves along the coast from one port in his dominions to another.[20] The attempt opened the door to protracted discussions in which the sultan took the frequently-to-be repeated stand that to cripple the slave trade was to undermine his own economic base. Of course, British influence was not solely dependent on negotiation and the sultan could not remain intractable in the face of persistent pressure. While the navy was only moderately successful in stopping dhows, it was still a powerful visible reminder of the British presence in the region and of the sultan's dependence on that power. While the sultan could hedge and delay, he could not afford to ignore the continuing requests of the consul given the British military paramountcy in the region. The first concession was gained by Playfair in June 1863. Majid finally agreed to the total prohibition of all transportation of slaves by sea from January through April each year. The proclamation came into effect on 1 January 1864.[21] The agreement represented progress in the campaign since the navy was given a free hand with the slavers during the prohibited months. Moreover, any limitation or restriction on the trade imposed by the sultan was seen as a positive development. However, the concession seemed better on paper than it did from the cruising ground. After only one season, officers were reporting that the only real result of the proclamation was increased suffering for the slaves who had accumulated during the prohibited period only to be crowded into the dhows as soon as the season opened. As Walker warned, while a step in the right direction, the concession was not a crippling blow. 'The northern slave trade is carried on with great activity from April to September and unless the removal of slaves be stopped during these months as well, this arrangement will have very little effect upon that traffic,' he said.[22] Among the more cynical navy observers was Captain Bedingfeld who dismissed the concession as 'a neat bit of Eastern diplomacy'. As Bedingfeld saw it, the Majid proclamation was negligible in practice because it banned exportation 'during the 5 months when it is next to impossible to bring the slaves over; the other 7 they have fair wind and weather'.[23] One thing is clear and that is that the concession had little impact on the numbers of slaves carried which, as has already been seen, increased after the proclamation.

It is not surprising that agitation for additional political measures was soon the order of the day and much of the pressure came from the navy officers on the scene. The Foreign Office recognised that some sort of additional agreement with the sultan was required although there was a reluctance to press for concessions too quickly. A series of memos by Wylde demonstrates the thinking in the Foreign Office following the Majid concession. In 1866, Wylde expressed the belief that the government would shortly have to bring pressure on the sultan to prohibit exportation from one port to another.[24] This prohibition was exactly what Rigby had been directed to obtain five years earlier. Nevertheless, there was still a cautious approach to the problem. One reason for delay was a reluctance to undermine the economy of the sultanate. The sultan continued to be useful as a symbol of control on the coastline and there was little doubt that precipitate action against the slave trade could destroy his economic and political bases of support.[25] Playfair warned of the dangers of premature action, citing economic reasons for moving slowly. He suggested that it was for the government to consider seriously whether the prohibition on transport within the sultanate

> . . . should be forced on the Sultan which must inevitably cause the downfall of his House, or whether we should not rather await the time when the natural resources of Zanzibar having been more fully developed, such a measure may be carried out with safety.[26]

Trade returns from Zanzibar superficially supported such arguments as, by 1863, the sultanate had become the world's chief market for the supply of ivory, gum copal and cloves. By 1864, cloves, the leading product, were producing in excess of $300,000 per annum.[27] Of course, the sinister fact was that the alternative products were dependent on slave labour in the Zanzibar system. Slave-grown cloves or slave-borne ivory hardly offered an acceptable alternative to the actual trade in the slaves themselves. Nevertheless, the hope that alternative products would become more significant continued to encourage delay. Another factor was the health of the sultan which was thought to be precarious. Wylde explained on 13 May 1867:

> We shall be compelled to interfere sooner or later, and the only question seems to be whether we should do so at once, or wait a year or two on the chance of our having to deal with another sultan.

The Foreign Secretary, Lord Stanley, favoured waiting.[28] Wylde's plan at this time was a grace period of from one to three years after which a total ban on exportation of slaves from the African coast would be enforced along with the obvious corollary — a ban on importation into Zanzibar.[29] From Zanzibar, John Kirk privately expressed the belief that the concessions that had already been gained were 'all that the sultan can safely grant'.[30]

While these factors were encouraging a cautious approach, however, others were combining to stimulate action. It is true that the East Coast slave trade and associated developments in the Indian Ocean continued to be of low priority in comparison with broader questions of strategy and diplomacy. Moreover, with ministerial attention focused on problems ranging from reform at home to international questions such as the Franco-Prussian War and the *Alabama* arbitration, slave trade matters were left largely to the slave trade department in the Foreign Office and to the Admiralty. However, at times backbenchers, abetted by the press, naval officers and the slave trade societies, forced the issue to the fore. All three were having an effect during the late 1860s and early 1870s. *The Times* began reporting the annual captures of the squadron and naval officers were among those using the paper's columns to campaign for new initiatives. As one letter, signed R.N., contended, 'about 18,000 slaves are taken every year; or, rather I should say, half that number, for quite one-half perish on the passage.'[31] Such public expressions of concern complemented questions in Parliament which helped to force the subject before ministers.[32] Also, public interest in East Africa and its slave trade was stimulated by exploration in the interior. As one historian has suggested, there was a particular 'pride of nationality' in the journeys of exploration with Livingstone contributing a Victoria Falls, Baker the Albert Nyanza and Speke his Victoria Nyanza.[33] The popular accounts of these travels prompted some bolder readers like Joseph Thomson to lead in their turn a new generation of explorers.[34] Most confined themselves to the role of armchair geographer, but did at least maintain a modicum of interest in the subject. Moreover, the evangelicalism and humanitarianism which stimulated the anti-slavery societies along with the missionary thrust in the region, also helped maintain public interest in East African questions. This interest was never overwhelming, but it was consistent enough to leave its mark on official policy.

Meanwhile, events in the Indian Ocean injected another factor into the equation. As has been seen, when the realm of Saiyid Said was divided to form the sultanates of Zanzibar and Muscat, the comparative wealth of Zanzibar tempted Saiyid Thuwaini to attempt to seize Zanzibar. The conflict was eventually settled by the award of a subsidy from the Sultan of Zanzibar to his brother in Muscat. This 'Canning Award', named after Lord Canning, the Governor-General of India, called on Majid to pay 40,000 crowns per year; he agreed to the plan in 1861. Instability in Muscat, however, provided an excuse for ending the subsidy in 1867. Saiyid Thuwaini's son, Saiyid Salim, killed his father and seized the throne of Muscat; Majid capitalised by terminating payment of the subsidy. When pressure was brought to bear on him to resume payment, he appealed to London against the necessity of subsidising his brother's murderer.[36] Wylde thought that the situation might open the door to resuming pressure on slave trade questions. In May 1868, he argued that Majid would be ready enough to end the trade if he could do it without ruining his own revenue and the possibility of releasing him from the subsidy seemed a good way to do just that.[37] Some months later, when another coup in Muscat put Saiyid Azan on the throne, Wylde returned to the idea and argued that by ending the subsidy 'we should be enabled to make terms with Saiyid Majid for the gradual abolition of the slave trade in his dominions'.[38] This argument was supported from other directions. When the change of government in 1868 brought Lord Clarendon to the Foreign Office, Sir Roderick Murchison, President of the Royal Geographical Society, immediately took up the case of the subsidy with him. He argued that release from the subsidy would prompt the sultan to 'at once give up his right (to maintain) . . . a slave market in his island'.

Murchison chided the new minister by suggesting that if Lord Palmerston were still alive he wouldn't have allowed such an opportunity to slip through his fingers.[39] Thus the subsidy question became another factor encouraging new political pressure on the Zanzibar slave trade.

It was against the background of this political debate that the criticism of the aggressive naval action in the spider's web took place. Alienation of the sultan could prove counter-productive if the carrot and stick approach over the subsidy were to be employed. As a result, the government took two steps. First, it moved to establish clear accountability at Zanzibar through the Vice-Admiralty Court. A second decision was to set up a committee to investigate the navy's slave trade operations and related matters. The committee included Churchill who was in England on leave, Rothery, the registrar of the High Court of Admiralty and legal adviser to the Treasury on slave trade questions, and Captain Henry Fairfax, who had served on the station in command of the *Ariel*, representing the Admiralty. Vivian and Wylde were also members of the group which sifted through the varied reports dealing with areas of controversy during the autumn of 1869. Rothery and Wylde, who exerted considerable influence, saw their role as one of checking the wholesale abuses they believed to have typified the squadron's activities.[40] They were major contributors in drafting the final committee report which led to a revision of the general instructions to the commanders on the station.

Foreign Office action on both these questions — the changes in the Vice-Admiralty Court and the instructions — caused progressive worsening of relations with the independently-minded Heath. A particular cause of trouble was extension of the jurisdiction of the Vice-Admiralty Court which was given full powers of adjudication in the summer of 1869 as a direct result of the complaints arising from the spider's web operation.[41] The fact that a Vice-Admiralty Court could finally hear all cases in Zanzibar and the requirement to bring captured vessels to the port of adjudication was important in shifting the navy's cruising ground back toward Zanzibar rather than the Arabian coast. The consul, who had an interest in maintaining as good relations with the sultan as possible, was placed in a position to discourage widespread captures on suspicion.[42] The most important single element in the changed circumstances was the new judge of the court, Dr John Kirk. Kirk was agency surgeon and vice-consul when he first took over the court for Churchill who was on leave. Soon he was consul in his own right and his long tenure in the post made Kirk the archetype of the British man-on-the-spot in East Africa. It did not take him long to assert his presence in his dealings with the navy.

The spark came when a dhow owned by the sultan's governor of Mombasa was captured by the *Nymphe*. It was not a question of arbitrary capture or of condemnation without evidence since the dhow clearly had domestic slaves aboard. But Kirk ruled against the captors asserting that the fact that the dhow carried domestic slaves was not sufficient to condemn it as a slaver under the law as it stood at the time. In other words, it was a test case on the general legality of carrying domestic slaves to sea. Heath was livid. He assailed Kirk in a report to the Admiralty in which he attacked what he saw as an impossible interpretation. Arguing that the instructions to navy officers clearly stated that the first criterion justifying a captain to conclude that a vessel was engaged in the slave trade was 'if you find any slaves on board' Heath believed Kirk had ruled on the basis of ignorance of the situation and of the instructions. He also offered a spirited defence against some of the broader complaints against his squadron. Probably the most repeated criticism was the destruction of dhows at sea which Wylde had viewed as intolerable. Far from intolerable, suggested Heath, it was absolutely necessary. Strong winds and currents frequently made it impossible to bring dhows into the port of adjudication, he claimed. Recalling recent captures by the *Daphne* and *Star*. Heath observed that between them they had captured 39 dhows but depleted coal supplies and the monsoon made bringing the dhows into port out of the question 'it being as much as the men of war could do to reach port themselves'.[43]

The unfolding confrontation might have recalled memories of Crawford and Rigby, but the commodore did not confine himself to a row with the new consul. In fact, before he was finished, Heath was feuding with all the civil supervisors of the slave trade patrol. He took criticism of the active prosecution typified by the spider's web patrols as a personal attack on his leadership. When Rothery criticised the fleet, Heath returned the criticism with biting invective. He wrote to the Admiralty:

I beg now to call attention to the . . . report forwarded to me in No. 318 'I must add that this case presents another instance of the irregular and arbitrary way in which the powers entrusted to Her Majesty's Cruisers for the suppression of the slave trade appear to be too often exercised on the East Coast of Africa.' I think I may fairly reply 'This sentence presents another instance of the irregular and arbitrary way in which Mr Rothery draws up his reports.'[44]

With this reply, Rothery was infuriated and the conflict became even more personal. 'A more insolent and outrageous letter . . . I don't think that I have ever before read,' Rothery retorted. He accused Heath of a host of indiscretions which he insisted 'is in keeping with Commodore Heath's generally insolent and arrogant character'.[45] Through the summer, Rothery continued to attack Heath at every opportunity.[46] If the Foreign Office seemed a likely referee in the confrontation there was a reluctance there to take up that role. Hoping the storm would pass, Vivian in the slave trade department suggested, 'I think we had better keep out of the quarrel'.[47] That, however, proved impossible since the conflict between Heath and Rothery soon put the Admiralty on the defensive and the issue produced a confrontation of ministries.

The man in the middle was the second secretary, Vernon Lushington, who found himself in an uncomfortable position. On one hand, a natural tendency to defend the naval personnel prompted Lushington to challenge some of the more serious charges against the squadron. On the other hand, the fact that Heath had acted in large measure on his own authority meant that Lushington was defending some actions which he thought to be questionable. The realities of lack of communication meant that senior officials in the Admiralty were forced to defend policy decisions taken without their blessing or approval. Lushington fumed at his position and minuted 'It is worth pointing out that the duty of sending full reports of each case to the Admiralty . . . has so far as I can ascertain, been persistently disregarded'.[48] It is significant that despite pique at being placed in such a position, however, the official Admiralty response was to support Heath on all points. Lushington's complaints again the anti-naval tone of the criticism levelled against the spider's web caused the Foreign Office to attempt conciliation. Lord Clarendon 'has never intended to impute blame generally to the naval officers,' the Admiralty was assured.[49] Significantly, no serious move was made to increase control from the Admiralty.

Meanwhile, Heath complicated matters even further. As has been seen, he had clear ideas about how to end the slave trade and lobbied for his phased end to the traffic through a government monopoly in a series of private interviews with the sultan. Such diplomatic activity by the naval commander was clearly a challenge to the consul's authority and provoked opposition in the Foreign Office and in the committee studying the slave trade as well. The committee noted the tendency of naval officers to assume diplomatic functions in East Africa and Vivian hopefully suggested that when the report reached Heath 'he will probably take the hint'.[50] In reality, however, the committee report only annoyed the commodore more. The instructions to commanders which resulted from the committee study were published 6 November 1869 and were prefaced by reference to 'serious irregularities and mistakes committed by Officers commanding H.M. Ships' on the East Coast. It was said that the document was not intended to replace the old instructions but was rather designed to clarify them. On the question of vessels liable to capture, the instructions gave a clear victory to Kirk in upholding the decision which had caused his original rift with Heath. Officers were warned that 'Slave Trade must for this purpose be carefully distinguished from slavery'. Finding slaves on a vessel was not sufficient reason to detain her unless they were clearly being transported for sale. Far from clarifying this point, however, the instructions actually confused the issue more. If a few slaves were working as crewmen or were domestic servants for passengers, the dhow should not be captured whereas if slaves were found crowded or chained together the vessel was subject to capture. The obvious difficulty was the many cases which fell somewhere in between. In these, the instructions suggested, 'It must rest with the officer to distinguish to what class any particular case belongs by a careful consideration of all the circumstances.' After all the discussion, committee study and conflict, the issue was still clearly up to the naval officer who had to rely on his own judgement in deciding which dhow to capture and which to release. Other equivocal clarifications suggested that Zanzibar dhows were not to be destroyed at sea 'without (if practicable) conferring with the consul'. Officers were charged with bringing captures to the port of adjudication and nothing would excuse their failure to do so 'except facts shewing satisfactorily that doing so would have involved serious danger to the lives of the prize crew'.[51] After all was said and done, the clarification could not fairly be said to have clarified anything at all. Responsibility for incorrect captures was still that of the commanding officers involved and the instructions made their judgement the only criterion for making those captures.

The fact that their action had been faulted without real assistance being offered was not lost on the officers involved. Sulivan, who was in the process of finishing his book in the aftermath of the committee's report, was understandably quick to take members of the body to task. He suggested that any mistakes had not been made by the officers on the station. Any errors were 'on the part of those who did not fully understand what orders and instructions the naval officers had been directed by in this service'.[52] Writing at about the same time, Colomb probably spoke for all the officers on the station when he noted with some frustration that commendation for the naval slave trade suppressors was unheard of 'but it is certainly common to receive more or less blame from the Foreign Minister for the time being'.[53] Colomb claimed that the officer had to stretch the wording of his instructions or he would be totally ineffective. He suggested that the officer had to 'take upon himself the responsibility of innumerable breaches of the technical law for the sake of carrying out its spirit'.[54] Nor were the captains who had recently returned from the station the only ones to echo this view. Writing while the committee was still sitting, Oldfield took a position very close to Colomb's. The captain, who had taken such forceful individual action almost ten years before, argued that the senior naval officer had to be able to respond in a similar fashion. The working of the squadron 'must be left to the officer in command of the station,' he told Rothery. On the question of illegal captures it was not a recklessness on the part of the officers Oldfield insisted. 'Many of the mistakes that have occurred in making seizures on the East Coast have occurred by officers reading the Treaties and slave instructions too *literally*,' he argued.[55]

The controversy prompted several officers to return to the longstanding sore point of measuring captures and the related lack of application of their general instructions to the peculiarities of the East Coast. The lament had been voiced by Captain William Bowden five years earlier when he complained of the inadequacies of the instructions in reference to empty vessels. A lengthy list of articles constituting slave fittings justified capture but the list had been drawn up for the West Coast squadron and conjured up images of the Middle Passage to the Americas in European or American vessels. Bowden complained that he had seen numerous slave dhows and none of them had ever had any sort of slave fittings at all. 'If they have cargo, they sit on it, and if not on the sand ballast,' he explained.[56] As Sulivan took up the argument, 'I have never seen a fettered negro in any of the dhows on the East Coast, and I doubt if any one else has'.[57] Colomb agreed that the slave trade instructions pertained almost exclusively to the defunct West African trade and said that guidance for measuring prizes had been designed for the large ships of European powers 'and are hardly at all applicable to the crazy old Arab dhow often guiltless of name, papers, books or flag'.[58] In the main, Sulivan concentrated on the instructions' uselessness for measuring the dhows which he thought were so strangely shaped that they looked more like sea monsters than ships. He insisted that the huge stern and unusual poop of the dhows required new measuring techniques because 'the usual method of ascertaining tonnage is inapplicable'.[59]

On top of all this, Heath was continuing his personal campaign. As might be expected, he was not pleased with the committee's references to improper seizures. Reflecting naval frustration, he chided the committee for damping the zeal of the officers who, he assured the Admiralty, would feel that their motives had been impugned and that they had been unjustly treated. Nor was his tone particularly diplomatic. In fact, Heath's criticism of the committee was sufficiently strong to provoke an official 'Reply of the Committee on the East African Slave Trade to Sir Leopold Heath's Observations upon their Report'. Their displeasure was obvious when they wrote that

> . . . the remaining paragraphs of the Commodore's letter contain a strong protest, conveyed in language which we think is neither proper nor justifiable, against our observations upon the subject of the improper seizures of slaves; the destruction of prizes prior to adjudication, &c.[60]

One aspect of Heath's attack on the report, however, could not be dismissed. The main thrust of his arguments was that the squadron would have to be increased. If the government did not like the way he was fighting the trade with the ships on hand, they would have to send him more ships to do the job efficiently. The slave trade committee had admitted a need for four additional ships on the station, but Sir Leopold, a man who could not be accused of a lack of ambition, claimed that 'at least 10 vessels besides the flagship should be appropriated for this service'.[61]

This claim represented over twice as many ships as were then on the station, and placed the Admiralty in another difficult position.

Through 1868, an economy drive led the Admiralty to review ship assignments on a global scale. Home waters and the Mediterranean were viewed as sacrosanct, but Imperial commitments were studied with a view to a cutback in expenses. The West Coast of Africa seemed an obvious area for reductions since the trans-Atlantic slave trade had been largely eliminated. For the same reason, it was thought that the North American and West Indies squadrons might also be reduced. The China and Japan squadron was seen as another possible area for pruning. There was never serious consideration given to increasing the size of any station, including the East Indies. In February, the suggested naval cuts were forwarded to the Foreign Office for review and Lord Stanley gave his approval to reduction in the West African and North American stations. He would not, however, sanction cuts for China and Japan. Plans were re-submitted after the Liberals took power and Clarendon concurred with Stanley's response. Granville, then at the Colonial Office, cautioned only that the seas off British Columbia and 'in the neighbourhood of Hong Kong and the Straits' should continue to receive adequate naval attention. No ministerial interest at all was shown in East African waters at this time. In the end, the relative strengths of the stations stood at 25 ships for the China Station, one stationary ship for the Cape, 5 for the south-east coast of America, 10 ships in the Pacific with 4 vessels designated for Australian waters, and surprisingly, still 11 vessels for West Africa. It was cold comfort for the East Indies Station which had only six vessels with 1,000 men assigned. Of these, three were generally on slave trade operations while three were left for the Bay of Bengal, the Arabian Gulf and the Red Sea.[62]

Interestingly, it was not the shortage of ships on slave trade operations, but rather the lack of vessels for the Persian Gulf which finally did result in a slight reinforcement of the station. In the autumn of 1868, the Shah of Persia approached Indian authorities with a scheme for a small naval force in the Persian Gulf which would be provided by him and manned by Persian seamen but commanded by British officers seconded for the service. The Government of India could see advantages in such a squadron, but only if it remained under their control. They thus endorsed the plan for a Persian Gulf presence but suggested that it should be a force like the then defunct Indian Navy. The Admiralty's reaction was that neither alternative was acceptable and that while the commander of the East Indies Station would, as far as possible, meet the demands for naval assistance in the area, ultimate control should not be vested in the Government of India or with the Shah. The establishment of a separate force, 'completely independent of the control of the Admiralty' was totally unacceptable. Finally a compromise of sorts was agreed in which the squadron was increased enough to maintain a Persian Gulf commitment. But, continually cost-conscious in the wake of prior cuts, the Admiralty insisted that the expense of the Persian Gulf operations should be defrayed by the India Office. Three ships were eventually designated for the duty and operating costs were put at £70,000 per annum. Control of the ships, however, was left to the discretion of the commander-in-chief of the East Indies Station and the additional vessels were sometimes diverted to the anti-slave trade patrol both in the northern reaches of the station and off East Africa. Problems of intense heat and deterioration of vessels helped allow this flexibility since eight months was seen as the longest period any ship could remain on station. In rotating the vessels, the station commander could sometimes divert them for more pressing requirements such as slave trade operations.[63]

Against this background of economy and the small increase already given to the station for Persian Gulf commitments, Heath's insistence on a further doubling of station strength was staggering. Yet it is indicative of the defensive state of mind within the Admiralty following months of criticism of East African operations that the suggestion was accepted. In the atmosphere of criticism and complaint there was sufficient sympathy for Heath's suggestions that the request for more ships was forwarded to the Foreign Office with a conditional endorsement. The condition, however, was a significant one as the Admiralty explained that there could be no justification for increasing the size of the squadron unless there were a new diplomatic offensive launched to restrict the traffic further at Zanzibar itself. The Admiralty hoped that if it were determined to increase the size of the force, 'political measures will be taken which may render the employment of that force thoroughly effective'.[64]

The frustration reflected by the Admiralty was in large part justified. After a decade of persistent naval activity, the slave trade was still in full vigour and aggressive naval activity had resulted only in criticism and censure both on the cruising ground and in London. The Admiralty's call for increased political pressure was a considered response to the situation recognising that the operating framework of treaties would have to be improved for naval suppression to be effective. Of course, as has been seen, that view was gaining support from a variety of quarters and the Admiralty was joining a growing chorus calling for a new initiative. Therefore, in 1870 matters were unsettled and the committee report coupled with the inhibiting personality of Kirk at Zanzibar seemed to be reversing the aggressive forward policy of Heath. Moreover, to complicate an already complex problem from a naval point of view, another question was assuming ever larger proportions. This problem was probably the most important of all. The cruisers had taken thousands of slaves but there was still no clear idea what was to be done with them after they had been taken off the dhows. Some went to Aden, some to the Cape and others to the Seychelles with the deciding factors generally being the position of the ship at the time of capture and the personal preference of the captain. There was no question that the discretion of the captain was decisive. The Foreign Office stressed this point in a note to the Colonial Office. In response to a request for information on possible landing sites, A. J. Otway asked the Colonial Office to supply information to the captains 'in order that they may be enabled to exercise their judgement as to which place it may be most desirable to send the captured Negroes'.[65] The question was certainly important to the navy as well as for the civil representatives where the slaves were landed. A capture of the *Star* in June of 1869 emphasised the nature of the problem. DeKantzow's ship had been cruising for 56 days and had boarded 112 dhows without finding any evidence of slaving. The routine was suddenly shattered when the cutter captured a dhow remarkably full by the standards of the East African trade — 236 slaves including 155 children were packed into the dhow. The dhow was reported to be unseaworthy, not to mention filthy, and after the slaves were transferred to the *Star* it was scuttled. With already reduced supplies, deKantzow had to leave his station immediately to land the slaves. His preference, like many of the other officers on the station, was the Seychelles. Any thought of making the Seychelles had to be abandoned, however, when smallpox broke out among the slaves soon after the capture. The only thing to do was make for the nearest possible landing site which was Aden. Fortunately the ship had already had a brush with smallpox and captain and crew had been vaccinated the previous year. It was less fortunate for the resident at Aden, however, who could not cope with such large numbers of slaves. That fact was clear from the previous time the *Star* had put in with smallpox among her liberated slaves. In December, she brought 134 slaves who were quarantined on an island in the inner harbour where they were all vaccinated. As the crisis passed, however, the *Daphne* entered port with another large cargo of freed slaves. The resident, Major-General E. L. Russell, finally informed the government in no uncertain terms that the situation was impossible. The influx of slaves was too great a burden for such an isolated settlement to bear, he insisted. Russell told the Secretary to the Government at Bombay that it was unfair to the glutted community and unfair to the slaves to try to locate them in Aden so he saw no solution but to send the whole lot, as well as any new arrivals which might be brought in, to Bombay where the government could decide what to do with them.[66] The result, as Russell undoubtedly expected, was to relieve the pressure on Aden.

The pressing question, however, was not answered. There was still no satisfactory alternative which could serve as a depot for the liberated slaves. It was not until 1869, on the prompting of Heath, that reports were required from such places as the Seychelles concerning the fate of the slaves landed there.[67] In June of 1869, Clarendon admitted to having no idea of the condition or distribution of the slaves liberated at Mauritius, Seychelles, Aden or Bombay.[68] Even without a regular reporting system, however, it was clear that the Seychelles also had problems in dealing with the numbers of slaves being released there. Difficulty in finding employment for the Africans led the Admiralty to order in July 1869 that no more slaves be released in the island group.[69] Wylde had previously argued that the Cape was a better place for them.[70] His suggestion failed to take into account the realities of operations after control of the squadron had been shifted from the Cape Station to the East Indies Station. Relocation at the Cape, questionable from the standpoint of the welfare of the freed slaves, was hopeless for the cruisers which would have been pulled off their stations to deliver the Africans there.

By 1869, Wylde had become less enthusiastic about relocation at the Cape and was leaning toward Zanzibar itself as the best place to release the slaves. While calling for supervision and protection at Zanzibar, he argued that the fact that the former slaves would go back into the labour market was a major advantage since the availability of cheap labour would reduce the demands for slaves.[71] Many disputed the argument. One of the more visionary plans for the former slaves came from Sulivan who thought that Britain owed them more than simple emancipation. Two years of instruction to adults and a broader education for children was a minimum the captain said. What was most needed in Sulivan's view was some sort of a mainland depot such as the one that had operated for years at Sierra Leone on the West Coast. 'Why not create a colony for them in their own country?' he wondered. One thing he was certain about was that Zanzibar was not a suitable place to liberate slaves recently shipped from the slave market there. 'I have no hesitation in saying that it would be better for the poor negroes to let them be taken without hindrance wherever the dealer wished than to leave them at Zanzibar,' Sulivan wrote.[72] Meanwhile, Heath was saying much the same thing to the anti-slavery societies about India. 'I doubt whether their future career as negroes in Bombay is a happier one than as a domestic slave in Arabia,' he suggested.[73] After all the discussion, however, there was no clear decision and the issue of disposition of freed slaves become one of the many open questions of 1870.

If indecision marked many aspects of slave trade policy, there was at least one clear new dictum laid down and it was not a popular one with the navy. The role of Kroomen on navy ships has been discussed and their service had gained them widespread respect in the fleet. One example which illustrates the quality of the black seamen involved the *Dryad* off Ras Madraka. The ship had closed on a dhow which was run aground to avoid capture. Three boats were sent to try to rescue the slaves. As the surf was heavy, one boat stayed to seaward of the breakers while the other two went in to collect the slaves. When the boats hit the surf, however, the smaller of the two was swamped. Nevertheless, the crews still managed to reach the beach and collect 58 slaves from the dhow. It was, of course, impossible to embark such a large group in the single boat so the slaves were shuttled to the third boat in groups. This worked smoothly for three trips and on the fourth all the remaining slaves and crewmen boarded. But after covering over half the distance to the cutter, the boat was hit by a large breaker which swamped and sank it. In the difficult swim back to shore an ordinary seaman, Henry Blake, and three of the slaves were drowned. For the men stranded on shore, the situation was perilous and the only way back to the ship seemed to be the swamped gig awash in the surf. Jim George, head Krooman, and Peter Warman, Krooman, offered to swim back into the surf to try to attach a line to the gig. The men succeeded in retrieving the boat only to find that the airtight compartments were filled with water which, coupled with the bad footing in the shifting sand, made it impossible for the men on shore to pull the boat on to the beach. As the men fought the surf, a wave caught the gig and threw it into the wreckage of the dhow where it was destroyed. A glimmer of hope appeared when the other gig, relieved of the weight of its passengers, was seen wallowing well out in the surf. George again went into the sea but was unsuccessful in two attempts to swim to the second boat. The men ashore thus faced the uninviting prospect of spending the night on the hostile shore without food or ammunition. In the meantime, Colomb had been watching the plight of the boat crews from the ship. Anxious to send some sort of supplies to the men, Colomb asked for volunteers for a hazardous journey to the beach in a canoe which had been taken off a previously captured dhow. Ben Coffee, second head Krooman, and Yellow Wheel, Krooman, stepped forward to make the trip. Rifles, ammunition, biscuit and water were securely lashed to the bottom of the canoe and the two Kroomen efficiently manoeuvred the small craft through the surf to the party ashore. Considerably safer with the arms from the canoe, the exhausted seamen camped on the beach for the night assisted in making camp by the remaining freed slaves. Next morning, Colomb decided that there was no way to rescue the party but that since they were now armed they could rejoin the ship by marching to its anchorage. Relying on his signal book, Colomb hoisted the flag signal 'March' and the party ashore rejoined the ship overland. Obviously, the contribution of the Kroomen was vital to the safe outcome of the episode. For his part in the action, Jim George was awarded the bronze medal of the Royal Humane Society.[74]

Such heroism by the black seamen of the Kru coast earned them the respect of their shipmates as well as their officers. It is not surprising then that a plan announced by the Admiralty on 7 April 1870 to end the service of the Kroomen on the East Coast was met with an outcry from the officers on the station. The move was prompted by the difficulty in bringing the West African Kroomen back and forth to the East African Station. The Admiralty decided that native Africans, referred to as 'Seedies' should be entered in the ships instead of Kroomen.[75] Lushington was sceptical and thought 12 Seedies to be roughly equivalent to 8 Kroomen.[76] Commodore Heath was totally opposed to the change as were most of the officers commanding ships on the station. Even long after the change had been given time to work, captains still lamented the loss of their Kroomen and lobbied for their return.[77] It proved to be an unsuccessful lobby and the colourful and significant contribution of the Kroomen on the East Coast came to an end in 1870.

By the beginning of 1870, the navy's record against the slavers looked reasonably respectable. The spider's web had netted 32 slave dhows and resulted in the release of over 1,000 slaves. The dhow totals meant that Heath's new ships, changed cruising strategy, and the commitment of virtually the whole of the East Indies squadron under his personal supervision had produced the best single season yet against the East African slave trade. The totals of captures for the new steam sloops were also impressive. Captures during its assignment to the campaign including the spider's web action, saw the *Nymphe* under Meara and his predecessor Captain Thomas Barnardistan take 29 dhows along with 577 slaves over a three year period. DeKantzow's *Star* managed 25 captures with the liberation of 363 slaves during a similar time span. Colomb's *Dryad* captured seven slavers having 365 Africans onboard. Also impressive were the totals from the *Daphne*'s list of captures. Sulivan and his ship took 20 dhows while stopping transport of some 600 slaves.[78]

The totals seemed to suggest an upswing in the navy's fortunes against the slavers. The cruisers had clearly enjoyed some success against their adversaries and had found changed cruising tactics to their advantage. It must be remembered, however, that there was tremendous ferment in London resulting from the operations of the cruisers. The captains on the station had tackled the slavers with vigour but their zeal had brought complaints which had prompted reappraisal in London. The conflicts between the commodore and civilian supervisors, the charges and counter-charges surrounding the committee and confusion over issues ranging from the disposition of freed slaves to the retention of Kroomen all combined to cast a pall over the apparent success of the squadron. Recrimination over inapplicable instructions and agitation for a new political initiative also added to an unsettled situation which further shook the uneasy balance between the major elements within the structure of British East African operations. The clearest lesson to emerge from the first full decade of persistent naval operations against the slave trade was that the treaty structure would have to be improved for adequate results to be achieved. It would be necessary to initiate the long-delayed political initiative against the trade.

Notes

1. Preston, Anthony, 'The End of the Victorian Navy', in *The Mariner's Mirror*, vol. 60, 1974; pp. 363–81; and Ballard, G. A., 'British Sloops of 1875', in *The Mariner's Mirror*, vol. 24, 1938, pp. 302–17.

2. Sulivan Papers, Sulivan to Secretary of Admiralty, private, undated draft, and Summary of Service, G. L. Sulivan; and ADM 196/13, p. 284.

3. ADM 196/13, pp. 438–9, service record, Philip H. Colomb; and Marder, Arthur J., *British Naval Policy 1880–1905* (London, 1941), pp. 47–8; and Schurman, Donald M., *The Education of a Navy* (London, 1965), pp. 42, 57–8 and 192. Schurman suggests, 'The great productive period of Colomb's life, and the real beginnings of his historical work, were coincident with his retirement from active service and his appointment as lecturer on tactics and strategy at the Royal Naval College, Greenwich.' Schurman claims that Colomb should share credit with such people as Lord Fisher and Churchill for what naval readiness existed in Britain in 1914. Among Colomb's significant books and articles are: *Naval Warfare* (London, 1891), *Memoirs of Admiral Sir Astley Cooper Key* (London, 1898) and Lecture on 'Naval and Military Signals', *Journal of the Royal United Service Institution*, 29 May 1863, vol. VII, 1864.

4. ADM 196/13, pp. 308 and 304, service record, Edward S. Meara, and service record, Walter deKantzow.

5. FO 84/1295, pp. 156–66, Commodore Heath to Admiralty, number 237, 2 September 1868; and FO 84/1292, Commodore Heath to Churchill, 25 August 1868.

6. See pages 69–71.

7. FO 84/1310, pp. 163–5, Commodore Heath to Admiralty, number 53, 1 March 1869.

8. Colomb, P. H., *Slave-Catching in the Indian Ocean* (London, 1873) p. 185.

9. ADM 127/40, Commodore Heath to Admiralty, number 42, 22 January 1870; and Sulivan Papers, Commodore Heath to Captain Sulivan, memo, 31 March 1869. The arrangement found cruising ships much nearer one another than was ordinarily the case on the East Coast with its shortage of vessels. The situation actually brought *Star* and *Daphne* near enough together at one time for boats from both ships to be involved in a set of captures. The result was a unique case of ships sharing bounties. See also HCA 35/81 and HCA 35/82.

10. Colomb, pp. 200–3 and p. 233. Latter passage quoted by Lloyd, p. 253.

11. ADM 127/40, Commodore Heath to Admiralty, number 42, 22 January 1870.

12. Sulivan, G. L., *Dhow Chasing in Zanzibar Waters* (London, 1873, reprinted with introduction by D. H. Simpson in 1967 and in 1968) pp. 159–63.

13. Ibid., p. 64.

14. FO 84/1307, pp. 241–2, Kirk to Secretary to the Government, Bombay, number 132/31, 12 April 1869; and ADM 127/40, Commander Meara to Commodore Heath, 5 May 1869; and Acting-Lieutenant Clark to Commander Meara, 16 April 1869. See also Clowes, vol. VII, p. 226.

15. Sulivan, pp. 167–9.

16. FO 84/1279, p. 77, Majid to Seward (acting consul), 20 February 1867.

17. ADM 127/40, Churchill to Secretary to the Government, Bombay, 12 December 1868; and Majid to Churchill, 1 December 1868.

18. Ibid., Majid to Churchill, 1 December 1868. See also ADM 1/6127, Foreign Office (Otway) to Admiralty, 10 March 1869.

19. FO 84/1292, pp. 300–3, memo, W. H. Wylde, 26 February 1869.

20. ADM 123/178 Russell to Rigby, number 1, 19 February 1861; and Rear-Admiral Walker to Admiralty, number 145, 16 July 1862.

21. FO 84/1204, p. 347, Playfair to Secretary to the Government, Bombay, number 21/42, 15 June 1863; and FO 84/1224, p. 182, proclamation, Saiyid Majid, 1 January 1864.

22. FO 84/1228, pp. 321–23, Rear-Admiral Walker to Admiralty, number 106, 24 May 1864; see also Commander Chapman to Rear-Admiral Walker, 30 June 1864.

23. FO 84/1281, pp. 117–18, Captain Bedingfeld to Commodore Hillyar, 1 December 1866.

24. FO 84/1267, pp. 275–7, memo, W. H. Wylde, 1 May 1866.

25. There can be little doubt that the sultan was in a difficult position and that major concessions on the slave trade would threaten his position. The problem will be seen more clearly in the following chapters. The fact was certainly not lost on Playfair who could see, as could the Arabs, the damaging economic impact of Rigby's freeing of slaves held by Indians in Zanzibar. For the fullest analysis of this impact, see Sheriff, *op. cit.*

26. PP, Accounts and Papers, 35, 1864, LXVI, (Slave Trade) extract of Playfair to Secretary to the Government, Bombay, 23 May 1863, pp. 72–3.

27. PP, Accounts and Papers, 42, 1863, LXX (3229), Report on the Trade of Zanzibar for 1860, 1 May 1860, pp. 239–51; and PP, Accounts and Papers, 30(1), 1864, LXI(I), Report on the Trade of Zanzibar for 1863, 20 December 1863, pp. 178–82.

28. FO 84/1281, pp. 259–60, memo, W. H. Wylde, 13 May 1867 and minute, Lord Stanley.

29. FO 84/1261, pp. 324–9, memo, W. H. Wylde, 26 January 1867.

30. Mss. Brit. Emp. S22.G.7, Kirk to the Rev Horace Waller, 29 November 1867. Waller, influential with the Universities Mission and the anti-slavery societies, was being supplied with information from Zanzibar by Kirk. The correspondence is interesting as Kirk felt obliged to get the 'truth' out in London but implored Waller not to let anyone discover that Kirk was his source of information.

31. *The Times*, 25 July 1867, p. 9–f. See also *The Times*, 3 June 1867, p. 11–f and 10 December 1870, p. 11–d.

32. For example, see Parliamentary Debates, 3rd Series, 1867–8 (190) 1687; 1868 (191) 1578, (192) 1130; 1870 (199) 119, (203) 1770; 1871 (207) 952; 1872 (210) 970–971; (212) 1608. Among members pressing on slave trade matters was retired publisher Charles Gilpin, Liberal MP for Northampton. Former chairman of the National Freehold Land Society and Parliamentary Secretary to the Poor Law Board, Gilpin was also an active spokesman for the Anti-Slavery Society. For a discussion of the

relationships and attitudes of the leaders of the anti-slavery movement during this period, see Temperley, especially pages 73 – 8.

33. Cairns, H. A. C., *Prelude to Imperialism* (London, 1965), p. 148.

34. For a discussion of the impact that the accounts of the early explorers had on Thomson, see Rotberg, Robert, *Joseph Thomson and the Exploration of Africa* (London, 1971), pp. 16 – 17.

35. FO 84/1179, p. 336, Majid to Rigby, 28 June 1861. The award might have been better called the 'Coghlan Award'. For details of the preliminary study and later difficulties surrounding the subsidy, see Kelly, pp. 541 – 53, 625 – 34, 666 – 71, 694 – 8 and 748 – 51.

36. FO 84/1279, pp. 233 – 41, Churchill to Secretary to the Government, Bombay number 310/59, 14 August 1867; and FO 84/1292, pp. 84 – 8, Churchill to Secretary to the Government, Bombay, number 7/39, 26 February 1868.

37. FO 84/1292, pp. 113 – 14, memo, W. H. Wylde, 28 May 1868.

38. Ibid., p. 311, memo, W. H. Wylde, 16 November 1868.

39. Ms. Clar. dep. c. 510, Sir R. Murchison to Lord Clarendon, 9 December 1868.

40. ADM 127/40, Foreign Office (A. Otway) to Admiralty, 21 July 1869; and HCA 36/5 bundles 6 – 7 (letter in separate envelope marked 'Misc. Correspondence') Wylde to Rothery, private, 28 July 1869.

41. P. P. Bills, Public, V, 'An Act to regulate and extend the Jurisdiction of Her Majesty's Consul at Zanzibar', (32 & 33 Vict.) 22 July 1869.

42. For an interesting discussion on backgrounds, methods of recruitment, etc., of consuls, see Platt, D. C. M., *The Cinderella Service* (London, 1971).

43. ADM 127/40, Admiralty (V. Lushington) to Commodore Heath, number M 127, 24 July 1869; Commodore Heath to Admiralty, number 29, 12 January 1870; and Commodore Heath to Admiralty, number 212, 22 September 1869.

44. Ibid., Commodore Heath to Admiralty, number 34, 14 January 1870.

45. FO 84/1328, pp. 385 – 9, Rothery to A. K. Stepney, 19 June 1870.

46. See, for example, Rothery to Treasury, 16 July 1870.

47. Ibid., p. 144, memo C. Vivian, 22 February 1870;

48. ADM 1/6174, minute V. Lushington, 18 November 1870.

49. ADM 1/6168, Foreign Office to Admiralty, 2 March 1870.

50. FO 84/1328, pp. 122 – 3. memo, C. Vivian, 21 February 1870.

51. ADM 127/40 and ADM 123/185, 'Instructions for the Guidance of Naval Officers employed in the Suppression of the Slave Trade', 6 November 1869.

52. Sulivan, pp. 258 – 9.

53. Colomb, p. 461.

54. Ibid., p. 191.

55. HCA 36/5, bundle 4, Oldfield to Rothery, undated.

56. ADM 127/10, Captain Bowden to Commodore Montressor, 30 June 1865. For purposes of comparison, a work dealing exclusively with West African naval activities is Ward, W. E. F., *The Royal Navy and the Slavers* (New York, 1969).

57. Sulivan, p. 55n.

58. Colomb, p. 70.

59. Sulivan, pp. 101–3, and p. 167.

60. ADM 1/6170, 'Reply of the Committee on the East African Slave Trade to Sir Leopold Heath's Observations upon their Report', p. 7, 12 September 1870.

61. FO 84/1328, pp. 390–406, Commodore Heath to Admiralty, number 85, confidential, 25 March 1870.

62. ADM 1/6072, Admiralty (Hammond) to Foreign Office, 20 February 1868, and Foreign Office to Admiralty, 26 February 1868; and ADM 1/6127, 'Amount of Naval Force to be maintained on the Several Foreign Stations', Admiralty position paper, f. 230/99, Foreign Office to Admiralty, 25 January 1869; and Colonial Office to Admiralty, 12 February 1869. The West African ships were seen as a short-term residual force to prevent any revival of the trade. All vessels were small with the total commitment of manpower being roughly equivalent to that on the East Indies Station.

63. ADM 1/6072, Foreign Office to Admiralty, 20 September 1868; Admiralty to Foreign Office, 26 September 1868; India Office to Foreign Office, August 1868 and 24 September 1868, and minutes on above; and ADM 1/6286, India Office to Admiralty, number 250A, 11 July 1873, minute, Augustus Spalding, 28 October 1873, Cumming to Admiralty, 8 August 1873; and minute, Lushington, 5 and 6 September 1873.

64. FO 84/1310, pp. 160–2, Admiralty (W. Romaine) to Foreign Office, 31 March 1869.

65. CO 167/522, Foreign Office (A. J. Otway) to Under-Secretary of State for the Colonies, number 6426 Mauritius, 5 June 1869.

66. ADM 127/40, Russell to Secretary to the Government, Bombay, number 480/1335, (extracts) 18 December 1868; and number 489/1370, 24 December 1868; and Commander deKantzow to Commodore Heath, 9 June 1869.

67. FO 84/1309, pp. 88–9, Foreign Office to Admiralty (draft), June 1869.

68. CO 167/522, Foreign Office (Otway) to Under-Secretary, number 6426 Mauritius, 5 June 1869.

69. ADM 127/40, Admiralty (V. Lushington) to Commodore Heath, number M209, 19 July 1869; and CO 167/522, minute, Sir F. Rogers, 15 December 1869.

70. FO 84/1267, pp. 267–8, memo, W. H. Wylde, 19 April 1866.

71. FO 84/1310, pp. 286–8, memo, W. H. Wylde, 28 May 1869.

72. Sulivan, pp. 273–4, and p. 278.

73. Mss. Brit. Emp. S22.G.7. Commodore Heath to Sir T. Fowell Buxton, 16 April 1868. There was a great deal of discussion in anti-slavery circles about the question of the relative comfort of slaves in Muslim societies. The truth of the matter seems to be that domestic slaves were frequently treated fairly well whereas plantation slaves in places like Pemba were less fortunate. A study of the general status of slaves in Muslim countries is Fisher, Alan and Herbert, *Slavery and Muslim Society in Africa*, (London, 1970). A particularly useful recent analysis of the question is Cooper, Frederick, *Plantation Slavery on the East Coast of Africa* (Yale, 1977). Cooper has also dealt with changing labour patterns in *From*

Slaves to Squatters: Plantation Labor and Agriculture in Zanzibar and Coastal Kenya, 1890–1925 (Yale, 1980).

74. ADM 127/40, Acting-Lieutenant Henn to Commander Colomb, 6 May 1869, and Admiralty to Commodore Heath, number P270, 21 September 1869, and Colomb, pp. 242–53. (The account in Colomb's book differs slightly in detail from the official report. Differences are easily attributable to Colomb's having forgotten the sequence of specific details in the interval between the events and the writing of the book. The above account is drawn from the official version where differences arise.)

75. ADM 127/1, Admiralty to Commodore Heath, number M73, 7 April 1870. The origin of the term probably stems from the word *sidis* for Negro slaves as opposed to *habshis*, or Abyssinian slaves. See Kelly, p. 413.

76. ADM 1/6220, minute, V. Lushington, 9 June 1871.

77. FO 84/1390, pp. 238–42, Captain Fairfax to Sir Bartle Frere, 21 January 1873; and ADM 127/1, Commodore Heath to Admiralty, number 109, 11 May 1870. The preference for the Kroomen over Seedies continued for a long period of time. For example, see Keyes, Sir Roger, *Adventures Ashore and Afloat* (London, 1939), p. 56.

78. Compilations of totals for captured dhows and released slaves are drawn from High Court of Admiralty documents, HCA 35/81 and HCA 35/82. Sulivan's capture totals include dual prizes taken with the *Star*. All totals for liberated slaves must be viewed as approximate, given the vagaries of adjudication.

4

The Frere Mission

On 7 October 1870, an emissary from the palace informed Churchill that the death of the Sultan of Zanzibar was imminent. The consul immediately notified Commander R. M. Blomfield who brought the *Teazer* close into harbour opposite the consulate to stand by in case of any civil disturbance. The consul also sent Kirk to fetch the heir apparent — Saiyid Barghash. As Majid died, his brother assured Churchill that he had mended his formerly rebellious ways and that not only would he take no action as sultan without consulting the consul, he would also give satisfaction on the ultimate suppression of the slave trade. Churchill was sufficiently satisfied to acquiesce in the accession of the new sultan.[1] The consul, however, was badly informed about the attitudes and base of support of the new sultan. After his abortive coup, Barghash had been allowed to return from exile in 1861. He then began a secluded, countryside existence during which he came more and more under the influence of the *mutawi'ah*, members of a movement which had begun in Muscat to espouse the religious fundamentalism of the Ibadi sect. While religion was the dominant concern, the philosophy of the *mutawwa* also produced strong anti-European attitudes.[2]

Barghash needed the consul's support to gain the throne, but after having secured his position, he quickly reacted against the increasing dependence of the sultanate on Britain and took up the anti-Western position of his supporters. Within three days of becoming sultan, Barghash had repudiated his agreement with Churchill and the consul angrily reported 'it is to be regretted that there should not be at the present moment in Zanzibar anyone to dispute the succession.' His anger at the new sultan's *volte-face* on

79

such questions as the steadily growing slave trade, Churchill actually began considering ways to depose Barghash a day later. Believing that another brother, Saiyid Turki, might dispute the succession, he suggested that the Foreign Secretary could plainly see 'how desirable it would be to unseat him on the first pretext'.[3]

Displeased with the new sultan, the staff at the consulate was also concerned with the state of the slave trade which Barghash seemed quite unwilling to check. Early in 1870, Kirk suggested that the total number of slaves introduced into Zanzibar was up over 2,500 from the previous year. What made the increase particularly remarkable was the fact that a cholera epidemic was raging on the island as well as on the coast and the mortality rate at Kilwa had been put at 200 deaths daily with slaves in the stricken area being offered for as little as one dollar each.[4] Nor was the navy well placed to check the increases. The new instructions stemming from the committee report required assessment and a measure of caution and, as has been seen, the cruising ground was forced back toward Zanzibar by the emphasis on bringing captures into the port of adjudication. There were, however, some positive developments from the committee report. One change was that Heath's successor as commanding officer of the station was to hold the rank of rear-admiral. In addition, the Admiralty hoped to implement the call for four additional ships to be added to the squadron. The Treasury, however, took a different view of priorities and, in an economy move, insisted that two of the gunboats be diverted to the China Station.[5] For once the Admiralty and the Foreign Office were united against the Treasury. In the Foreign Office, Vivian fumed about the fact 'that the hesitation of the Treasury should obstruct the carrying out of the proposals of the East Africa Slave Trade Committee.'[6] Wylde was even more upset and attacked the Treasury suggesting

> . . . the position assumed now by the Treasury makes them practically the arbiters of the destinies of the country for however expedient or requisite a measure may be it is liable to be thwarted by a refusal of the Treasury to sanction the expenditure for carrying it out.[7]

Lushington was displeased and observed that it would still be possible to have only two ships available for slave trade duties.[8] The issue finally came to the floor of Parliament with Lord Campbell moving that an address should be sent to the Queen 'that such measures as are necessary to assist the cruisers employed in the repression of the Slave Trade on the Eastern Coast of Africa may be adopted.' He explained that 'it has become a struggle between the Foreign Office and the Treasury,' and suggested that it was clear that while the former was attempting to strengthen the naval posture, the Treasury 'are not disposed to second the exertion.' The government, however, stood by the decision and Lord Stanley spoke against the motion, arguing that information concerning kidnapping of Fiji islanders by British subjects required a strengthened naval presence in the Pacific. He contended that the situation meant it was likely that ships would be transferred from East Africa, not to it. The real issue from the government's point of view was that, 'the Government . . . might be trusted to do that which was just and necessary without further instigation on the part of the House.' The motion was defeated and the intended increases in the cruiser squadron were checkmated.[9]

In the meantime, the navy was making do with the ships on hand. An early action after the accession of Barghash helped reestablish Majid's proclamation of 1864. Feeble as it may have been, the five-month prohibition was seen as a useful addition to the treaty structure and Kirk was disturbed by Barghash's refusal to re-issue the proclamation. Since no one was sure if the document was still valid, Kirk was anxious for a test case. He was presented with one by Captain Richard Adams who had taken command of the *Nymphe*. Adams captured a dhow with 268 slaves which he brought into Zanzibar. Unfortunately the dhow had sailed within the grace period of the old proclamation so Kirk released the dhow. In explaining his action to the sultan, however, he said it was released only because it had sailed before the expiration of the grace period provided in the proclamation of 1864. The sultan responded by thanking Kirk for his decision and without questioning the original right of capture.[10] Apparently Barghash was pleased that the dhow had been released and Kirk was certainly happy that the Majid proclamation seemed to have been accepted by the new sultan and thus retained as a part of the slave trade law. Adams and the crew of the *Nymphe* were less pleased, having lost a considerable sum in bounties on the release of what was clearly a slaving dhow.

Meanwhile, Commander F. P. Doughty of the gun vessel *Magpie* was sent into a northern cruising zone. Despite difficulties in dealing with captured vessels, the station commander felt it necessary to keep at least one slave trade cruiser patrolling the northern approaches to the Persian Gulf. As a result, Doughty was stationed off Ras al Hadd where he found himself in the same sort of situation that had confronted Sulivan and Colomb two years before. For example, on 30 May 1871 the *Magpie* approached a becalmed dhow two miles off the cape. The dhowmen had already seen the ship approaching and put out a small boat which they were using to tow the dhow ashore. By the time the ship could dispatch her own boats, the dhow had landed and the crew made off with the slaves, Nevertheless, the boat crew struck inland to cut off the fleeing Arabs and managed to retrieve 61 of the slaves.[11] The cruising was extremely difficult for the *Magpie*'s crew, fresh from Britain and unaccustomed to the heat which hovered around 90 degrees, even at midnight. In less than a month during the summer, there were 59 attacks of sunstroke treated on the ship. Not only did the heat take a toll, strong gales had damaged the ship's boats. The old problem of numerous boardings with sparse results also hampered Doughty who inspected 86 dhows before making his first capture.[12] Difficulties plagued other ships on the station including the *Columbine* under Commander John Tucker. In December of 1871, a boat was dispatched to board a dhow but the boarding party was repulsed with heavy casualties. Two able-seamen, Henry Radley and J. Barrett, along with an ordinary seaman, J. Thomson, were killed and two other members of the boarding party were seriously wounded.[13]

The failure of the navy to achieve its objective was plain. The coastal blockade was barely making a dent in the slave trade figures. Kirk estimated that during the last half of 1871 a total of 14,392 slaves had been shipped from Kilwa and that approximately 3,000 had been sent from other ports within Zanzibar dominions including Dar-es-Salaam. The total of over 17,000 slaves represented revenue at the Zanzibar custom house of more than £9,000 and Kirk believed that something like 7,000 of the slaves must have been exported as far north as Arabia or Persia.[14] Kirk was quick to emphasise the navy's difficulties. A report which he sent to Churchill in September of 1871 is worth quoting since it helps stress the ill-will which was growing between Kirk and the navy officers on the station. Kirk, as judge of the Vice-Admiralty Court, suggested to the consul:

As to slave trade it is a farce to see as now one cruiser prowling about and professing to blockade 1000 miles of coast. I expect to see this vessel come in soon with a poor fishing boat and some intricate case while thousands and thousands have been packed as regular slave cargoes and shipped off.[15]

While arguing against Kirk's imputations, the navy would have been the first source of agreement that there weren't enough ships to do the job. When the Treasury re-directed the gunboats intended for the station, the new admiral commanding, Rear-Admiral James H. Cockburn, despaired of being able to prosecute the slavers effectively. 'I cannot see any prospect of stopping the slave trade by half and half measures,' he complained.[16]

Cockburn, who had been sent to the station to exert the added experience and prestige of a rear-admiral, was appalled at what he found there. After visiting the slave market in Zanzibar, he described it as the most disgusting thing he had ever seen with some of the slaves being living skeletons and others, while well fed, being pulled around with a crooked stick like so many sheep in a market. Even more frustrating for the admiral was his squadron's inability to stop the traffic with the resources on hand. He believed that every new plan the navy employed was countered by the Arabs who were aided and abetted by the sultan himself. He informed the Admiralty that the naval effort was 'a matter of sneer and jeer by the Arabs.' So Cockburn insisted that something must be done and suggested two proposals. One was to use economic leverage in the form of a subsidy to force the sultan to abandon the slave trade while the other was to employ a radical new naval initiative. Of course the call for economic pressure was nothing new although it may have helped stimulate plans which were already being developed. What was more important was his suggestion for locating a stationary guard ship to serve as a permanent depot in Zanzibar harbour. Equipped with steam launches and commanded by a captain experienced in slave trade matters, this permanent ship would become the centre of the anti-slavery patrol.[17] As will be seen both parts of the plan soon came to fruition and the guard ship concept radically transformed the navy's approach in the region.

Pressure for a new political initiative was certainly not limited to Cockburn or the Admiralty. Far more significant was the fact that the slave trade was continuing to attract Parliamentary attention with a major investigation into slave trade questions conducted by a Select Committee in July 1871. The appointment of the committee was in part due to lobbying by humanitarian forces, notably the Church Missionary Society and the Anti-Slavery Society which had jointly worked to secure Parliamentary action. Their position was strengthened by the heightening of interest in East African matters which accompanied growing concern for the missing David Livingstone, the mounting of the official Dawson relief expedition, and finally Stanley's successful search. The cause was also helped by a series of public meetings designed to further stimulate public interest through speakers including Sir Bartle Frere, former Governor of Bombay, and Horace Waller who were being supplied with information by both consul and naval personnel.[18] Frere is particularly significant since he was attempting to generate public interest as a means of stimulating a more forward East African policy. The Select Committee was also a useful tool for the government during a period in which policy goals in East Africa were becoming more and more muddled. With renewed public attention adding to the already growing consensus for a new political initiative at Zanzibar, the committee appeared a good way to gain the mandate of the House of Commons in case force were to become necessary in dealing with Barghash. It might also clarify questions of policy which were dividing the Indian government. Bombay continued to maintain its traditional support for a more forward policy in the region through encouragement of trade and alignment with local rulers who appeared open to trade initiatives. The Indian government at Simla, on the other hand, was loath to provide funds for Bombay initiatives and preferred to adopt an aloof acceptance of local rulers regardless of legitimacy, policy or trading position. The division was clear on the question of the Muscat subsidy with Simla strongly disinclined to pay the bill and preferring to sever the link with Zanzibar altogether rather than incur the additional expense of paying the subsidy from Indian funds. Questions of who ought to finance the Zanzibar consulate itself added to the difficulty. The situation has been described by one historian as a series of steps 'into administrative chaos and confusion.'[19] Another factor arguing for a Select Committee from the government's point of view was that it could force the humanitarians in the House to shoulder a larger share of the burden of responsibility for the decisions which were going to have to be taken.

The 15-man panel drew heavily from the vocal humanitarian spokesmen in the House. The chairman was Russell Gurney, Liberal MP for Southampton whose Quaker family had a long association with the humanitarian movement. Membership also included Gilpin along with Sir John Hay, Sir Robert Anstruther and Viscount Enfield. The committee called a wide range of witnesses including Colomb and Heath as well as Rigby and Churchill. Some of those testifying saw their appearance as a chance to propagandise for intensified actions. Rigby, for example, confided privately that his purpose would be to point out how the trade had grown and that 'the time has arrived to put an entire stoppage to it.'[20] Naval issues were naturally of high priority. Rigby, recalling the *Gorgon* era, argued that the ships used on the station were old and inefficient while Heath insisted that such vessels as the *Nymphe* were new and well designed for the service. Rothery suggested that it was essential to bring question-able dhows into the port of adjudication while Colomb argued that if doubtful vessels had to be towed into port the effect would be that all doubtful vessels would always be let go. Important allegations were made against the navy by the Rev Edward Steere, soon to become head of the Universities Mission, who accused the boat crews of everything from drunkenness and debauchery to harassing commerce. On this score it was Rigby who took up the navy's cause and refuted the allegations as did Colomb who, on the question of commerce disruption, suggested 'a violent disease requires a violent remedy.'[21] Rear-Admiral Charles Hillyar joined Heath in arguing that the squadron would have to be increased but Heath went further saying that the trade could never be stopped by the navy alone and that while ten ships would be a minimum to attack the trade, there was no guarantee that even that number would succeed. 'I think we have gone on for 25 years and have done no good whatever,' was his sweeping conclusion.[22]

Sir Leopold was not alone in feeling that the navy could not extinguish the trade as long as slavery was maintained as a legal institution all along the East African and Arabian coasts. Officers on the station were reporting the same view that was being expressed before the committee. Commander R. B. Cay of the *Vulture* told Cumming that the trade was being carried on in driblets and that unless some sort of controls were placed on the dhows, 'I do not see how the slave trade can be suppressed.'[23] At almost exactly the same time, Captain H. R. Wratislaw reported, 'I would submit unless slavery, including domestic, is entirely put an end to in the territory of Zanzibar no number of cruisers could prevent the continuation of the Slave Trade.'[24]

The Select Committee was inclined to agree and the report

outlined plans for a major new offensive against the trade. The committee suggested that 'all legitimate means should be used to put an end altogether to the East African slave trade.' The major thrust of those means should be aimed at the sultan in the committee's view. The report suggested that the sultan should be told that in view of the systematic evasion of the treaty provisions limiting the trade, the British government would be forced to abrogate existing treaties and take the necessary steps to stop the slave trade completely. In addition, the committee agreed that the naval squadron off Zanzibar should be increased for the time being. This proposed boost to the navy's strength was gratifying to the naval witnesses, as was the committee's vote of confidence on the question of control of the squadron which they said must be left to the commanding officers. The committee recommended such specific additions to the squadron as steam launches for in-shore operation and tried to deal with the problem of disposition of freed slaves. Slaves taken by cruisers should be released at Zanzibar only if the sultan complied in a new treaty, otherwise they should be taken to the Seychelles.[25]

Support for a new political initiative had been growing for several years and the committee report helped to assure new action despite a measure of indecision within the government. Vivian privately explained to Kirk that the Gladstone government was hesitant about undertaking the massive responsibility for completely eliminating the trade. He explained:

It is not to be wondered at that govt. should hesitate to commit themselves to the policy recommended by the House of Commons committee involving an increased expenditure estimated at nearly £80,000 a year until they can see their way to some adequate results.

According to Vivian the government was not willing to accept that the situation on the East Coast was analogous to the earlier case of the West Coast which had been stimulated by Europeans and Americans and carried on in European-design vessels. But the whole question had been taken up by Parliament and Vivian assured Kirk that the government could not ignore the question for long. 'Something must be done soon, as the subject is sure to be raised again when Parliament meets,' he concluded.[26] As things developed, Vivian was right. The Queen's Speech of 1872 included reference to the question of the slave trade and Gilpin kept the matter before the House. In June of 1871, he went so far as to move that a new treaty should be negotiated with the sultan that 'will relieve Her Majesty's Government from existing arrangements, by which they are made parties to the Slave Trade.'[27] Lord Granville, now Foreign Secretary, confided to Gladstone that 'we must not let the question of the East Coast of Africa Slave Trade sleep.'[28]

Through late 1871 and into 1872 the problem of the slave trade enjoyed new prominence as it became a full-fledged item on the agenda at cabinet meetings.[29] The approach emerging from these cabinet sessions was for a special mission to go to Zanzibar and to Muscat to negotiate a new treaty for the suppression of the slave trade. Not only could a special mission exert added pressure on the sultan, it would also serve as a graphic demonstration that the government was doing something about the whole question. A helpful addition would be for the mission to be headed by a recognised leader in the British anti-slavery ranks since this would reduce the public criticism for inactivity which had begun to grow after publication of the Select Committee's report. By September of 1872, Granville thought he had just the man for the job — Sir Bartle Frere who had been in the forefront of the agitation for a forward policy on the coast. The only question was whether Frere would accept the post and Granville slyly suggested to Gladstone that if it were offered correctly it would be hard for him to refuse. 'He may object on the point of dignity but having proclaimed the suppression of the Slave Trade as the great object of his life, he could only refuse with a bad grace,' Granville observed.[30]

As it turned out, Frere did view the mission as being beneath his dignity. When Wylde met with Frere and Sir Henry Rawlinson he was told that the job hardly required a man of Sir Bartle's calibre and that they thought that the resident at Bushiri, Colonel Lewis Pelly, would be a good man for the post. Frere did of course say he would undertake the mission if he were ordered to do it. Wylde's revelation must have caused the Foreign Secretary a smile since he had already written the letter which he was sure Frere could not refuse two days before.[31] In the end Granville's plan worked to perfection; the special mission was headed by Frere and the government could bask in the anti-slavery societies' adulation of Sir Bartle. It was immediately apparent that the choice was a popular one within anti-slavery circles and with the press. As it was put in the columns of *The Times*:

No one knows more of such questions than Sir Bartle Frere, and no one is more highly endowed with those cautious and conciliatory qualities which tend so much to success when difficult and disagreeable duties are to be performed.[32]

In the meantime, the attitude in the Foreign Office was hardening. In May of 1872, Kirk reported 'never since coming to Zanzibar have I seen so many large dhows come in crowded with slaves and seldom have the slaves imported been landed in a worse state.'[33] Wylde decided that it would be necessary to insist on the sultan's total surrender of the right to carry slaves along the coast or all the exertions against the trade would be thwarted.[34] Frere was of the same opinion and confided his belief that beyond attacks on the northern slave trade, the draft treaty should include prohibition of the transit of slaves for sale between the African mainland and Zanzibar as well.[35] The Admiralty took the same hard line and informed the Foreign Office that to stop the general slave trade the limited traffic between Zanzibar and the mainland would also have to be stopped. The Admiralty view was based primarily on the advice of Oldfield who had been consulted on the question. Oldfield believed 'that it is quite impossible to stop the general slave trade unless the more limited trade be also stopped.'[36]

As the planning for the mission continued, additional members of Frere's staff were named including Pelly, the Rev G. P. Badger as interpreter, and Major C. B. Euan-Smith as Frere's private secretary. The Admiralty was anxious to be involved in preliminaries for the mission and wanted to assure naval representation. Suggesting that Frere should have an experienced cruiser captain to advise him on naval questions, the Admiralty recommended Captain Charles Jago who was on the station in command of the *Briton*. Frere was pleased with the recommendation and the appointment was made. Jago, however, broke a leg and was forced to the Seychelles to recuperate. He was replaced on the mission by Captain Fairfax from the flagship who had served as the naval representative on the 1869 slave trade committee.[37] The navy was also charged with transporting the mission on the final leg of the journey and the yacht *Enchantress* was assigned to carry Frere and his staff. Rear-Admiral Cumming was ordered to rendezvous at Zanzibar with his flagship and all the other ships available on the station at the time.[38]

Frere and his party arrived at Zanzibar on 12 January 1873 and found Cumming in the flagship *Glasgow* along with *Briton* and

Daphne already in harbour. The mission began auspiciously in an air of ceremonial pomp which shook the normal routine of the town. The first meeting at the palace seemed to Frere to be the time to impress the Zanzibaris so he arrived with the Admiral accompanied by all his off-duty officers. To add to the impact of the visit, Sir Bartle invited officers from the United States vessel *Yantic*, also in harbour, to accompany the group which was swelled to 48 men including Kirk and the consular staff. The streets were lined with the sultan's troops and naturally large crowds gathered to inspect the visitors. Frere was especially pleased when he arrived at the palace and was met by Barghash some thirty yards from the door. 'He has never before been known to advance so far in welcome of any visitor,' Frere noted confidently in his report. A salute was fired as the party arrived which was dutifully returned by the *Glasgow*. The highlight of the first meeting was Frere's presentation to the sultan of a letter from Queen Victoria. And the ceremonies had only just begun since the sultan returned the visit by arriving among the British ships in his barge with equal pomp. It was a far cry from boat cruising after dhows for the seamen who were pressed into spit and polish formation to welcome Barghash. The boats formed double lines to escort the sultan, the yards were manned, and the inevitable royal salute was fired.[39]

The ceremonial success seemed to presage good fortune for the mission but it soon became clear that the omens had been inaccurate. Barghash was ready to be a good host and to respond with official correctness; he was not ready to end the slave trade. His position is, of course, understandable in light of the strength of *mutawwa* support among his advisers. In addition to the anti-Western sentiment of the *mutawi'ah*, a number of leading figures in the sultanate, including the sultan, had a large financial stake in the slave trade. It is hardly surprising that six days after his arrival, Frere was reporting that the pressure from the sultan's advisers was greatly against his signing the draft treaty.[40] Frere, who had trouble enough with the sultan and his court, also found that he was receiving cold comfort from the American and French consuls as well. He reported that the United States consul, W. G. Webb, seemed determined to thwart the goals of the mission but that the greater problem was probably Captain Byron Wilson of the *Yantic* who was equally determined to achieve the goals for himself. The captain had a companion travelling as a sort of private secretary who was also a special correspondent for the *New York Herald*. Wilson seemed intent on duplicating the recent East African coup of Henry Stanley by obtaining a treaty for the United States before Frere could negotiate the document for Britain. The captain's main problem was his anti-treaty consul, for, unable to speak Arabic, Wilson had to rely on Webb to translate the document. The consul changed the whole point of the treaty in the translation and turned it into a simple assurance of goodwill from the United States.[41] The American machinations thus succeeded only in confusing the issue. Probably even more damaging was the coolness to the mission of the French consul, de Vienne. Returning to Zanzibar while negotiations were in progress, the consul not only failed to offer active support to Frere, he also left Barghash with the impression that he could look to France for support to maintain his independence.[42]

Against this background of difficulties, Frere's discussions with the sultan continued. There were, in fact, two rounds of talks with the first set collapsing in early February. Frere's position was simply that the sultan had to sign the treaty in order to maintain friendly relations with Great Britain and that the predominant British influence in the region meant that the sultan could not do without that friendship. Barghash did not dispute Frere's contention but pointed to a recent hurricane which he said had ruined the island and made any further economic losses unthinkable at that time. The sultan referred to Zanzibar's dependence on agriculture and said that its agriculture could not be carried on without slaves. 'All our people have become as a sick man full of pains, and requiring a skilful physician to treat him with gentle medicines until his disease is cured,' Barghash told Badger at one stage of the discussions. Frere countered by suggesting 'that to continue the importation of slaves is to administer to the sick man more of the poison which has made him sick.' Then Frere tried to use the navy as his trump card by telling the sultan that anyone could see that the navy was able to cripple the trade with a very small squadron and that if necessary a larger squadron would be called on to crush it altogether but that such action would have an even more detrimental impact on legitimate commerce.[43] Of course Barghash, who could see the force of Frere's arguments, hoped through delays to pacify his advisers and minimise the damage to his revenue. His delaying tactics of asking for time as well as a release from the Muscat subsidy to rejuvenate the economy were the same that Majid had used in prior years. The persistent hostility of his entourage left him with little room for concession without completely undermining his local support. Nevertheless, Frere was still hopeful that some sort of arrangement could be achieved. In an effort to give the sultan a little more time to consider the case and change his mind, Sir Bartle left for an inspection tour of the southern slave ports, such as Kilwa, in February and was hopeful that on his return, Barghash would prove more amenable.[44]

The delay had little effect. As the second round of talks began, it was clear that Barghash was under tremendous pressure from his advisers and relatives to resist the treaty.[45] Barghash remained convinced that adherence would be impolitic under the circumstances and a renewal of discussions had little impact on that outlook. The sultan had already summarised his position by saying, 'we have considered what has been said, and we are convinced it involves destruction to us. It is quite in your power to destroy us, but you ask us to destroy ourselves, and that we cannot do.'[46] Despite the definite nature of the refusal, however, as Frere left Zanzibar having failed to gain the treaty he harboured no animosity and showed considerable insight into the situation there. He informed Granville that while the sultan seemed to have forgotten that such a question as the slave trade existed or that he had ever received a mission on the subject, Barghash 'is by no means a frivolous or thoughtless man.' The envoy believed that the sultan had only tried to pacify the strong slave trade interests in his retinue and was awaiting the next move of the British government. 'He knows we shall not bombard him into obedience, and hopes we will not dethrone him.' Frere explained. He went on to express the belief that Barghash would really be pleased if the British government would settle the question for him. At any rate, 'he had rather rely on our forebearance, if we do use any form of compulsion, than on the loyalty or reasonableness of any of his family or subjects.'[47] Other members of the mission were less charitable. As Euan-Smith fumed, 'he has made his bed and must lie upon it.'[48]

The next leg of Sir Bartle's mission was easier, as expected. He arrived in Muscat on 12 April and four days later reported that the accommodating Saiyid Turki, who had little to lose in the exchange and who had already been well schooled by the British resident, had agreed to prohibit all import or export of slaves, to abolish all public slave markets, and to confer freedom on all slaves setting foot in his territory. The Muscat Treaty was signed on 14 April 1873 and the Frere mission was effectively at an end.[49]

There were of course results from the mission besides the Muscat Treaty. Frere had taken action while on the coast and later suggested more changes in a wide-ranging report. One of the most remarkable of his immediate actions was an attempt to provide additional assistance for the consul. Feeling that the need was too urgent to wait, he authorised the hiring of two men who in his own words 'happened to be at Zanzibar.' One of Frere's retainers was Captain Frederic Elton who had seen service with the army in India. The second was Frederic Holmwood, 'a young English gentleman of apparently good education who has been travelling for his amusement.'[50] Despite a relative lack of experience, they proved to be invaluable additions to the staff. As will be seen, Holmwood, whose sole qualification seemed to be that he was on the scene and available, proved to be one of the more effective men on the coast. Frere also turned his attention to the navy after soliciting information from officers including Cumming and Captain G. J. Malcolm of the *Briton*.[51] The officers managed to win Frere over to several of their ideas. Most important, Frere was led to recommend a permanent guard ship at Zanzibar which conformed to the specifications Cockburn had already sent to the Admiralty.[52] He also argued for securing the right to search and detention of vessels under foreign flags including French vessels.[53] Moreover, Frere tried to deal with the old problem of disposition of slaves captured by the cruisers. He recommended that most be turned over to the missions which were beginning to develop within Zanzibar dominions.[54]

All these recommendations and initiatives were, however, only sidelights. The main point was that the Sultan of Zanzibar had refused the treaty and in doing so had flung the gauntlet at the authorities in London. The consequence was a conviction within the government that the issue could not be allowed to rest and that if persuasion had failed, intimidation would have to be used to force the sultan to sign. As Lord Halifax advised Gladstone, 'we can hardly now withdraw from the undertaking.' The plan which Halifax thought best was to blockade all the major Zanzibar ports to force the sultan to submit.[55] It did not take long for the machinery for just such an action to be set in motion.

Wylde was sure that a show of force would prompt immediate capitulation of the sultan who would then 'do whatever we tell him.' After conversations with Badger, Wylde confidently believed that the smallest warship could overawe the entire town of Zanzibar which he described as 'entirely at the command of the guns of a ship of war.'[56] In May of 1873 the plan was set in motion. Kirk was told that the government would not acquiesce in the sultan's refusal and that he was to re-submit the Frere treaty to the sultan. He was also informed that Cumming had been ordered back to Zanzibar and if the treaty had not been signed by his arrival, he would blockade the island.[57] The blockade was no idle threat. Cumming was telegraphed his orders which directed him to proceed to Zanzibar and, if the treaty had not been accepted before his arrival, 'you are to establish Blockade of Island Zanzibar and enforce it according to the Law of Nations.' In response to instructions contained in orders to advise the Admiralty of the ships which would be involved in the blockade, Cumming unreeled an overwhelming force of the flagship *Glasgow*, along with *Wolverine*, *Nimble*, *Vulture* and *Magpie* which would accompany him and *Briton* and *Daphne* which were already at Zanzibar.[58] The imposition of the blockade would clearly constitute an act of war and the Foreign Office was under no illusions on the point. The Admiralty was advised that if the response to the demand was unfavourable 'a public notification of war will be issued, accompanied with a notification of blockade.'[59] The Law Officers cautioned that the Vice-Admiralty court would have to be suspended 'whilst Great Britain is at war with the sultan.'[60]

The government had plainly decided to flex its muscles with the sultan and that could only be done with naval force. It is significant that the ultimate sanction was the navy and that execution of the blockade was totally in naval hands. Goschen, who had succeeded Childers as First Lord, privately and confidentially conveyed Granville's desires to Admiral Cumming. The government did not want the naval force to wait for notification of war or further action from London. 'The notification of blockade is to be issued by you . . . and no reference home is necessary,' the admiral was informed. 'We have of course been anxious while leaving a great deal to your discretion to obtain for you all possible assistance to enable you to arrive at just conclusions in the delicate circumstances in which you are placed.'[61] The final act in the initiative with Barghash was clearly in the hands of the men-on-the-spot.

Captain Malcolm in the *Briton*, a large, new sixth-rate steamer, was senior officer on the East Coast and his orders were sent through the resident at Aden when the broader instructions were sent to Cumming. He was advised that the consul would show him the orders from the government. If the treaty were signed he was to cooperate with the sultan but if not he was directed to await the arrival of the fleet.[62] Malcolm was, however, in the position of

man-on-the-spot in his own right, and he and Kirk immediately
set about putting as much pressure on the sultan as possible. The
Briton's boats were despatched to serve as a small anti-slave trade
squadron which Kirk credited with paralysing the trade. Only one
small cargo of slaves managed to escape the *Briton*'s mini-blockade
and Malcolm's success gave Kirk an important lever in his
negotiations with Barghash which actually began before the
specific instructions from London had been received. A new and
more helpful United States consul, F. R. Webb (not to be confused with W. G. Webb his predecessor), had taken over and was
able to offer the United States consulate as neutral ground for a
meeting between Kirk and the sultan on 27 May. Kirk reported
that he reminded the sultan of the success of the *Briton* and warned,
'if so much could be accomplished and so efficient a blockade
carried out — I argued — by a few determined sailors in open
boats, how easy for us at once to stifle the bulk of the trade.'[63] The
argument was reinforced when the terms of the government's
ultimatum arrived five days later. While the threat of total
blockade strengthened the consul's negotiating position, it also
increased his fears that the sultan might attempt some desperate
ploy. A major cause of concern was the rumour that a French
man-of-war would soon arrive at Zanzibar, and the consul feared
that the sultan might try to claim protection on the French vessel.
Kirk had, however, already discussed that possibility with
Malcolm who decided that if a French vessel approached the port,
he would immediately proclaim a blockade of the town. Kirk
explained to the sultan that the navy would impose the blockade
and that the consul could not delay it for even a single day. As
Barghash listened to the disastrous implications of a blockade, he
recognised that resistance to naval pressure on such a scale was
futile. 'Now I understand,' he said, 'you may consider the treaty
signed.'[64]

On 5 June 1873 the sultan ratified one of the most significant
additions to the treaty structure on the East Coast. All export of
slaves from the coast as well as transportation from one part of the
sultan's dominions to another was banned. Any vessel involved in
transportation or conveying of slaves was liable to seizure and
condemnation. In addition, all public slave markets were to be
closed, the sultan agreed to protect liberated slaves, and no natives
of Indian states were to be allowed to possess slaves.[65] On the
following day, a well-pleased Kirk reported that the slave market
at Zanzibar had been cleared and closed.[66]

In the euphoria which greeted the signing of the treaty, Kirk heaped praise upon Malcolm and the men of the *Briton* to whom he gave credit for convincing Barghash and his advisers of the hopelessness of resistance. He praised Malcolm's 'skilful management of the slender means at his disposal (which) paralysed the Arabs.' In a report to the Foreign Office, Kirk gave due credit when he wrote:

> I should however fail in my duty when speaking of the means concerted to bring about so startling a result, did I not also bring to your Lordship's notice the energy, endurance, and high moral courage displayed by the junior officers and men of H.M.'s Navy — upon whom the toil of carrying out these measures has devolved — short handed and throughout a rainy season all have patiently done their duty in open boats without even the excitement of active resistance or the incentive of prize captures, whilst Her Majesty's Ships have at no previous time, and with such reduced crews, without even boats in case of accidents, ventured into such intricate channels and dangerous waters, upon this difficult and imperfectly surveyed coast.[67]

Notes

1. FO 84/1325, pp. 243–4, Churchill to Acting-Secretary to the Government, Bombay, number 75/277, 7 October 1870.
2. Kelly, pp. 629 and 742; and Gavin, R. J., 'The Bartle Frere Mission to Zanzibar, 1873', in *The Historical Journal*, V, 2, 1962, pp. 123–4.
3. FO 84/1325, p. 250, number 77, 10 October 1870 and p. 254, Churchill to Foreign Secretary, number 47, 11 October 1870. See also Coupland, pp. 87–90.
4. Ibid., pp. 76–83, Kirk to Foreign Secretary, number 2/20, 1 February 1870.
5. FO 84/1329, pp. 125–8, Admiralty (V. Lushington) to Foreign Office, 20 October 1870, and pp. 276–7, 17 December 1870; ADM 1/6170 Admiralty to Dacres and Childers, 23 September 1870; and ADM 1/6198, Foreign Office to Admiralty 22 March 1871.
6. FO 84/1329, pp. 278–9, memo, C. Vivian, 20 December 1870.
7. Ibid., memo, W. H. Wylde, 22 December 1870.
8. ADM 1/6198, memo, V. Lushington, undated.
9. Parliamentary Debates, 3rd Series, CCXII, 23 July 1872 (Lords), motion, Lord Campbell, response, Lord Stanley, 1608–1620.
10. FO 84/1344, pp. 100–1, Kirk to Foreign Secretary, number 8, 8 January 1871.

11. FO 84/1346, pp. 125–31, Commander Doughty to Rear-Admiral Cockburn, 11 June 1871.

12. DTY/2, Commander Doughty, Letter Book HMS *Magpie*, Doughty to Rear-Admiral Cockburn, 15 June 1871 and 31 July 1871.

13. FO 84/1358, pp. 161–9, Sub-Lieutenant Archibald Harene to Commander Tucker, 18 December 1871.

14. ADM 127/41, Captain Wratislaw to Rear-Admiral Cumming, number 20, 1 July 1872; and FO 84/1357, pp. 88–94, Kirk to Foreign Secretary, number 11, 25 January 1872.

15. FO 84/1344, pp. 481–4, Kirk to Churchill, 25 September 1871 (extracts).

16. FO 84/1345, pp. 209–11, extracts of letter from Rear-Admiral Cockburn, 3 March 1871.

17. FO 84/1346, pp. 78–83, Rear-Admiral Cockburn to Admiralty, 31 May 1871. Extracts from above quoted by Lloyd, p. 256. Lushington had already reached much the same conclusion, see ADM 1/6170, memo, V. Lushington, 23 September 1870.

18. *Church Missionary Society Intelligencer*, VIII, 1872, p. 354. The public meetings concerning the East African slave trade held during the early 1870s, supported by such activists as Frere, attracted large and influential audiences. a notable example was a large and particularly important meeting at the Mansion House which followed the committee report. Chaired by the Lord Mayor, it included Frere, Rigby, and no fewer than ten members of Parliament. Business included unanimous acceptance of Frere's resolution for 'the entire abolition of the slave trade in Eastern Africa.' Press coverage of the meeting is in *The Times*, 26 July 1872, p. 10-e.

19. Gavin, pp. 134–5. For a discussion of financial considerations, especially the question of whether the majority of the expense of the Zanzibar consulate should be shouldered by the Foreign Office or the India Office, see Gregory, Robert, *India and East Africa* (Oxford, 1971) pp. 22–4.

20. Mss. Brit. Emp. S22. G7, Rigby to T. Fowell Buxton, 15 July 1871; see also Coupland, pp. 165–70.

21. PP, Reports from Committees, 6, 1871, XII, Select Committee's Report on East African Slave Trade (C. 420 of 1871), printed 4 August 1871.

22. Ibid., p. 53, Q692.

23. ADM 127/41, Commander Cay to Rear-Admiral Cumming, 31 December 1872.

24. Ibid., Captain Wratislaw to Rear-Admiral Cumming, 31 December 1872.

25. Select Committee, pp. viii–ix.

26. FO 84/1344, pp. 66–67B, Vivian to Kirk, private and confidential, 12 December 1871.

27. Parliamentary Debates, 3rd Series, CCVII, 30 June 1871, 952–7; see also CXCIX, 10 February 1870, 119; and CXC, 16 March 1868, 1687.

28. ADD 44169, ff 80–83, Granville to Gladstone, 16 September 1872.

29. ADD 44639, f. 67, memo, cabinet agenda, 24 June 1871; and

ADD 44640, f. 6, memo, cabinet agenda, 22 January 1872; and f. 187, 12 October 1872; and ADD 44641, f. 106, memo, cabinet agenda, 10 May 1873. It should be noted that for a government under pressure on such issues as the Education Act of 1870, an active slave trade policy could appear to be a very appealing political diversion. Forster's bill which doubled the state grant to established church schools succeeded in alienating the nonconformist support which Gladstone relied on so heavily. These normally Liberal voters had expected a system of publicly controlled schools supported from public funds. An active slave trade suppression policy seemed one way to try to rally some of this non-conformist support which was so significant in anti-slavery circles.

30. ADD 44169, ff. 80–83, Granville to Gladstone, *op. cit.*

31. FO 84/1386, pp. 116–19, memo, W. H. Wylde, 26 September 1872.

32. *The Times*, 24 October 1872, p. 10-c. Frere was continually conspicuous in anti-slavery gatherings. See, for example, note 18. His prestige was further enhanced by his position as Vice-President of the Royal Geographical Society. For further press reaction to Frere's appointment and his general position among the anti-slavery spokesmen see *The Times*, 26 July 1872, p. 10-e, 25 October 1872, p. 9-e, 5 November 1872, p. 4-a through e, and 13 November 1872, p. 9-f. For a life of Frere, see Martineau, J., *Life of Sir Bartle Frere* (London, 1895).

33. FO 84/1357, pp. 295–300, Kirk to Foreign Secretary, number 40, 23 May 1872. Quoted by Coupland, p. 182 and Lloyd, p. 263.

34. Ibid., pp. 235–6, memo, W. H. Wylde, 27 July 1872.

35. ADD 44169, ff. 120–3, memo, Sir Bartle Frere, 3 November 1872.

36. FO 84/1387, pp. 42–5, Admiralty (R. Hall) to Foreign Office, 8 November 1872.

37. Ibid., pp. 16–19, 4 November 1872, and pp. 122–7, 18 November 1872. Correspondence also appears in ADM 1/6240.

38. Ibid., pp. 1–4, 1 November 1872. The Foreign Office would have preferred that the flagship *Glasgow* be turned over to the mission — an idea rejected by the Admiralty; see ADM 1/6240, minute, Lushington, 26 October 1872.

39. FO 84/1389, pp. 148–57, Frere to Granville, number 8, 14 January 1873.

40. FO 84/1389, p. 164, Frere to Granville, number 10, 18 January 1873.

41. Ibid., pp. 182–6, extracts from a private letter from Sir Bartle Frere, 1 February 1873; and Bennett, N. R., *Studies in East African History* (Boston, Mass., 1963), pp. 35–8.

42. FO 84/1390, pp. 1–14, Frere to Granville, number 38, 26 March 1873; Coupland, pp. 195–6; and Gavin, p. 145.

43. FO 84/1389, pp. 260–4, Frere to Granville, number 22, 13 February 1873; and FO 84/1390, pp. 45–53, Frere to Barghash, 19 January 1873 (enclosure in Frere to Granville, number 38) 26 March 1873; and pp. 26–8, extract of letter from G. Badger (enclosure in Frere to Granville, number 38).

44. FO 84/1389, pp. 260–4, Frere to Granville, number 22, 13 February 1873.

45. FO 84/1390, pp. 1–14, Frere to Granville, number 38, 26 March 1873; and enclosures to same, especially pp. 21–3, Kirk to Frere, 16 January 1873 for background of the sultan's advisers.

46. Ibid., pp. 117–22, note, Sir Bartle Frere, 1 February 1873. Quoted by Coupland, p. 189.

47. FO 84/1389, pp. 365–75, Frere to Granville, private, 25 March 1873.

48. Mackinnon Papers, vol. 10, Euan-Smith to Mackinnon, confidential postscript, 11 February 1874.

49. FO 84/1390, pp. 274–7, Frere to Granville, number 52, 16 April 1873; and p. 298, telegram, Sir Bartle Frere, 18 April 1873. For an example of preliminary work in Muscat, see R/15/3/A/5, Lewis Pelly to Lieutenant-Colonel Ross, 23 July 1872.

50. FO 84/1389, pp. 320–1, Frere to Viceroy of India, 20 March 1873. Quoted by Coupland, p. 201. See also Etherington, Norman, 'Frederic Elton and the South African factor in the Making of Britain's East African Empire', *The Journal of Imperial and Commonwealth History*, IX, 1981, No. 3, pp. 255–74.

51. ADM 127/41, Captain Malcolm to Frere, 24 March 1873; and FO 84/1390, pp. 228–30, Frere to Granville, number 47, 4 April 1873.

52. FO 84/1391, pp. 175–80, memo, Sir Bartle Frere, 24 May 1873.

53. Monk Bretton Papers, box 42, Frere to Lord Enfield, 25 November 1873.

54. FO 84/1390, pp. 207–9, Frere to Kirk, 1 April 1873.

55. ADD 44186, ff. 18–24, Lord Halifax to Gladstone, 13 May 1873.

56. FO 84/1393, pp. 217–21, memo, W. H. Wylde, 3 June 1873.

57. Ibid., pp. 79–82, Foreign Office (draft) to Kirk, number 12, 15 May 1873.

58. ADM 127/41, Admiralty to Rear-Admiral Cumming, number M133, 4 June 1873, and answer to same.

59. Ibid., Foreign Office (Enfield) to Admiralty, 5 June 1873.

60. FO 83/2362, Law Officers (J. Colleridge, G. Jessel and J. Deane) to Granville, 22 May 1873.

61. ADM 1/6281, George Goschen to Cumming, private and confidential, 6 June 1873. For other correspondence relative to the blockade see Admiralty to Admiral Yelverton (C-in-C Med), 15 May 1873, Admiralty (Hall) to Cumming, 15 May 1873; Foreign Office (Granville) to Admiralty, 15 May 1873; Foreign Office (Hammond) to Admiralty, 15 May 1873; and Foreign Office (Granville) to India Office, 15 May 1873.

62. ADM 127/41, cypher to resident at Aden to be forwarded to the senior officer at Zanzibar, 16 May 1873.

63. FO 84/1374, pp. 163–9, Kirk to Foreign Secretary, number 36, private and confidential, 27 May 1873. Malcolm's hand had been strengthened by Frere's authorisation to bring any slave taken at sea before the consular court. See FO 84/1390, p. 216, Frere to Captain Malcolm, 28 March 1873.

64. FO 84/1374, Kirk to Foreign Secretary, number 49, 5 June 1873.

65. FO 84/1374, Treaty signed by Kirk and Nasir-bin-Said-bin-Abdallah and ratified by Barghash, 5 June 1873.

66. FO 84/1374, Kirk to Foreign Secretary, number 47, 6 June 1873.

67. ADM 127/41, Kirk to Cumming, 11 June 1873; and FO 84/1374, Kirk to Foreign Secretary, number 39, 31 May 1873.

5

The Sulivans and the *London*

With the signing of the treaty of 1873, there was widespread hope among government officials and navymen alike that a death-blow had been struck against the slave trade. There is no doubt that the treaty was an important addition to the framework of East African operations and that the position of both the navy and the consul had been significantly improved. There had also been an obvious heightening of British influence and prestige after Barghash's capitulation. The end of the slave trade, however, was not to come overnight. Reports from cruiser captains and Rear-Admiral Cumming quickly changed from elated optimism to questioning whether the new treaty had really done any good at all. The great fear was that while the seaborne trade could be effectively checked under the new treaty, there was no provision for stopping the overland trade which seemed to be growing up to replace it. In the year following the treaty, an intense blockade was imposed to try to strangle the vestiges of the trade. The initial success of the attempt was reflected by Commander Foot of the *Daphne* whose boats boarded nearly 250 dhows without finding even a single domestic slave on board. Foot confidently, if somewhat unrealistically, proclaimed 'the Slave Trade by sea from the Sultan of Zanzibar's dominions to the Arabian Coast and Persian Gulf is at an end.'[1] The *Briton* and *Vulture* were also meeting similar results and two survey vessels, the *Shearwater* and *Nassau*, helped keep would-be slavers off balance by poking into bays and creek mouths while trying to chart the coast more accurately.[2] By June of 1874, however, confidence at the success of the blockade was being eroded by reports of the growing inland trade. Captain Lindsay Brine, then commanding the *Briton*, reported to Cumming that the treaty had succeeded in suppressing the export of slaves by sea with extraordinary completeness but that 'it has brought into existence a very greatly increased transport by land.' Brine, in suggesting boat patrols in the rivers to counter the new trade, reported that most of the slaves were marched from Lake Nyasa to the coast at Kilwa and then northward along a route usually several days inland from the coast. The land route did, however, approach the coast at several places such as Dar-es-Salaam and Brine thought he might be able to intercept the caravans there.[3] Cumming was unhappy about a plan for boats up uncharted rivers, but was convinced that some action was required. He assured the Admiralty that 'unless stringent and immediate measures are taken to stop this, our work by sea is practically thrown away.'[4]

Confirmation for Cumming's view was coming from the interior where Frere's consular retainers were already doing good work. The new vice-consul Elton was sent to the mainland to register and free slaves held by British Indians as provided by the treaty. Accompanied by a sub-lieutenant from the *Shearwater* and 19 porters, Elton surveyed the mainland and found clear evidence that the slaves who could not be shipped by sea were simply being marched off overland.[5] In the meantime, Holmwood was making a survey of his own in which he attempted to determine the extent of the land trade from October 1873 to October 1874. He put the number of slaves arriving at Pangani, across the channel from Pemba island, at a staggering, and unrealistic, 32,000 and suggested that something like 15,000 of those were absorbed on Pemba itself. Holwood's grim estimate was that the mortality rate among the slaves was 25 to 30 per cent on the first leg from Kilwa to Pangani and that on the northern reaches of the inland route it might soar to as high as 75 per cent.[6] Of course these claims were discussed among cruiser captains off the coast. Foot used Elton's report as the basis for asserting that the slavers were claiming that the treaty had been the best thing possible since they were saving the custom duties and freight charges previously paid to ship slaves by sea. He told Cumming that the slavers 'simply laugh at the idea of the English putting down the slave trade.'[7]

If the reports of the growing inland trade caused a reaction verging on panic among some officials on the scene, the issue was viewed more dispassionately in the Foreign Office. Wylde calmly observed that 'it is only natural to expect that if one channel is dammed, the stream will endeavour to find another outlet.' He was convinced that eventually the government would have to prod the sultan into establishing some sort of post on the inland route. The Foreign Secretary was not sure that was necessary. Derby believed that the navy was the only real tool the government had and that it could be used since the inland route still provided for a short transit by dhow. 'It is only at the seaports that we can interfere effectively — and to some seaport they must be sent, whether nearer or farther,' he reasoned.[8] For the time being, at least, the emphasis would remain on naval suppression despite the rising inland trade.

While the problems of the overland route were growing, the navy was having difficulties with the remaining seaborne traffic as well. One problem, involving two young sub-lieutenants of the *Daphne*, unfolded only four months after the signing of the treaty. Midshipman Percy Hockin had been sent to the ship after disciplinary problems on the flagship. He was quickly sent out on boat cruising duties under the guidance of Sub-Lieutenant Marcus McCausland. As one of Hockin's contemporaries later recalled, 'the idea of sending away one of the "bad hats" from the flagship rather pleased the captain, so Hockin was sent away under McCausland, one of the *Daphne*'s senior subs.'[9] The decision to use McCausland as a moderating influence on the younger Hockin was a remarkable one — if there was ever a case of the blind leading the blind this was it. McCausland had become a midshipman in July 1862 and by December 1865 he had been deprived of three months service time for misconduct. Within four months he was disciplined again losing four months service for misconduct in the process. The ensuing six months saw him disciplined twice more with the loss of another four months of service time. The climax came on 9 February 1867 when McCausland was dismissed from the Royal Navy by court martial. He was ultimately restored in September 1867, but forfeited all his service time dating from the first offence over two years before. The record obviously did not look promising for the McCausland-Hockin partnership, but their boat cruising was initially successful. Their two boats were forced into a river mouth about 40 miles north of Lamu by squalls and after making contact with the local Arab chief, the two officers decided that the river was a perfect place to lie in wait for dhows. As luck would have it the river turned out to be a watering place for dhows and they made a quick capture. After returning to the ship with the prize, they immediately volunteered to go out again and returned to the same place where they again pounced on a passing dhow. More mature or cautious officers would have recognised that they were pressing their good luck and that by interfering with the dhow trade they were costing their 'friends' at the river mouth considerable revenue. Obviously, however, neither McCausland nor Hockin had been known for prudence in the past and true to form they returned to the same spot to try again for the third time. On the way, the two decided to race to the river and McCausland's cutter won easily. Arriving well ahead of Hockin, McCausland was welcomed by the local chief who invited him to the village. Incautiously taking only his interpreter and the captain of a dhow flying British colours which had put in for water, McCausland left his boat and crew on the beach and accepted the invitation. When they arrived, he was given the customary seat of honour next to the chief who told him that a meal would be served shortly. Suddenly one of the men who had been standing behind McCausland ran him through with a spear. The terrified interpreter and dhow captain ran to the beach just in time to meet Hockin who had finally arrived in the second boat. Taking the crews of both boats Hockin quickly advanced to the village only to find that the wooden stockade gates had been closed. As crewmen began cutting down the pallisades, others opened fire through the gaps in the wooden fence. At this point the villagers offered a deal — McCausland for a cessation of the sailors' fire. Hockin, who thought McCausland might still be alive, accepted and the villagers capitalised on the pause in the firing to slip into the jungle behind the village. When the seamen entered the village, they found McCausland's body, marked not only by the initial spear thrust but also with slashes on the head and several gunshot wounds. The discovery was a sobering one for Hockin who wisely withdrew since falling tides might have beached his boats and he was some 200 miles from his rendezvous. It was not necessary, however, to cover the entire distance because the boats met two boats from the *Briton* under Lieutenant Arthur Phillpotts on the way. Phillpotts took charge of all four boats and returned to the village where a contingent of seamen tried unsuccessfully to block the rear of the village while the rest of the boat crews launched a frontal attack. In the ensuing melee, one villager was shot and the village was burned to the ground. In the aftermath, the man identified as the one who actually struck the fatal thrust was imprisoned at Zanzibar where he died less than a year later. For his part, Hockin matured as a result of the experience and went on to serve in four other ships on the station. However, he never entirely lost his flare for recklessness and in 1889, while a commander on the flagship of the Pacific Station, he died of pneumonia after jumping into icy water to save a man who had fallen overboard.[10] For the navy, the McCausland episode was an unfortunate one which underlined the potential dangers of the great responsibility which devolved on to the young officers in charge of boats, especially if they were lacking in judgement in the first place.

While mistakes by junior officers tended to be excusable, similar lack of judgement by senior officers reflected very badly on the navy as a whole. At about the same time the McCausland affair was unfolding off Lamu, an even more serious situation was developing in the Red Sea. Captain Thomas Ward, in command of the *Thetis*, was in transit to the China Station and should not have been involved with slave dhows at all. Nevertheless, Ward decided to do some slave trade suppression on his own initiative while passing through. Coming upon ten dhows, he dispatched the ship's boats to inspect them for slave trade violations. Not surprisingly, the dhows attempted to flee the approaching boats only to be forced in and captured. Ward, totally a novice in questions of slave dhows and not even in possession of the slave trade instructions or the slave trade warrants routinely issued to ships assigned to the East Indies Station, mistook the black seamen for slaves and the stores for slave provisions and promptly ordered the dhows to be burned. Subsequent investigation by the political resident in Aden showed that Ward had burned ten totally innocent pearl fishing boats, had liberated several black seamen who felt no need of being freed, and most unfortunately had had three dhowmen killed in the action. On top of that, the political repercussions were soon felt as the *Thetis* had brought both Egyptian and Ottoman sovereignty into question by its actions. A court of inquiry was established at Aden and Ward and the *Thetis* were ordered back from the China Station to answer the charges. The court found that Ward's actions were completely illegal but remarkably did not take any decisive action against him. With court martial seeming a likely result of the episode, the Admiralty only disapproved Ward's action.[11]

Despite the Law Officers' concurrence that Ward's action were totally unjustifiable,[12] the Admiralty's view was that Ward had simply misunderstood his general responsibilities in interfering with the dhows in the first place and had honestly, if incompetently, misinterpreted the evidence after the capture. The Foreign Office was less disposed to be charitable and Wylde, while admitting that further action against Ward was the Admiralty's concern, angrily noted 'such conduct to say the least shews a great want of judgement and discretion.'[13] If the Foreign Office was angry, the Treasury was furious since they had received the bill which totalled over £1,000. The Treasury attacked the whole affair and informed the Admiralty of their regret that an officer 'should have been so wanting in judgement and discretion as to allow himself to be led into perpetrating an outrage, which . . . brings discredit on the efforts of this country to suppress the slave trade.' The letter continued that the action had been so inexcusable that they would have insisted on Ward paying the whole amount of the damages himself had the sum been a moderate amount. In view of the size of the claim, however, the Treasury would submit a supplementary estimate to Parliament for the amount but only if 'every effort will be made to ensure, in future, the exercise of proper caution on the part of officers in command.'[14] The Admiralty weathered the storm and even adopted the novel approach of assigning the *Thetis* to the slave trade patrol. The rationale seemed to be that if Ward were so anxious to chase dhows, they would assign him where he could do so legitimately. In general, however, the navy's credibility was damaged both on the scene and in the view of the government.

In addition, the *Thetis* affair was only one aspect of a protracted struggle between the Treasury and the Admiralty over slave trade issues, principally the payment of tonnage bounties. As has been seen, criticism of Heath's forward policy produced a defensive reaction among navymen. The attitude continued to affect thinking within the Admiralty. The issue which persistently rankled most was the Treasury's routine downgrading of tonnage bounties and a frequent refusal to pay any bounty at all if the dhow had been destroyed at sea. When the Treasury refused to pay part of the bounty thought due to the *Peterel*, Lushington had had enough. He attacked the 'very unsatisfactory course of proceeding on the part of the Treasury,' and suggested that 'they are aware they are acting in an arbitrary manner.' When bounties were refused on captures by the *Star*, Lushington was 'sure that this deduction cannot be maintained' and complained to the Treasury.[15] Dacres, at the Admiralty as Second Naval Lord agreed that the Treasury was 'acting in a most high handed manner.' For Lushington it was a graphic demonstration of the inferior position of the Admiralty in dealing with the Treasury or Foreign Office. 'This case illustrates the unsatisfactory position of the Admiralty with reference to all these bounty cases.'[16] The bickering between the two ministries continued with the Admiralty complaining about general Treasury procedure and the specific judgements being handed down by Rothery.[17] Nevertheless, the Treasury was in the stronger position and had the last word. Rothery was supported to the hilt and the Treasury announced that it was 'not disposed to limit the discretion at present vested in this Board with respect to determining the amount of tonnage.'[18]

With such a situation in London adding to the difficulties being experienced on the coast, there is little doubt that the euphoria which had greeted the signing of the treaty had evaporated within the year. The rise of the inland trade promised a continued long period of slave trade suppression, and the *Thetis* and McCausland affairs undermined the seamen's standing. There was, however, one bright spot for the navy. Invariably the senior officer on the East Coast shaped operations on the station. When an Oldfield or Sulivan was on the coast the navy's stock soared and during the period of the treaty negotiations and after, Malcolm was in that sort of position. The praise which Kirk lavished on Malcolm during the negotiations for the treaty has already been noted and the captain continued to make his presence felt. For example, during a visit to the Somali town of Mogadishu, the *Briton*'s interpreter was jostled and spat upon while carrying the captain's greetings to the Imam. The interpreter was too ashamed to report the incident to Malcolm who heard nothing about the affair until his next visit to the Somali coast when he learned that the treatment of the interpreter was being viewed as a great coup against the Royal Navy. Recalling such incidents as the loss of the *Penguin*'s boat crews on the same coast several years before, Malcolm decided that the affront could not be allowed to stand. Since the town was near enough to the coast to be easy prey for the cruiser's guns, Malcolm felt safe in pursuing an impressive if somewhat daring indulgence in theatricals. He had a boat crew take him ashore then stand well off to sea leaving him unguarded on the beach, resplendent in dress uniform. When a delegation from the town arrived, they were informed that the Imam of the town would have to come to the beach with his whole entourage and apologise as well as promise to punish the parties who had insulted the interpreter. 'If I feared you I would not come alone amongst you to make you ask pardon,' Malcolm informed the astonished Somalis. Horrified at the suggestion, they insisted that captains always went to the Imam, not the other way around.

Malcolm replied, 'This captain will not do it and the Imam must come to him to the water's edge.' The very brashness of the move aided its success and the Imam and his senior advisers promptly hurried to the beach to comply with the demands.[19]

The colourful Captain Malcolm, with his flare for well-staged performances, helped stem the criticism which the navy received from the *Thetis* incident. But even Malcolm was not immune to criticism and the honeymoon between him and Kirk proved to be a short one. One source of friction was two dhows captured by the *Briton*'s boats under Lieutenant J. G. Blaxland. The first, a dhow called *Hassarah*, was found to have several black crewmen one of whom insisted that he was a slave being carried for sale. The claim prompted scrutiny of the passengers and discovery of a boy who was also a slave being taken for sale. Since the passengers did not appear to be implicated, Blaxland landed them and their belongings, put the slaves in the cutter, and put a prize crew on the dhow to bring it and the *nakoda* to Zanzibar. On the way, however, the dhow began to wallow and Blaxland decided it was unsafe to bring it any further. He destroyed the dhow and as the cutter was full, he let the captain go after making him sign a confession. The decision to release the captain was a questionable one although technically within his instructions. Shortly thereafter, Blaxland took a second dhow, the *Bora Salaam*. Finding another boy being carried for sale, he took the vessel but this time had room in the cutter and brought the captain back to Zanzibar where he was imprisoned. The row began after a complaint from Kirk led the government to censure Malcolm for having failed to bring in the captain or crew from either vessel. There had clearly been a misunderstanding but Malcolm exploded with an angry 15-page report to Cumming in which he insisted that the called-for action of bringing the captain to the port of adjudication had been impossible in the first instance and had been done in the second. Kirk had approved the action and then had confused the dhows in his report, Malcolm insisted. Continuing his irate letter, he wrote, 'the duties to be performed were arduous, the means to perform them at my disposal were insignificant.'[20] In the end, both the Admiralty and the Treasury accepted the report and reversed themselves by approving Malcolm's actions, but the episode was just one amongst many as relations between the consul and the captains deteriorated again.

The real beginning of the difficulties had predated the treaty and involved Kirk in a series of charges against the *Wolverine* under Captain H. Wratislaw. The allegations included a charge of rape lodged against a boat's crew and another charge of petty theft. The rape charge was dismissed after investigation by a court of inquiry. The charge of looting, however, proved more substantial. It has already been shown that at times looting did go on and in this case the issue could not be proven although the irregularities of the boarding procedure were sufficient to result in censure for Wratislaw and the boarding officer.[21] The result of the charges was an overdue revision of boarding instructions which Cumming issued in July of 1873. The major change was the requirement for the boarding officer to leave a written record of boarding with the captain of the dhow while retaining a duplicate of the form for the ship's records. The form was to include any complaints by the *nakoda* as well as his signature.[22]

The case of the *Wolverine* was a serious one and the charges clearly demanded investigation. Some of the later difficulties between Kirk and the navy were, however, of a different nature, and seemed to indicate more than a little pique on the consul's part. One month after lauding the navy's role in gaining the treaty, Kirk was dismissing the cruisers' presence as an irrelevancy in his reports to the Foreign Office.

> The favourable result thus far attained is however as much owing to the assistance rendered by His Highness the Sultan, the pressure brought upon the trading community and the employment of secret agents, in the pay of the consulate, as to the exertions of our fleet which, unsupported the slavers would not have found it difficult to evade.[23]

Malcolm, on the other hand, was ready enough to credit Barghash for living up to his agreement but clearly thought the rest of the credit ought to go to 'the vigilance of the cruisers (sic) and their boats.'[24] On at least one point Malcolm seems to have been correct. While Kirk was to build up a rather formidable intelligence network, it can hardly be credited with much success during mid-1873. Kirk's claims for his secret agents seem inflated in view of a report made by Captain W. F. Prideaux, who took over the consular duties while Kirk was in England in 1874. Prideaux set out to ascertain why the people Kirk had procured to report on treaty infringements and provide additional information 'have omitted in every instance to do so.' The conclusion was that with only two exceptions, the persons who had agreed to function as secret agents 'had apparently never seriously intended carrying out that promise.'[25] While the usefulness of the agents seems to have been nil, it could also be argued that the pressure brought on the trading community was in large part naval pressure, but regardless of the true complexion of the situation it was undeniable that Kirk had stopped being charitable in his dealings with the navy. It was also clear that improvements in the treaty structure had not removed the potential for conflict between the consul and the captains.

A major difference between Kirk and the navy concerned interpretation of the land slave trade. Kirk did not share Cumming's fear that the inland trade threatened to undermine the whole agreement. Kirk, writing while in London, suggested to Lister that the reports were nothing to worry about since the slaves being transported only represented the residue left at Kilwa when the treaty was signed. He confidently suggested,

> I fully expected and knew that these would be taken by land to the coast settlements within the sultan's dominions but I am not satisfied that when these are fully worked off it will pay to bring down more slaves than are actually needed by the Arab residents on the coast.[26]

His position was challenged by Cumming who quite rightly cautioned against the dangers of allowing a time period to 'work off' the slaves as recommended by Kirk. The admiral suggested that there would be no way to set such a time limit since 'so long as the dealers find no opposition is made to the traffic of slaves by land, so long will they continue to transport them to the coast.'[27] It was Kirk's view which prevailed, however, as the Foreign Office was prepared to dismiss the naval warnings and the reports from people such as Elton. Wylde expressed confidence that estimates from the coast were much exaggerated[28] and entirely concurred in the view which Kirk had expressed. It would indeed be premature, Wylde suggested to attempt to interfere with the land traffic at present.[29]

There was one area, however, in which Kirk and the navy authorities were in agreement and that was the lack of clear instructions or guidance offered to the men-on-the-spot in East Africa. The difficulties with the slave trade instructions have already been discussed but the problems were compounded by the treaty of 1873 despite the positive achievements embodied in that document. Many of the old provisions had been made inapplicable by the new treaty and there were a number of areas in which interpretation of the document was by no means clear. For example, there was continuing confusion concerning when and if domestic slaves could accompany their owners on dhows, Employment of slaves as crewmen was another problem. It was also unclear whether slaves could be taken on short journeys by dhow within the territorial waters of a particular portion of the sultan's dominions such as Pemba. If navy officers were in the dark before the treaty, they were even more so after it had been signed, since the government was remarkably slow in clarifying the issues or applying any sort of guidance at all to the men responsible for executing the new document. In January of 1874, Malcolm underlined the problem in a report to Cumming dealing with the status of slaves employed as seamen. Charged with the naval enforcement of the treaty for some eight months, Malcolm still had not received a copy of the document. He complained:

> I cannot quote the words of the Treaty of the 5th of June as up to the present moment a copy of it has never been communicated to the senior naval officer on the East Coast of Africa.[30]

Kirk, who had the treaty, was not much more pleased with his situation. Exactly one week after Malcolm lodged his complaint with Cumming, Kirk, on leave in London, wrote to Rothery about problems of interpretation. Kirk complained that the Foreign Office had done absolutely nothing about the questions of interpretation of the treaty and he was unsure about how to proceed in Vice-Admiralty cases in Zanzibar.

> I told Bourke my position on my return will be difficult and I think a very unfair one, he said they should not allow me to do anything *illegal* but he did not in the least enlighten me in what the law is.[31]

The reluctance in the Foreign Office began to assume startling proportions. Six months after Malcolm and Kirk had complained, Wylde noted that some sort of further instructions ought to be issued to guide the consul but it was quite impossible to frame the instructions until decisions were made 'in regard to the interpretation to be put upon the treaty.'[32] The point was that the government was not clarifying the difficult questions because it had not decided what the answers to those questions were.

In the meantime, the Admiralty was anxious to provide its

officers on the scene with guidance for the changed set of circumstances. From the Admiralty point of view it was not a question of increasing control from London, but simply of helping the officers. On 18 November 1873, an 'immediate' correspondence was sent from the Admiralty to the Foreign Office and the Treasury forwarding draft proposals for a new set of instructions. The Admiralty wanted to promulgate the instructions quickly and expressed the hope that the draft would be approved so that it could be sent out on the next week's post.[33] Two months later, after an involved round of discussion of legal technicalities with the Law Officers, nothing had been done and the Admiralty tried to stimulate some sort of activity by writing, 'My Lords will be glad to have the approval of Earl Granville to the Instructions at as early a date as possible as they are anxious to communicate them to the officers concerned.'[34] That correspondence was followed by a plea for action in April and then on 11 June, almost exactly six months after the initial correspondence, the Admiralty again wrote a 'pressing' note urging action 'with as little delay as possible, as it is important that the instructions should be promulgated as soon as practicable.'[35] Over two months later, the Foreign Office was still trying to decide how the instructions should be worded on such questions as French dhows, fugitive slaves and domestic slavery. A major problem in the eyes of the Law Officers was that of dhows 'entitled to claim the protection of the flag of a foreign state.' In practice the foreign state causing the most concern was France because use of the French flag seemed to offer a way for dhowmen to continue the seaborne trade. The Law Officers wanted to make it clear that officers could not board vessels only to investigate their nationality, unless such boarding was specifically sanctioned by treaty.

> Whatever suspicions they may entertain with respect to a vessel bearing a foreign flag as to her just title to claim its protection, if their suspicions should ultimately prove unfounded the visitation, search or detention will be unjustified and unjustifiable even though the vessel should be proved to be engaged in the slave trade.[36]

Wylde suggested that if the Law Officers' recommendations on this and other related points were accepted, the instructions would be legally correct but would be so restrictive that they would cripple the anti-slavery patrol. The opinion was then expressed that the best approach would be to wait until something went wrong and to deal with problems as they arose.[37] As Derby minuted 'I think the instructions may stand as they are for the present.'[38] On 7 September 1874, almost a year after the Admiralty request for clarified instructions had been sent, one of the most remarkable documents in the slave trade series was drafted in the Foreign Office. 'Lord Derby is of opinion that it will be better to postpone any changes in them until some practical inconvenience has been shown to be caused from adhering to them in their present form,' the Admiralty was advised.[39] After a year of discussion in which the Law Officers and the Foreign Office experts could not agree on what the cruiser captains ought to do on specific points of procedure, the government totally abdicated the responsibility and left it to the captains on the station to make the best of the situation and use their judgement without precedents or new instructions. The guidelines in hand pre-dated the treaty which had completely changed the whole East African situation and in many cases the officers did not even have copies of the treaty to guide them, but it would still be up to them to execute the treaty as best they could.

It is difficult to explain the reasons for the government's lack of action. The fact that the final decision had been taken by Derby may have been a factor. Granville had once described Derby by saying 'the fault of his character (irresolution) was developing itself every day . . . he would die the most irresolute old man in England.'[40] Derby's indecisiveness, however, is not enough to explain the remarkable governmental inertia, since he was aided and abetted by counsellors like Wylde, and the initial delay was Granville's own. In the final analysis, one answer is probably that the questions facing the cruiser captains were extremely delicate and doing nothing to clarify the situation was simply following the line of least resistance. If the government waited for something to go wrong, the captain's intuition might be good enough and there would be no need for any action at all. More important is the fact that inaction in Whitehall might actually stimulate a forward policy on the East Coast. The government could hardly sanction activities such as stopping vessels under the French flag on the high seas. But a committed cruiser captain forced to rely on his own judgement might do just that. If he got away with it well and good; a blow had been struck against the slave trade. If there was a complaint, it was simply a case of an officer misunderstanding his instructions. It was an easy way out for the government but a difficult one for the navy officer who faced censure for illegal capture. Nevertheless, the officers on the station were to be left to their own devices despite the fact that lack of clarification produced confusion and the possibility of consular-naval conflict over inter-pretation, especially in the Vice-Admiralty Court. The men-on-the-spot were to be left to sort matters out for themselves as the government failed to provide the guidance needed to demark their spheres of responsibility or the clarification required to regulate their activities.

It was Sulivan who described the situation best from the naval viewpoint. He lamented the fact that the decisions of the Law Officers which formed the precedents for slave trade proceedings were never communicated to the ships on the station. There were difficult questions such as who were slaves under the meaning of the treaty; when was a domestic slave travelling with his legal owner subject to release and when not. 'The onus of the construc-tion to be put on such passages falls on the unguided judgement of persons little accustomed to the interpretation of the law,' Sulivan said.[41] A Foreign Office memo at about the same time fitted in well with Sulivan's argument but also partially explained the problem. Suppose a Mombasa landowner goes to Kilwa and buys 50 slaves for work on his own lands and then takes them to his estates by dhow, questioned the memo. Is the dhow subject to capture?[42] No one in the Foreign Office was quite sure, but the officers on the station were confronting just such situations all the time.

There was another East African question attracting government attention during the 1870s which diverted the attention of the Foreign Office East African experts. The situation involved mail contracts to Zanzibar. In the autumn of 1871, the Cabinet decided to subsidise mail service by steamers to Zanzibar at least partially in the hope that improved communication and stimulation of private shipping in the area would discourage the slave trade while boosting legitimate commerce. Initial planning suggested that the Union Steamship Co. (Ltd.), which held the contract from England to the Cape, should handle service from the Cape to Zanzibar. In the meantime, the British India Steam Navigation Company would provide service from Aden to Zanzibar. Both lines were to be subsidised and the Union Company persuaded the government to treat the East Coast contract as one with the West Coast agreement. This move brought opposition from several sides including the Postmaster-General who objected to using postal funds to pay for the Zanzibar contract which he viewed as political, not postal. Residents of the Cape also objected since they would be paying increased rates under the new Union contract. In the furore following, the England to the Cape contract was abandoned. The Union Company responded by saying that they would require a higher subsidy of £29,000 for the Zanzibar service. Feeling some responsibility for the reversal that the company had had on the West Coast leg, the government accepted despite the fact that the British India Steam Navigation Company had offered to provide the same service for a subsidy of only £16,315. Finally the whole thing blew up into a matter requiring a Select Committee which found that the government's approach 'was questionable in policy, and in the result unsatisfactory.'[43] The situation was yet another cause for confusion in the already complicated arena of policy decision concerning East Africa.

It was in this atmosphere that one of the major innovations in the navy's anti-slavery campaign HMS *London*, came to Zanzibar to take up her position as a stationary depot ship and the centre of the anti-slavery activities around Zanzibar. In the unsettled situation caused by the lack of instructions and difficulties between Kirk and the navy, as well as the Admiralty and the Treasury, it was important that the navy send a capable man to command the ship. At first, rumours pointed to Oldfield, then in command of the *Achilles*, for the post.[44] In the end, Oldfield did not receive the position, but the choice for captain was still a fortunate one. The first commander of the *London* was another officer who had made a major impact on the East Coast, Captain George Sulivan. As has already been discussed, when Sulivan relinquished command of the *Daphne*, he was among the most experienced of the East Coast captains and his captures of slave cargoes had made him one of the most successful in terms of slaves liberated. Moreover, experience and proven ability combined with another much needed attribute — Sulivan was diplomatic enough to get along with John Kirk. The captain had certainly helped his cause with his book which had been published in 1873, the year before he took over the *London*. Charges against Kirk by Henry Stanley in connection with supplies which the then acting-consul had been unable to forward to Livingstone in the interior brought a shower of criticism which nearly cost Kirk the appointment as consul. Sulivan took Kirk's side in the matter and referred to the pleasant hours he had spent with the doctor and the fact that he had 'witnessed, to some extent, his anxious endeavours and indefatigable exertions in all matters related to the celebrated African explorer Dr Livingstone.'[45] That passage certainly did not hurt Sulivan with Kirk nor did his unique background of experience which grew from a length of service well in excess of the normal three-year assignment off East Africa. Easier relations between the captain and consul removed a major obstacle to smooth operations off the coast.

Sulivan's ship was a veteran campaigner in its own right. Built at Chatham dockyard in 1840, the *London* had taken part in the bombardment of Sebastopol in 1854. In 1858 she had been converted to steam and a screw propellor was added. The Admiralty plan for the ship, after Sulivan brought her round the Cape from Devonport, gave it several roles to perform. The *London* was to serve as a receiving ship incorporating the role of hospital ship with that of prison ship. She had also been fitted with appliances to serve as a floating factory for repair of the fleet's engines. Several large boats were assigned to the ship but some of the lessons of independent boat cruising had been learned and Cumming was advised that the boats should always work in pairs so they could provide mutual support.[46] There were several incongruous features about the different tasks to be performed, but Sulivan quickly set about insuring that his ship functioned properly. One of his early goals was to move the forge off the ship and a small island opposite the town of Zanzibar struck him as a good place to locate it. A bit of personal diplomacy won the sultan's approval for a virtual cession of the island of Bawy and Sulivan was able to move the forge as well as some of the workshops onto the island.[47] While there had been nothing in his instructions about establishing a shore installation at Zanzibar, Sulivan was only beginning and quickly turned his attention to entrenching the navy's presence even further. One problem was manpower and arguing that his allowance of 18 seedies was insufficient, Sulivan petitioned for an increase to 33. He also observed that he would be pleased to have Kroomen instead: he did not gain the Kroomen but the seedie allowance was increased. The request was typical as Sulivan bombarded the Admiralty with a series of requests for more stokers than his rather small initial complement of ten, more senior officers for boat patrolling duties and more officers to be put in charge of stores on the ship. He also interceded for his men, including over 200 seamen, by requesting extra pay for stokers, artificers and other men employed in difficult jobs.[48] These requests met with varying degrees of success but Sulivan never allowed the Admiralty to forget the *London* on its isolated station. A junior officer who reported to the ship shortly after Sulivan's departure described the vessel with the changes which the captain had initiated. She was moored in the bay opposite the consulate and towered over the town 'dominating the whole seascape.' The main deck with the gun ports serving as ventilation had been fitted as the hospital for three-quarters of the length from forward. The factory section was in a large specially built deckhouse and a machine shop had been set up on a portion of the quarterdeck which extended across the ship.[49]

By July 1875, Rear-Admiral Reginald Macdonald, who succeeded Cumming in command of the station, made an inspection tour of the *London*. He reported that due to the factory on deck and a lack of ballast, the ship could no longer be looked on as a sea-going vessel but was well pleased with the general arrangements. 'I had every reason to be satisfied with the extreme cleanliness both of the ship and men,' he said. Macdonald did find the concept of a steam factory located over a hospital to be an odd one but he felt that the plan would work satisfactorily. 'She is as well arranged as circumstances will allow,' he concluded.[50]

It did not take Sulivan long to assert the *London*'s presence as a major military factor in the area. After signing the treaty of 1873, the sultan found that his influence had been undermined in several parts of his dominions. A major crisis came in January 1875 when the *akida*, or military commandant, of Mombasa revolted and declared the independence of the city. The sultan's governor, however, remained loyal and a confrontation developed with the governor holding the town while the commandant and his troops controlled the nearby fortress, Fort Jesus. As the situation deteriorated, Sulivan dispatched Commander Stratford Tuke, commanding the *Rifleman*, to report on the situation. His findings indicated that Mohammed ibn Abdallah, the *akida*, held the fort with some 400 men while the governor had a much inferior force in the town. On 15 January a dhow arrived at Zanzibar bringing news that hostilities had broken out and that three days before the *akida*'s troops had opened fire on the governor's house and had then attacked and plundered the town. Much of the town had been burned although the arrival of 200 reinforcements still loyal to the sultan forced the insurgents back to the fortress. Caught in the middle of the conflict were the British Indian merchants who were forced to flee after losing large amounts of property in the fire. The report of the deteriorating situation prompted Barghash to seek naval intervention to restore his authority. Prideaux, who was acting consul in Kirk's absence, approached Sulivan to provide the necessary support.[51]

The *Rifleman*, one of the brand new composite gun vessels, was already off the coast standing by to protect British Indian subjects. After receiving Prideaux's request, Sulivan quickly organised an additional force to proceed to Mombasa in the *Nassau*, a surveying vessel commanded by Lieutenant F. J. Gray. Two companies of small arms men from the guard ship, a field piece and the party to man the gun were all loaded onto the survey ship along with the *London*'s steam cutter which was designated to serve as a rocket boat. At noon on 16 January, Prideaux joined the company and the ship sailed with Sulivan himself taking overall command. The following morning they arrived off Mombasa and were told by Tuke that the situation had worsened with the *akida* using the 49 guns mounted in the fortress to harass the sultan's forces in the town and causing considerable property damage in the process. Tuke said that most of the town had been burned and that the governor's house and the custom house had been badly damaged. He also estimated that some 25 houses belonging to British subjects had been destroyed. The fortress was set back from the mouth of the bay facing over an inlet but the ships were able to anchor in the bay within shelling distance of the fort. Sulivan and Prideaux, acting on their own authority, decided that on the following morning an ultimatum would be delivered to the *akida* demanding his surrender. Failure to comply would result in the ships attacking the fort. The ultimatum was delivered by Lieutenant Gray who promptly returned with the *akida*'s refusal to submit. As Sulivan described the situation, 'on receipt of this reply the Acting Consul General placed the matter in my hands with a request that I would take the necessary steps for the reduction of the fort.'[52]

The fort, while weakened by age, was still a formidable building with the lower section of its stone walls some twelve feet thick; the mortared upper sections were approximately three feet thick. In preparation for the attack, Sulivan transferred one company of the *London*'s small arms men to the *Rifleman* and positioned the cutters to serve as rocket boats under the command of Lieutenant W. M. Annesley. On Sulivan's signal, the ships and their boats opened fire simultaneously and the fire was immediately returned from the fort. After about an hour exchanging fire from the harbour, the ships were ordered to close on the fort. The *Nassau* led the way and after a slow approach of about 30 minutes anchored between 350 and 400 yards from the fort. The *Rifleman* followed and took a position outside the other ship. The small arms men began firing on the fortress and were quickly followed by the large guns of the ships. The fort's defenders returned the fire but attempted to concentrate their shot at the rocket boat which Annesley was bringing around a reef which formed a narrow channel forcing the boats directly under the batteries of the fort. Fortunately for the boat crew, the fire from the fort was erratic, in large part due to the pounding of the ships' guns led by the 6½-ton gun of the *Rifleman*. After an hour of the bombardment, the guns on the sea face of the fort had been silenced so Sulivan gave orders for the ships themselves to pass the reef and press the attack. Since the large gun of the *Rifleman* provided the best means of breaching the walls, that ship led the second advance which brought the ships to within 200 yards of the fort. As the vessels advanced, the steady fire of the small arms men made it impossible for the fort's defenders to train their guns on the ships. Meanwhile the heavy fire from the *Rifleman*'s large gun was having devastating effect. One shell lodged approximately six feet below the turret at one angle of the fort with such force that it knocked the whole angle of the wall down. Another shell passed through the upper portion of the sea face of the fort, lodged in the fort's granary and blew up two floors opening a twelve foot hole in the wall of the building. With his vessels in position, Sulivan began preparations for advancing his forces to storm the fort when the *akida*'s colours were suddenly hauled down. The ships immediately ceased firing and anchored. That evening the *akida* came aboard the *Nassau* and surrendered to Sulivan. The captain allowed the *akida* and his men safe passage and on 20 January formally took possession of the fort with the naval force on hand. Sulivan then turned the fort over to Prideaux who in turn delivered it to the sultan's Governor of Mombasa. Losses among the defenders of the fort were put at 17 killed and about 50 wounded; the British force had no casualties.[53]

The results were welcomed in Zanzibar and in London. Prideaux delightedly reported that 'the results of this expedition have been in the highest degree satisfactory.' He assured the government that if decisive action had not been taken at Mombasa, the *akida*'s example would have been followed all along the coast destroying the sultan's authority and increasing the difficulties in enforcing the anti-slavery provisions in the treaty. 'Tranquility and confidence have been completely restored at Mombasa, the sultan's authority re-established, and British prestige maintained, without a single casualty on our side,' he reported.[54] Prideaux's report was forwarded by the Foreign Office to Disraeli and to the Queen, and Wylde commended the 'sound policy' of supporting the sultan's power in view of the loss of authority he had suffered from the slave trade treaty.[55]

The action at Mombasa was significant from several points of view. British power supported the sultan and in underlining Barghash's dependence strengthened the government's hand in its slave trade policies. The navy also re-asserted its position as a strong tool of government policy in the region. Moreover, in asserting his man-on-the-spot prerogatives to achieve a military victory, Sulivan forcefully impressed on the whole of the coast the new strength of the navy operating from its home base at Zanzibar. The immobile *London*, with its pool of guns, boats and manpower, was the key to the success of the Mombasa police action and the power of 'gunboat diplomacy' in the dominions of Zanzibar had clearly been greatly enhanced by its arrival. This development was significant since after the treaty, more force was required to maintain the sultan's authority. Of course there had always been a tendency to rely on force when it was available; with the establishment of the *London*, the military option was permanently at hand.

Similar actions on a smaller scale were repeated. A case in point was later in 1875, shortly after Sulivan left the *London*. Two of the ship's boats landed to arrest a dhow that had gone aground near Tanga, but an attack by men from two nearby villages forced them to withdraw. Kirk, who had returned to Zanzibar, demanded that the sultan take some sort of action so Barghash sent his steam yacht, *Star*, with the governor of the district, accompanied by two of the *London*'s boats, to bring the village chiefs to Zanzibar. The now seasoned Lieutenant Annesley was sent in charge of the boats assisted by Lieutenant Lloyd Mathews. The chiefs refused to come to Zanzibar so the navy was again called on to assert the sultan's authority. Attacking with shot, shell and rockets, some 40 small arms men quickly cleared and burned both villages as well as the beached dhow which had caused the trouble in the first place. Again, the navy served as an intimidating influence enforcing the sultan's authority and British policy at the same time. Probably the most important consequence of this minor action was the commendation of one of Sulivan's proteges. 'Lieutenant Mathews who had charge of the skirmishers handled them in a most efficient manner,' the captain was advised.[56] As will be seen, it was not the last time that Mathews would lead forces within Zanzibari dominions.

Of course, the *London*'s men were only infrequently involved in actions ashore since their primary duty continued to be boat cruising against dhows. As a consequence, despite the new treaty, the *London* managed enough captures to inject a continuing number of liberated slaves into Zanzibar and other regions. The old unsettled question of proper disposition of former slaves was still an open one and the slaves captured by the *London* as well as the other cruisers on the station continued to pose problems. The difficulty stemmed from the continuing lack of any sort of receiving system for the slaves at any of the possible landing sites. The long-standing criticism of the situation by the navy led some seamen to go to great lengths to correct the problem on their own initiative. One example involved men from the *Columbine* who, in mid-1871, actually returned six slaves to their former owners. The slaves had been kidnapped by dhowmen but told the sailors that they were happy with their former master and that they had been virtually free with him. Believing that conditions at any of the receiving stations were unsatisfactory, the seamen sacrified their £30 bounty and ran the risk of official censure by taking the slaves back to the original owner. In reporting the incident, Kirk, who had a low opinion of facilities at other points of disposal wrote that their action 'was certainly better than depositing them at Aden or Seychelles to be treated worse than slaves.' That view caused a reaction in the Foreign Office where an incredulous marginal notation pointed out that 'these are British colonies!'[57] Colony or not, many captains shared Kirk's opinion on this point. The location for the slaves was still largely up to the captain and at one point Malcolm opted for the difficult location of Natal where he delivered 113 slaves.[58] It is questionable whether their lot was much improved in Natal where adults were apprenticed to employers for a period of five years at an initial rate of pay of one shilling per month increasing at a rate of one shilling per month each year. Children were apprenticed for a period of seven years.[59] It was a far cry from Sulivan's call for a return to their own country. Devereux added his assessment of the sad state of the situation in a letter to *The Times* in which he admitted, 'we are to blame in not having provided schools for them before committing them to the inhabitants for service; then they would have done credit to their freedom.'[60]

The situation in Zanzibar itself was being criticised as well. A pamphlet prepared by the Universities Mission to Central Africa suggested that 'it is a question whether those slaves whom we capture and free are benefitted by our interference on their behalf.' Contrasting the condition of a slave in the north with that of a liberated African in Zanzibar, the report challenged Kirk by pointing to conditions in Arabia and then suggesting 'contrast this with those set free by, and living under, the so-called protection of the British Representative, and the finding will not be to our national credit.'[61] There was certainly room for criticism. Some slaves landed at Zanzibar were apprenticed to the sugar estates or oil mill owned by Captain H. A. Fraser, who had formerly served in the Indian Navy. The apprenticeship was a broad one. Kirk, who had expressed the belief that the freed slaves would have to be compelled to work through severe discipline, advised Fraser that 'I transfer all matters of reward and punishment in ordinary cases into your hands.' Kirk suggested that the slaves ought to be free to work as they pleased after they had learned 'what freedom is,' but that knowledge would 'in ordinary cases not come about under five years.'[62] The power over the free slaves given to Fraser is even more surprising since he had already been cited for employing slave labour. The Law Officers had argued that he should be informed in terms that would leave no doubt in his mind that he had 'had a very fortunate escape from the penal consequences of an illegal act.'[63] The peculiar arrangement with Fraser only ended in 1874 when he became involved in bankruptcy proceedings under circumstances which led Prideaux to accuse him of fraud.[64]

Another and better alternative was, however, becoming available through the growth of missions in and near Zanzibar. In fact, the freed slaves were one of the stimuli for the developing missionary thrust into the region.[65] But despite the commitment of the missionaries and the obvious advantages of their stations over apprenticeship programmes such as the one operating with Fraser, there were problems between Kirk and the leaders of some of the missions. Criticising the head of the Universities Mission over his preference for children of a teachable age, Kirk claimed that 'Bishop Tozer eagerly asks for all children under three feet high but seems disinclined to undertake the care of older people.'[66] For his part, Tozer chided Kirk suggesting that in the case of liberated Africans under consular protection, 'the slaves landed at Zanzibar, will be free in some subtle political sense of the word, but for all practical purposes, they will be slaves still.'[67] The consul seemed on better terms with the French Holy Ghost Mission which he felt seemed ready to take anyone.[68] A Church Missionary Society station near Mombasa, to be known as Freretown, seemed to be an alternative after July of 1875 when the Rev W. S. Price announced that he could accommodate 200 freed slaves immediately. 'Whilst we should prefer to take charge of freed slaves who are of a teachable age, we are quite prepared to take them, as they come,' he suggested.[69] The prospect of locating released slaves in or near Zanzibar was welcomed in the Foreign Office where it was believed that cheap labour would offset desires for importation of new slaves. There seemed to be no reluctance to use the liberated Africans in this way. Wylde explained the position by stating, 'it is to our interest in the suppression of the traffic that free labour should be supplied in Zanzibar in the place of the slave labour fresh supplies of which are not now procurable.'[70] There were, however, observers who fought the trend toward releasing the slaves at Zanzibar. Prideaux for one counselled against disposition at Zanzibar and believed that either Natal or Seychelles would be better.[71] The most eloquent anti-Zanzibar spokesman was Sulivan who still entertained a grander design for the Africans. In attacking disposition at Zanzibar to Cumming, Sulivan wrote:

> The system of giving negroes 'tickets of freedom' and letting them remain in Zanzibar is not less absurd than to write on a card 'I'm no longer a fox' and to hang it round the neck of one, and then send him into a kennel amongst hounds.[72]

Sulivan's view of a future for the liberated slaves was only one example of his insight into the affairs on the coast. Whether supporting the sultan, imposing anti-slave trade blockades, or attempting to provide better treatment for the liberated Africans, Sulivan was a dominating force on the coast. The fact makes it especially unfortunate that Sulivan was superseded as captain of the *London* due to a conflict with the ship's chaplain, E. L. Penny. The nonconformist Sulivan had a series of difficulties with Penny, a high churchman. The trouble started as the *London* rounded the Cape on the way to Zanzibar. Squalls in the stormy latitudes nearing the Cape caused Sulivan to shorten Sunday services held on the quarterdeck. He suggested to Penny that he should cut down the service by reducing the amount of chanting. The chaplain responded with a show of great indignation saying that the service was his exclusive concern. He then began to snub the captain at every opportunity. The situation was an obvious challenge to Sulivan's authority and in a later defence of his actions, he explained his attitude only to later cross out some of the angrier passages. What did Penny expect, he wondered? 'Was it with a view to get me to send for him, apologise to him for giving orders I considered advisable,' Sulivan questioned. He then answered the rhetorical question with the later amended, but still legible, response that if Penny were looking for such a response when

> . . . squalls may be expected, top gallant masts go over the side and a line of battle ship is about to round the Cape with her lower deck port 5 feet from the water line. If so Mr. Penny had mistaken who he had for a captain.

By the time the ship reached Zanzibar, the situation had deteriorated further with Sulivan taking issue over such things as the vestments which the chaplain insisted on wearing. The chaplain, however, did not confine himself to annoying Sulivan. The captain noted that 'The French and English consuls declined an invitation to the ward room mess giving as their reason that they would not meet Mr. Penny whose conduct towards them on former occasions had been so insulting.' A report on the situation was finally passed by Rear-Admiral Macdonald back to London where in an apparent effort to appear fair, the Admiralty surprisingly failed to support the captain and decided to remove both the captain and the chaplain from the ship. Sulivan was furious and demanded a court martial to enquire into the altercation. When the demand was refused, the issue came to the floor of Parliament with Evelyn Ashley introducing a motion on Sulivan's behalf. In the meantime, Sulivan sent a memorial to the Queen trying to gain the court.[73]

In the end it was all to no avail and the decision stood. Sulivan had, however, become something of a *cause celebre*. Even the provincial press such as the *Newcastle Daily Chronicle* took up the cause of 'a gallant captain who has been superseded in his command of one of Her Majesty's ships at an important naval station.'[74] The *Telegraph* warned that 'it is in the power of the Admiralty to prevent the seamen of Her Majesty's navy from regarding their religious instructor as a species of Jonah by choosing Naval Chaplains among the clergymen of strictly moderate views.' The paper continued that chaplains ought to look after the men 'instead of offending one third of the crew, making another third laugh, and bewildering the remainder by an antic liturgy.'[75] *The United Services Gazette* claimed that, 'a few more cases of miscarriage of justice such as the one represented by the case of Captain Sulivan, and public opinion will prove too strong for even a Conservative Admiralty.'[76] *The Scotsman* raged that 'it was obviously the duty of the Admiralty to support the captain.'[77] In the view of *Punch* the chaplain should have been taught, 'that to set Roman candles ablaze on the main, is sheer theological arson.'[78] The most important and definitive press comment came in *The Times* which regretted that the Church of England should have been represented on the ship by a man who on finding himself on board with 50 nonconformist crewmen 'makes it his business to insist most on the points on which they are disagreed.' The paper attacked Penny saying he 'persistently and with increasing rigour did the things most certain to irritate and estrange.' The conclusion of *The Times* was that 'Captain Sulivan has so just a cause of complaint . . . that England will hold him fully justified in his appeal to Parliament, and rather to be commended for his courage than guilty of aggravating his first offence.'[79] The reaction to the affair underlines the continuing public interest in East Africa as well as the widespread public concern generated by the combination of anti-slavery and theological issues. It also reflects the depth of the dissenting commitment of some naval personnel.

In the end, while Sulivan gained no satisfaction in his attempts to have the decision reversed, his career was not badly damaged by the episode. He went on to take command of the *Sirius* off the coast of West Africa, where, acting as senior officer on that coast, he directed a blockade against the King of Dahomey. He later took command of the *Repulse*. He was promoted to rear-admiral on the half-pay list in 1886 and became a vice-admiral in 1892. He was promoted to admiral on the retired list on 16 September 1897 and held that rank until his death in 1904.[80]

The biggest loser in the affair was the squadron off the East Coast which was robbed of one of its most accomplished commanders as a result of the proverbial tempest in a tea cup. By failing to support Sulivan, the Admiralty lost one of its most effective officers in the region. Nevertheless, Sulivan clearly left his mark on the East Coast. With 49 dhows captured and nearly 700 slaves freed by his three commands on the station[81] Sulivan was second only to Oldfield in the former category and second to none in the latter. His importance, however, went far beyond dhows captured or slaves freed. Sulivan became one of the best examples of the positive impact possible by a dynamic officer acting as the navy's man-on-the-spot. By efficiently beginning the

London's operation, he provided a model for the next decade of the navy's slave trade activities and by the skilful prosecution of such actions as that at Mombasa, he reasserted the navy's position as a powerful tool available to the government in maintaining British objectives in East Africa. In addition, Sulivan was an articulate and concerned spokesman for the navy and for the slaves being freed by his boats.

In his final report on the slave trade, Sulivan listed details of the traffic which he had fought for so many years and cautioned against the rising inland trade. After dealing with station routine he returned to what he considered to be the central issue in the suppression of the slave trade — providing for the freed Africans. Questioning whether the slaves were better off after being taken by the navy, he suggested that the answer was no. He warned:

No treaties and no efforts however great will lessen the traffic
to any extent until the question of what is to become of the
liberated African receives its due attention and consideration
and a better and more certain freedom is ensured to him.

The nonconformist captain shared with humanitarians at home a visionary concept of the development of Africa and suggested to Rear-Admiral Macdonald, 'Religion, Education, Trade and Agriculture must go hand in hand in their advance towards the interior of Africa.'

Sulivan assured the admiral that the slave trade would be abolished 'not by the capture of slaves or slavers, nor the acquirement of new slave treaties but by the intermingling of races and their dependence on each other.'[82] Captain George Sulivan left the *London* on 18 December 1875 but there was a continuity of sorts in the command since he was relieved by his cousin, Captain Thomas Sulivan.[83] For Penny, who had not yet left the ship, the change brought very cold comfort indeed. Thomas was a strong nonconformist like his cousin George and the chaplain's remaining time on the ship was far from triumphant.[84]

Several problems confronted the new Captain Sulivan but the main underlying one was that which had troubled his predecessors — a lack of clear instructions from London. The government's decision to withhold revised instructions to the navy and to await developments was beginning to have the result which might have been expected. Confusion on the coast translated into difficulty for the government at home. As early as June 1875, for example, the

problem of territoriality and its application to the treaty ban on
seaborne transit was causing problems. Captain Ward warned that
the majority of the remaining slave trade by dhow was between the
mainland and the islands of Zanzibar and Pemba. The nearness of
the islands to the coast compounded by numerous narrow passages
between the reefs off Pemba made the suppression of this branch of
the trade 'almost an impossibility.'[85] The legality, as much as the
difficulty, was of concern to the Foreign Office since some of the
captures were being made on smaller islands near Pemba and if
the islets were within territorial limits, it was questionable whether
the ban technically applied. Lister sought a report from Kirk
showing the distance of one of these islands, called Makungwe,
from Pemba as he was afraid that interference with the trade there
would be in violation of the treaty if it were within territorial
waters. The extent of the difficulty on the still partially uncharted
coastline was shown by Kirk's reply; he informed the Foreign
Office that 'as the island of Pemba has not been accurately
surveyed, I am not in a position to answer fully your Lordship's
question.' The best that could be offered was Lieutenant
Mathews' guess that it was about a mile and one half from Pemba.
Nevertheless, the lieutenant suggested that it should be treated as a
separate entity because it was being used as a depot for dhows.[86]
Again naval pragmatism seemed the only alternative in a situation
where legal precision, not to mention geographical detail, proved
elusive.

Mathews was involved in another question of interpretation
when he captured a dhow as a habitual slave runner. The vessel
was known to have carried slaves on several occasions in the past
and the navy had been keeping an eye out for it. When Mathews'
boat finally seized the vessel it had neither slaves nor proof of
slaving on board but Kirk had already condemned one 'habitual
slaver' and the case was routinely forwarded to London. After the
second capture had been brought in for adjudication, however,
word was received in Zanzibar that Rothery had reversed the
decision and said that habitual employment as a slaver could not
condemn a dhow without additional evidence. On that basis,
Mathews' capture was released. Kirk himself was disconcerted by
the decision and again sought enlightenment on interpretation
from the Foreign Office. What happens now if a vessel lands
slaves, then takes on a cargo of coconuts, and is then captured
without actual evidence of slaving on board, Kirk wanted to
know.[87] The newly arrived Captain Sulivan was sure he knew

already and protested vigorously to the consul that the situation was 'contrary to the fair, legitimate, and generally accepted reading of the Treaty of 5th June 1873.'[88]

While such matters of interdiction within territorial waters, necessary evidence, and related questions were troublesome, perhaps the most difficult single problem facing the government through the navy was the question of fugitive slaves. These fugitives were slaves who fled from their owners and claimed protection on a British ship or at a mission or other British shore station. The tendency of cruiser captains and boat officers was to receive the escapees, but the Foreign Office questioned the legality of the receipt and Derby tried to stop the practice with a circular issued in mid-1875. The move failed to take the sensibilities of the anti-slavery interests into account and Disraeli, recognising that an uproar was likely from these quarters, quickly had it cancelled.[89] Withdrawal of the circular, however, put the matter back into the hands of the navy officers who were again forced to rely on their own judgement. As a result, a whole series of fugitive slave cases were presented to the government. In January 1876, for example, five fugitives sought refuge in the *London*'s cutter off Pemba. Lieutenant Henry O'Neill was in charge of the boats and took the slaves believing that he would be right to receive them 'being without any definite instructions regarding slaves presenting themselves in this manner.'[90] A similar situation confronted Lieutenant W. R. Creswell later in the year when two men sought refuge in his boat. One showed the marks of a 'barbarous flogging' so Creswell took them back to the *London*. With reports of such activities filtering back to the Foreign Office, there was a growing fear that by taking these slaves off in territorial waters from a country where domestic slavery was legal, the navy was placed in a position of stealing private property. However, the pragmatic approach of supporting the navy's action quietly while being ready to pay compensation if it were claimed seemed to be the best response to most of the Foreign Office slave trade advisers. Julian Pauncefote suggested that if there was a danger that a slave was being cruelly treated that in itself might justify a commanding officer in removing him. He observed, 'we may assume that the commander in his discretion thought this to be the case.'[91] The discretion of the officer was left as the deciding criterion and there was a willingness to rely on that discretion even when the Foreign Office questioned the legality of naval proceedings. Frere's general criticism that the government 'think that, by shutting their eyes

127

and doing nothing, they can avoid the diplomatic entanglements and the outlay of money which they so much dread,' seemed particularly appropriate.[92]

The approach was, however, challenged by the opposition. Being out of power, the Liberals were critical. Privately, Granville confided to Gladstone that he couldn't really remember if the Liberal government had issued any fugitive slave instructions at all. He also admitted that he was happy he had not campaigned in the recent election on the fugitive question since, 'I should probably have put my foot into it.'[93] Nevertheless, he was adamant that international law was clear despite public opinion. 'A man of war ought not to receive slaves *within territorial limits,*' he insisted.[94] On the other hand, the nonconformist, humanitarian elements were vocal in taking exactly the opposite position. Anti-slavery writer Edward Hutchinson, for example, decried the circumstances surrounding the circular and included a word of concern that navy officers had been put in a difficult position as a result. The present situation, he wrote, 'has rendered some departmental instruction necessary for the protection of the navy.'[95]

Soon the uproar Disraeli had hoped to avoid was in full force and found its way to the floor of Parliament. In February of 1876, a motion by Samuel Whitbread called for approval of the proposition that:

A slave once admitted to the protection of the British flag should be treated while on board one of Her Majesty's ships as if he were free, and should not be removed from or ordered to leave the ship on the ground of slavery.

The motion also called for the withdrawal of any instructions which contravened that position. In the long debate which followed, many members supported the bill. In the end, however, the question became one of party. As J. E. Gorst warned, 'there was no doubt that a motion of that kind involved censure upon the government.' Disraeli himself cautioned the House that the suppression of the trade depended on immense labour and tedious negotiation based on the condition 'that their territorial waters should be respected and that the institution of domestic slavery should not be interfered with.' Disraeli urged restraint and then asked for time to establish a Royal Commission to study the matter. He then assured that the vote was taken on party lines with a rousing conclusion which had nothing to do with slaves or the slave trade.

I have sometimes succeeded in divisions: perhaps oftener failed; but I never, when I struck at my foe, pretended that it was not a Party question; and I cannot believe that such dastardly schemes can ever succeed in a House comprised of English gentlemen.

In the division, the government was supported by 293 votes to 248.[96]

In the next two months, the question of slave trade suppression arose with some regularity. For example, in April Sir John Kennaway gained approval for a motion urging the sultan to assist in the suppression of the inland slave trade.[97] However, by March, the Royal Commission had been established and was working on the fugitive slave question in detail.[98] Among the members of the commission were the Duke of Somerset, formerly First Lord of the Admiralty, and the two old protagonists — Rothery and Sir Leopold Heath. Among the witnesses were many who lauded the navy's activities on the coast. Sir Bartle Frere told the commissioners:

I think that you may rely very greatly upon the discretion and the judgement of our officers commanding men-of-war. They generally seem to me . . . to exercise any power of the kind with great judgement and with a very strong wish not to get their country into any difficulty.

George Sulivan could not resist decrying the general evils of domestic slavery which he suggested was just 'another name for general slavery.' He also returned to his favourite theme of providing for the slaves freed. When asked by the chairman if he thought a liberated slave was better off after being freed and landed in Seychelles, Sulivan replied 'I should say that he is very much worse off.' A place for them on the mainland, a sort of East Coast Liberia, was the only way of ever treating the former slaves fairly or of reducing the trade, he insisted. In the end, the commission concluded that 'Naval officers should be instructed that although ships of the Royal Navy should not be made a general asylum for fugitive slaves, they are not debarred from using their own discretion in retaining such fugitives on board.' If that sounded vague, it was meant to be. The commissioners also reported that 'the cases that present themselves to naval officers vary so much in character that it would be inexpedient, even were it possible to lay down any strict rules for their guidance under all the different circumstances which may occur.'[99]

The decision obviously failed to offer the definitive clarification which the navy might have hoped for. The clear guidelines many would have liked were described by Sir George Campbell in giving his reasons for dissenting from the report. 'Once admitted on board, I would hold those officers to be in no case bound to surrender any slave; on the contrary, I would prohibit their doing so.'[100] Such a position was strongly challenged by the Lord Chief Justice, A. E. Cockburn, who said that any such idea was an erroneous one which could lead to disregard of international law and which would almost certainly cause trouble with local authorities.[101] While the commission supported the Cockburn view, there is little doubt that the weight of naval opinion favoured Campbell's position. A clear example is found in Sulivan's printed copy of the commission report where he angrily scribbled his disagreement with Cockburn and the general findings of the committee. Alongside the statement that 'an officer who declines to give up a fugitive does to some extent interfere with the local institution of slavery,' Sulivan scrawled a marginal note questioning, 'Are we to recognize the human being as a marketable article as well as the pig or sheep?' Sulivan's notes on the general report are so useful they are worth quoting at length:

> The authorities apply to you to give up the slave refugee. He is our property say they. We are English, we don't acknowledge the existence or right of human property. But it's the law of our land that they become our slaves. But it's not the law of his land say we that they should become your slaves. But being in our land he is our subject. He cannot be your subject for you have forced him against his will from his country to yours and he is no more your subject than an Englishman travelling in it and not so much amenable to your laws as he would be if he would be there voluntarily. But he is under our flag and rule — no he is not for he has escaped to ours and we should be able to say we never give up refugees either political or negro.[102]

The fact that the navy would have preferred to be able to give the unequivocal reply envisaged by Sulivan, is reflected in developments while the Commission was grappling with the problem. Early in 1877, a letter to the Admiralty from the Foreign

Office sought explanation for Thomas Sulivan's actions in retaining certain fugitive slaves and officially inquiring what instructions he was acting under. The reply produced the startling revelation that the Admiralty had taken the initiative in trying to provide officers with some sort of guidance on the question. The reply was at ministerial level. G. W. Hunt, writing privately to Derby, suggested that 'this is a question that I do not think can be answered officially and I would suggest its being withdrawn.'[103] He explained that after Cabinet opposition had been expressed to surrendering slaves and pending the report of the Commission, the Admiralty had privately advised Rear-Admiral Macdonald to act accordingly and the letter had been submitted to Disraeli for approval. On this question at least, the Admiralty had given guidance to the fleet while circumventing the Foreign Office entirely. Hunt's confidential letter advised the admiral that the institution of slavery in any form was abhorrent to the government and 'that the restoration to his master whether directly or indirectly of a slave who has got on board one of Her Majesty's Ships, is an act which they wish to see avoided by all possible means.' The letter continued that there would be no new official instructions forthcoming at least until the Commission had reported. Therefore, the First Lord suggested 'I should be obliged to you if you would intimate confidentially to the officers on your station in command of ships . . . that they will best merit my approbation by acting in the spirit of this letter.'[104] Naturally Macdonald assured his compliance and that the guidance would be treated 'as *most confidential*.'[105] A displeased Foreign Office had no choice but to accept a *fait accompli*. 'Clearly we had better withdraw our letter,' Derby agreed.[106]

However, the rather obscure commission report, when it was finally produced, clouded the issue once more and the situation continued to cause problems. In March 1877, an eclipse of the moon provided a macabre setting for an episode which re-opened the whole question. A boat from the *Philomel*, under Boatswain George Downer, was hailed by four slaves in Pangani harbour. They said they had been cruelly treated by their owner who had confined two of them in chains, but the confusion attending the eclipse had allowed them to escape. Downer saw the scars on the bodies of two of the three women who had been assisted in the escape by a male slave, and agreed to take them aboard his boat. When the four arrived at the *Philomel*, Commander Henry Boys received them as fugitive slaves and promptly turned them over to Sulivan on the *London*. In the meantime, the owner went to Kirk to complain about the loss of the slaves. He openly admitted that he had put two of the women, his concubines, in chains for 40 days 'for going out at night.' Nevertheless, because domestic slavery was legal and there had been no treaty violations, Kirk wrote to Sulivan concerning the slaves and advising him that taking them had been an 'irregular action.' A somewhat shocked Kirk found, however, that the whole question had become a purely academic one. Partially on the basis of the instructions from Macdonald but also on the strength of his own inclinations, Sulivan had already sent them to Natal as immigrants. Sulivan would not even argue the point with Kirk. He informed the consul:[107]

> With regard to the legality or not of the reception of these slaves . . . I am not prepared to give an opinion, but having once been taken under the protection of the British flag, no other course but that pursued could be adopted.

Kirk appealed to the Foreign Office where Wylde observed, 'I have no hesitation in stating that the proceedings of the Naval authorities in this case are unjustifiable.' Not only that, he recommended 'that instructions should be sent to the commanders of our cruisers on the East Coast of Africa to desist from similar proceedings in future.'[108] There were two main objections to the navy's actions. Kirk stated the case by citing the irregularity of the removal of the slaves in the first place since the classification of fugitive hardly applied if the boat came into territorial waters to carry them off. He further argued that the protection of the flag did not apply to boats in the same sense that it did to ships. 'I think that boats under such circumstances occupy a very different position from a ship of war,' he reasoned.[109]

The eclipse episode became a test case not only on the fugitive slave question but also on the independent action of the naval authorities. In the end the old system was upheld. Pauncefote summarised the conclusions to the case which largely repudiated Kirk's position. 'The boats of men of war clearly enjoy the same measure of exterritoriality as the Public Vessels to which they belong,' he suggested. He continued that the ultimate responsibility for exercising discretion over taking a slave under the protection of the flag was the commanding officer's alone. In other words, Boys could have repudiated his boatswain's action. Since the captain elected to receive the slaves, Pauncefote felt that

Sulivan 'was right in his reply to Dr Kirk.' Of course, the government was obliged to pay compensation when it was claimed. The upshot of the case was that the government was willing to allow the navy officers to free the slaves in violation of the accepted interpretations of the law. As Pauncefote summarised the situation, with Derby's approval, 'the case therefore is one of compensation. We must pay for indulging in the luxury of illegality as regards the liberation of slaves.'[110] Wylde, too, had somewhat reluctantly come to the same conclusion. He suggested, 'I suppose as long as we receive no complaints of the proceedings of our officers in carrying away fugitive slaves from territorial waters we may let the cases pass without comment.'[111]

There was yet another factor complicating matters on the East Coast and that was the slavers' increasing use of the French flag as a means to avoid capture. The French refused to allow search of their vessels and were remarkably free in issuing French colours to potential slavers. As a consequence, more and more dhows were operating under the tricolour in an effort to resume their profitable slave trafficking. The problem assumed major proportions by 1875 when the political agent in Muscat reported that not many slaves had arrived that year but no fewer than three of the cargoes that had been landed had come in dhows flying the French flag. Commander Foot was worried by the same problem during the season of 1875.[112] Unlike many of the other questions confronting the slave trade suppressors, the issue of boarding French ships or dhows was plainly covered in the slave trade instructions. An officer could board to verify nationality but could make no inquiries beyond that. However, even this dictum allowed enough room for manoeuvre to bring the Foreign Office into the matter again. One of the most important cases in point occurred on Christmas Day, 1878, when the *London*'s steam pinnace under O'Neill found a dhow near Pemba. As the boat approached, the dhow made for the nearest land where it anchored and hoisted the French flag. O'Neill boarded to verify the nationality and after finding the papers in order was happily told by the *nakoda* that he had ten runaway slaves on board who he was taking back to their owners at Pemba. O'Neill observed that the dhow had been on the high seas and that French vessels weren't supposed to carry slaves against their will at sea. The *nakoda* wasn't interested and tauntingly reminded the lieutenant that even if it were so, there was nothing he could do about it since he had no authority over a French vessel. O'Neill was well aware that he was powerless under the law and started to leave the dhow when the terrified slaves ran to him imploring him not to leave them on board. The slaves told him that the dhowmen had been regaling them with horror stories of what would happen to them when they returned to Pemba and assured them that they would be flogged to death as an example when they returned. O'Neill, who had been on the station for three years, had heard

> . . . so many reports of cruelties practised by the Arabs toward fugitive slaves who had been recaptured, notably one in which a fugitive was burned alive in the presence of his fellow slaves as a warning, that I saw no reason to doubt the truth of their statements.

As a consequence, despite his lack of authority, he again tried to convince the *nakoda* to take them back to Zanzibar instead of to their owners at Pemba. When he refused, O'Neill threw caution to the wind and took all ten off in the pinnace.[113] The captain of the *London* recognised that the action was illegal but hopefully suggested that the French government 'Will be most grateful at this attempt to prevent the prostitution of their flag.'[114] In reality, he knew better than to expect the French to overlook the incident and, true to form, a complaint was quickly sent by Paris to London. The reaction in the Foreign Office is an especially interesting once since the issue was clear in terms of the illegality of the action. Still the response was mild. Pauncefote noted in preparing the government's response to O'Neill's actions that 'the case is hardly deserving of *censure* . . . (but) those rules must in future be strictly observed whatever may be the circumstances of the case.' That would have been an expected reaction; O'Neill could be vindicated on humanitarian grounds but the navy would be cautioned strictly to observe the rules in hand on the issue. But Lord Salisbury, the new Foreign Secretary, toned down the response even further. Crossing out Pauncefote's reference to strict observation of the rules in the future with his red pen, Salisbury suggested, 'I would leave him to draw his own inference.'[115] Even on questions like the sensitive one of boarding French dhows, where there were instructions which were unusually clear, the Foreign Secretary still wished to give room for manoeuvre to the officers on the station. Again the impulsive action of the navy on the coast could result in a more forward policy than could ever be officially sanctioned in public guidance from the government.

Since this continuing devolution of responsibility to the naval men-on-the spot is clearly of primary significance, the question of the calibre of these men is central to the success and methods of the anti-slavery patrol. Not only were cruiser captains trusted with major decisions; young junior officers sent away on boat cruising patrols were also forced to use considerable judgement in situations where they could not solicit assistance or advice. The abdication of responsibility for clarifying instructions under Derby and the continuing tendency to allow maximum discretion under Salisbury could place these junior officers in the role of jurist, diplomat and soldier. If it was a generally safe assumption that men senior enough to command a cruiser would exercise good judgement, the same did not always hold true for the younger men in charge of a detached boat. As has been seen in the earlier McCausland incident, the backgrounds of some of the junior officers on the station were not conducive to confidence in their abilities or judgement. The disciplinary action which appeared in McCausland's as well as Hockin's records was not unique to them alone. A survey of junior officer records for the station reveals, for example, J. P. O'Neill (not to be confused with Henry O'Neill of the *London*). As a sub-lieutenant on *Philomel*, he had been cashiered from the ship and deprived of two years' seniority by court martial because of drunkenness. He was transferred to another East Coast ship, the *Nimble*, but in August of 1876 resigned to avoid a second court martial.[116] On the *London* itself, Sub-Lieutenant Neville Legh served as a boat officer after having been deprived of seniority while on the *Excellent* and was then deprived of another 18 months by court martial after service on *Swiftsure*. He was finally forced to retire for reason of unfitness.[117] The conclusion might be drawn from these men that the slave trade campaign was drawing the fleet's hard cases as a sort of court of last resort. The implication would, however, be unfair and inaccurate.

The remarkable potential quality of the junior officers in the slave trade campaign is reflected in the *London*'s three principal boat officers in the late 1870s. Lieutenants Lloyd Mathews, Henry O'Neill and William Creswell presented a remarkable triumvirate of talent. Mathews' first ship as a lieutenant was the *London* but despite his relative lack of experience he quickly made an impression on authorities at Zanzibar with his zealous prosecution of the slavers coupled with an ability to command men in the field. As will be seen, Mathews left the navy to assume command of the sultan's forces and as 'General' Mathews became one of the dominant personalities in the development of British East Africa. O'Neill also attracted the attention of higher authorities in London and he too left the navy to take over duties as the British consul at Mozambique. Creswell, who learned boat cruising from O'Neill, later recalled that while serving as consul his mentor had been assisted by H. Rider Haggard's brother, and Creswell insisted that Captain Good in Haggard's *King Solomon's Mines* was really none other than O'Neill. Creswell, who had exchanged duty to join the *London* as a possible means of advancement, continued to do well too. After moving to Australia, he became Naval Commandant of Queensland in 1900 and Director of Naval Forces in 1905. The agreement at the 1909 Imperial conference for an independent Australian Fleet Unit opened the door for Creswell, then a rear-admiral, to take command of the force. He directed the unit until his retirement in 1919 and earned himself the title 'founder of the Australian Navy'. Both Mathews and Creswell were to receive knighthoods for their efforts. The three young officers, who went on to gain flag rank in two cases and a consular post in the other, demonstrate how competent the junior officers on the station could be.[118]

The obvious point is that there was a wide range of ability among the officers of the squadron. A junior officer like Mathews, Creswell, or O'Neill under the direction of a captain like Sulivan, could be immensely effective and could well utilise the independent judgement being forced on him by lack of control from London. On the other hand, a less qualified officer might require a tighter rein to avoid making serious errors and would suffer from the lack of guidance. Given the range of ability on the station, the government could expect the execution of the anti-slavery patrol by the naval men-on-the-spot to be very good at times. It could also be expected to be erratic with serious lapses.

Erratic or not, the situation continued. A case in point occurred when a native chief at Tullear Bay in Madagascar plundered the property of an English missionary and the Norwegian agent of a British firm. Captain William Selby of the *Vestal* intervened by imposing a £130 fine on the chief, leaving him with the option of paying or having his village burned down. When the ultimatum came to the attention of the Foreign Office, Wylde suggested:

We are practically left to the discretion of our naval officers who usually show considerable discretion and judgement in dealing with cases submitted for their decision and I think it would be to be deprecated that their hands should be too stringently tied.[119]

Pauncefote agreed with Wylde.[120] In general, Salisbury too supported the concept of naval discretion as he had in the past but wisely added, 'I have my doubts whether burning villages is altogether the most appropriate mode of introducing a missionary to the notice of the natives.'[121]

Activities ashore were always potentially dangerous for the navy and even the most competent officers sometimes found themselves in serious difficulties after landing. In November 1876, Creswell was in charge of the *London*'s boats off Pemba. The 24-year-old lieutenant had only recently joined the ship and was on his second solo foray with the boats when he was told that 100 slaves had been landed the previous night. Creswell had failed to capture anything on his first turn in charge of the boats and the thought of missing 100 on his second try proved too much for him. He decided to go ashore and try to recover the slaves in what he would in later years describe as a 'hare brained dash'. Looking back on the incident, the mature Creswell would admit that 'had an older head after weighing the consequences "landed to catch 'em" a Medical Board would have made short shrift of him.' Taking four men plus his interpreter, Creswell assigned a boat keeper to anchor off in deep water. The house where the slaves were supposed to have been taken was some seven miles inland up a river but Creswell and his group set off undaunted. After locating the house, he knocked on the front door asking for the owner of the house who, in the meantime, absconded out the back door. To make matters worse, all but seven of the slaves had been moved the night before. The seven were, however, taken to the local chief's house. Since the chief was technically an officer of the sultan, Creswell decided he could leave the slaves there. He recognised, however, that some attempt might be made to recover them so he stayed behind, keeping only the interpreter, while the crew returned to the beach to signal the steam cutter to come up river to the village.

Only minutes after the seamen left, however, Creswell heard gunfire and, running to investigate, he found that the sailors had been attacked by a large number of Arabs; two had been wounded. Falling back to the chief's house, they dressed the wounds and tried to barricade the dwelling. The prospect of holding the place seemed remote since the house was a tinderbox surrounded by other houses and trees. With only two uninjured men, Creswell decided that the only hope was to try to force their way to a small dhow anchored in the river. Pressing two of the chief's servants into carrying the most badly wounded seaman, Levi Hewlets, Creswell left the slaves in the chief's keeping and, positioning the other seamen around the stretcher, started for the dhow. There was no fire from the Arabs and the seamen easily reached the river. But the interpreter, Phros, had been left in the house in the confusion and a falling tide made it impossible to retrieve him. Creswell 'requisitioned' the dhow and, leaving one of her crew with a canoe to collect the interpreter, started down the river. As it turned out, the only member of the group having a narrow escape was Phros. The local chief decided that in the circumstances he would rather not have charge of the slaves after all and sent them with the interpreter after the seamen. On the way, they were surrounded by a group of Arabs who immediately recognised the interpreter. Phros took their recognition as his cue to make a run for it and, although shots were fired after him, he managed to reach the river where he found the canoe but no crewman and no oars. With the irate Arabs behind him, he made the best of the situation and after about an hour, the boat crew on the dhow saw the canoe coming down river after them, being madly paddled by hand by the interpreter.[122]

In the end, Creswell managed to return with all his crew which under the circumstances was more than might have been expected. He had not, however, succeeded in freeing any of the slaves. When Wylde composed the Foreign Office's response 'that his zeal in the execution of his duties had carried him beyond the bounds of discretion,' he was not telling Creswell anything he had not decided already.[123] There were two rather positive sidelights to the affair. Creswell had certainly learned what not to do and he was a fast learner. As he later recalled, 'much experience was compressed into a very few hours.'[124] In addition, the man who had landed the slaves, Mohammed ibn Rashid, was put in irons for a month despite an appeal by 40 of the most influential men of Pemba.[125] The object lesson for the slave traders was obvious.

Dangers ashore were not the only difficulties facing the navy since the problems associated with boat cruising were much the same as they had been 15 years before. A case in point was a southerly cruise by the *Vestal* in which her boats were detached to patrol near Madagascar. The pinnace was capsized in a squall and five seamen were killed. The surviving crewmen still had a perilous journey after reaching the beach without food or water. They were lucky, however, and managed to march some 40 miles overland to a village where they were rescued.[126] The men on the *London* did have some advantage in boat cruising duties since the depot ship had been specially equipped with boats designed for independent patrol work. There were five 40-foot launches which were named for the ladies of the Royal family. Four of these boats, *Helena, Beatrice, Louise* and *Alice*, were whaler-built cutters with a small 7-pound muzzle loader. A painted canvas aft served as officers' quarters while a forward canopy was rigged for the men. The senior boat of the *London* was a 42-foot, schooner-rigged sailing launch appropriately named *Victoria.* As Creswell remembered her, 'she had dignity, her silhouette was splendid; with her long raking masts in profile she looked the ideal slave catcher, but her virtues were static.' The main feature that put the larger launch in a class to herself was a cabin which ran for eight feet amidships and contained two berths. 'Superfluous to add that the cabin was scorned as effeminacy,' Creswell insisted and suggested that if the officer in charge of the boats stayed in the *Victoria* it was taken as proof that 'his heart was not in the job.' Another innovation for the *London* was a steam pinnace which greatly increased the range of the boats if not the comfort of the crew. Sailors on the pinnace quickly became black after being forced to sit, eat and sleep on coal bags. But Creswell's favourite was another small steam boat, the steam cutter. 'Officially she was the "steam cutter". Unofficially she was the "Wilful Murder" and the "Sudden Jerk" . . . to put it mildly she was an adventurous contraption,' he recalled. The steam cutter was to be especially lucky for the future architect of the Australian fleet. 'We should have had her as our mascot; in spite of her name she proved she was the luckiest of floating things if only by remaining on the surface, apparently against all the laws of physics and naval architecture,' he suggested. It was in this fleet that the *London*'s boat officers, dressed in battered pith helmets, trousers rolled up to the knees and barefooted, went after the slavers.[127]

By April 1877 fever had increased as a problem on the *London* and when cases reached as many as six a day, Sulivan decided to shift the ship to a new position some three miles from shore. The number of cases declined but illness remained a problem. One impact of fever was on boat crews; the recommended programme of one month away in the boats followed by two months on the ship frequently became one month on and one month off.[128] As

Lieutenant C. S. Smith was to recall, the brilliant exploits of the boat crews were far surpassed in merit 'by the unrecorded patient performance of dull duty in boat work, under the depressing influences of bad climate, poor food, and monotonous loneliness.' Smith spent one year and nine months on the *London* and estimated that during that time he spent 52 weeks on detached boat service covering some 7,200 miles while boarding 420 dhows.[129] An innovation which allowed the boats to make extended cruises was the establishment of a coal depot on a small island in the Pemba channel. The depot was designed for the steam boats working in the channel and allowed them to remain away for even longer periods of time.[130]

Utilising the extra range of the steamers, Creswell was able to make amends for his escapade inland on Pemba. Cruising in the 'Sudden Jerk' he boarded a large, becalmed *mtepe* dhow. Just as he boarded the vessel, Creswell saw that the hold was full of slaves. At the same instant the interpreter shouted for him to look out; one of the crewmen was about to fire on him. Creswell quickly stepped back aboard the boat while shouting full astern. The cutter, true to its name, jerked back suddenly and swung clear of the dhow before the slavers could fire. Deciding to bring in reinforcements, Creswell manoeuvred to a sailing boat which was in company and took it in tow back to the dhow. A sudden squall, however, blew up and the dhowmen ran up their sail and, in a desperate move, ran right at the approaching navy boats. Creswell responded by firing a rocket at the dhow. This proved too much for the dhowmen who lowered their sail again and surrendered. When Creswell went back on board, he found that he had managed to capture not only 18 armed Arabs but also 178 slaves, the largest single capture yet made by the *London*.[131]

Some of the greatest problems from the boats came when they were detached under senior enlisted personnel. The practice of sending boats out under petty officers had been regularly prohibited by successive station commanders in an effort to curb abuses but had been done just as regularly by captains who did not have enough officers to send away. In April of 1877, the steam cutter was on the beach being repaired, and, since it was not cruising, it seemed perfectly logical to leave a captain of the forecastle in charge. In the meantime, a dinghy came ashore from the launch with three ordinary seamen onboard. The two groups of seamen, with no officers on hand, noticed a fishing canoe going by and decided to obtain some fish. One of the men fired a pistol to attract the canoemen who came in hoping to sell their wares. One of the sailors from the cutter took some of the fish and later insisted that he had paid for them. But as Sulivan was to point out afterwards, 'it appears very evident from the vehement manner of the natives that he had not paid enough.' While this altercation with the cutter crew continued, the men in the dinghy tried to shove off. A number of villagers, however, thought the offending seaman belonged to the dinghy and tried to prevent the boat from leaving. The sailors in the dinghy panicked in the confusion and one of them decided to fire a shot over the heads of the villagers to frighten them away. Unfortunately, while firing over the heads of his assailants he accidentally hit and killed a man standing on the high ground behind them. The shot did have the effect of dispersing the crowd and both groups of seamen got away, but the authorities were understandably upset at the whole affair. Sulivan set up a court of inquiry on the *Diamond* which laid the blame on the men from the *London* and recommended the payment of a sum of 'blood money' in keeping with the tribal customs of the man who had been killed. Sulivan delivered the amount of 125 dollars to the sultan but Barghash would not accept the payment, saying they could give the money to charity and insisting on closing the case.[132]

If the sultan were disposed to dismiss the recklessness of the seamen, however, the consul was less forgiving. Kirk's criticism of the naval presence continued and at times the points he raised were extremely valid ones. The example of a villager killed by wild firing was a case in point as was the consul's repeated call for improving boarding procedures to counter charges of looting. This concern grew when Kirk heard the case of a boarding by men from the *Lynx*. He attacked the steps leading to a charge of theft of 131 dollars. While the charge could not be proved in court, the consul suggested that 'what here gave rise to the difficulty was the frivolous cause of detention of the dhow in the first place and the vexatious manner in which the search had been conducted.' He attacked the action of not following a routine procedure and was especially upset at 'unnecessary violence by the sailors.'[133]

Kirk did not, however, limit himself to trying to correct specific abuses or indiscretions. His reports continued to reflect a general hostility to the whole range of naval suppression as he attempted to minimise the navy's importance while stressing the role played by his consular establishment. His earlier praise for the navy's assistance in the treaty negotiation was replaced by an increased emphasis on the 'action taken in this matter by me.'[134] Some of the consul's private correspondence at this time seems shockingly egotistical. After having deprecated the dangers of the apparent revival in the trade reported by his own vice-consular observers, Kirk unblushingly told William Mackinnon that renewed vigour in the trade had come when 'the dealers saw I had other things to attend to, and to my disgust all I had warned the government of came about.' Saying that all the problems would have been averted had his consular establishment simply been enlarged, he claimed, 'the government will have to pay a few thousand pounds as prize money for capture of ships that never would have sailed had they given me what I asked in time.'[135] Of course, Kirk deserved credit for his part in the negotiations and general suppression on the coast; he ultimately received a knighthood for his efforts. The naval authorities never questioned Kirk's contribution. But the consul in his turn regularly minimised the navy's treaty and post-treaty significance. He suggested that 'whilst slavery exists in Zanzibar, our Navy is powerless to stop it.'[136] Contending that the navy could not act without consular support and information, he wrote, 'the Navy is of itself when single-handed the most inefficient and at the same time costly means employed.'[137] The general situation at this time was probably best stated by Creswell, who as a junior officer was in an excellent position to observe the consul and his relations with the senior naval officers. Suggesting that Kirk was the dominant single figure on the coast, Creswell was convinced that he overshadowed the sultan himself. As regards relations with the navy, he wrote:

There was at times a feeling that in the official reports . . . there seemed failure to appreciate the Navy's share of the work . . . It would perhaps have been expecting too much of human nature for Kirk and the consulate staff to have accorded us first place, and yet, without being quixotic, the Navy would readily have accorded that place to Kirk's share in the general achievement of suppression.[138]

Certainly Kirk was a dominant personality, and his significance in a man-on-the-spot role has been presented in detail elsewhere.[139] To the navy, Kirk's main role was as judge of the Vice-Admiralty Court in Zanzibar and procedures in that court give a picture of both consular and naval activity in the city in the late 1870s; Creswell paints a perhaps somewhat fanciful but still instructive picture of Kirk as judge. If matters had progressed from the scene described by Devereux with seamen swearing on dictionaries, procedures still lacked some of the niceties of the law courts in Britain. As the lieutenant put it, 'the procedure was not quite as formal as in the Court of Chancery or the House of Lords.' The most unusual fixture in the courtroom was a leopard which Kirk and his wife had raised from a kitten. Apparently, the consul liked to keep his leopard just inside the doorway to the courtroom where witnesses could not miss him on their entry. Creswell related that after establishing that a new witness had seen the beast, the consul would delight in informing him, 'Now if you speak the truth, he won't touch you, but if you tell any lies,' frowning severely, 'he'll have you as you go out.' In a masterful piece of understatement, Creswell suggested, 'This open intimidation of witnesses shows that our Prize Court was not of the most formal order.'[140] At times proceedings were so dubious that London became involved. For example, a dhow owned by a British subject was seized for having a slave on board. The seizure was, however, improper since the man was receiving wages as a seaman and there was no question of the vessel actually being a slave trader. Kirk, as the judge of the Vice-Admiralty Court, dismissed the case, but because the dhow had been rebuilt without being re-entered under the Merchant Shipping Act, he immediately transferred the case to the Consular Court with himself still sitting as judge. After this deft bit of legal sleight-of-hand, he found the vessel liable for all costs, expenses and damages and declared it forfeited due to the discrepancies in its papers. The horrified Law Officers, in reviewing the case, commented, 'It is difficult to conceive anything more absolutely illegal and unjustifiable than the conduct of Dr. Kirk in every stage of the transaction.'[141] Exercising proper control was difficult, however, when proceedings were in far-flung Zanzibar and, in the main, the men-on-the-spot continued to be left to their own devices.

One of the most long-standing disagreements between Kirk and some members of the naval establishment concerned the interpreters who served on the ships. In one sense it was easy to make the interpreter a scapegoat for questionable activities, but Kirk seems to have been genuinely convinced that the interpreters, themselves generally Arabs or coastal Swahilis, were totally unreliable. As early as 1869, he had come to the conclusion that 'as a class, those who embark in our cruisers as interpreters are an illiterate and worthless set.'[142] It is especially interesting to note that many captains tended to agree in general while stoutly defending their own interpreters. Some disputed the fundamental premise. While not dealing with general desirability, George Sulivan characteristically supported the interpreter who had worked for him. While still commanding the *Daphne*, Sulivan commended his recently deceased interpreter and suggested that he 'did not at all answer to the description of the class given by Dr. Kirk.'[143] Bedingfeld also commended his interpreter, 'whose great experience, sound common sense, and tact in procuring information I found invaluable.'[144] At least one interpreter received the Royal Humane Society medal for saving two children who had been thrown overboard by a dhow and Creswell believed that 'the native interpreters were, for the most part, a fine, courageous lot.'[145]

Nevertheless, Kirk continued his general criticism of the interpreters. Some criticism came from the navy as well; Cumming attacked the interpreter of the *Wolverine* as a man 'on whose word not the smallest reliance can be placed' and noted in confirmation that the man was promptly gaoled as soon as the ship returned to Zanzibar.[146] In 1873, Kirk had the *Daphne*'s interpreter dismissed and, convinced that he had accepted bribes, had him publicly flogged then turned over to the sultan.[147] Of course, one problem was that many of the interpreters were simply afraid of reprisals for their interference in the slave trade. Wratislaw believed that the interpreters were 'very inferior and but of little use,' but thought that the main reason was that 'they are afraid to give information as they belong to, and live in the island.'[148] By 1874 the Foreign Office took up agitation for reform of the general system. Wylde suggested that 'the sooner some plan is adopted for providing the navy with interpreters the better it will be. At present we are getting daily into difficulties for the want of them.'[149] The final basis for a reformed interpreter corps incorporated recommendations from several people including Frere who had included the subject among his reports. The plan, which was first formulated in 1874 and continued in theory into 1878, called for the establishment of an interpreter corps consisting of three grades. First-class interpreters were to be able to speak, read and write English, Swahili and Arabic and were to be paid at a rate of 8 shillings per diem. Second-class interpreters were to be able to read and write English and Swahili or Arabic and speak all three languages. They were to receive 6 shillings per day. Third-class interpreters, paid at the rate of 3 shilling per day, were to have a colloquial knowledge of English and Swahili and be able to speak enough Arabic to be understood.[150] The plan was, however, strictly theoretical. By April 1876, Kirk observed that there were no qualified first-class interpreters on hand and he doubted that there ever would be; the confidential Arabic writer at the consulate had only managed to qualify as a second-class interpreter and he was the best available. Two men had been employed in the third-class and they were deployed with ships at the time of the report.[151]

While the plan for a qualified native interpreter corps was failing, however, another approach was meeting with considerably more success. Shortly after the signing of the treaty in 1873, Malcolm had argued that the only way to ever solve the problems presented by unqualified interpreters was for the officers themselves to learn the local languages. This suggestion was forwarded to the Admiralty by Cumming who endorsed it and recommended that financial rewards should be offered as an incentive to officers to qualify in native languages. Cumming reminded the Admiralty that pecuniary incentives were already being offered by the Indian government to officers who qualified in the Arabic, Persian or Hindustani languages.[152]

The plan was endorsed in London and in November 1873, Navigating-Lieutenant Edmund Nankivell of the *Daphne* became the first officer to qualify in the Swahili language.[153] Shortly after Nankivell's qualification the incentive was increased to 100 rupees per month and his example was followed by several other officers on the station.[154] By the time the *London* was well-established in the late 1870s, Mathews, O'Neill and Creswell were all competent in Swahili and the knowledge of the language of the coast tremendously increased their effectiveness by allowing them to solicit information from the local population without having to use interpreters. The officers' knowledge of the language and their ability to monitor the native interpreters certainly had a salutary effect. By April of 1879, Kirk was able to commend an interpreter of the *London* who, when offered a bribe by the *nakoda* of a boarded dhow, immediately turned the money over to the boat officer who was able to use it in court to help condemn the dhow.[155] By the beginning of 1885, the navy had no fewer than 25 officers fully qualified in the Swahili language.[156]

Another major change on the station occurred in July 1878 when the Sulivan era came to an end as Thomas[157] was relieved as commander of the *London* by Captain Hamilton Earle. The period when the guard ship was commanded by the two Sulivans had established it as a major political and military focus for the region and had clearly placed it at the centre of the naval campaign against the slave trade. After slightly over five years operation, the *London* was responsible for the capture of some 150 dhows with over 1,000 slaves on board. During the same period, individual cruisers, now able to patrol further away from Zanzibar, also contributed captures. For example, the *Columbine* commanded by Commander John Tucker took 11 dhows with 412 slaves aboard. One of the most remarkable single captures came on 9 July 1875 when Ward's *Thetis* took a dhow with the startling total of 338 slaves on board. But the key was clearly the *London* which had accounted for some 75 per cent of dhow captures and the majority of the slaves freed.[158] By concentrating a large naval presence at Zanzibar which included a number of well-adapted cruising boats to operate in nearby waters especially off Pemba, the guard ship helped to bottle up the slavers at their source. Moreover, it gave the commanders of individual cruisers more freedom of action since they were no longer tied to Zanzibar and could patrol the long East African coastline in both directions. As a consequence, the station commander could better utilise his still limited resources. The approach now was to divide the station into four major cruising zones with two of those — East Africa and the Red Sea — having clear slave trade responsibilities. The *London* provided the permanent presence necessary to support the sultan and British policy objectives in Zanzibar while the two or three other vessels in the East African zone could freely patrol the coast toward Kilwa in the south or Ras al Hadd in the north. In the meantime, the small Red Sea squadron, generally comprised of two or three vessels, could keep watch for slave dhows that had managed to elude these efforts and arrive in the Persian Gulf. It is clear that the *London* gave a powerful boost to naval efficiency and that the work of the Sulivans in establishing it effectively was a major contribution to the slave trade campaign.

Notes

1. FO 84/1404, pp. 34–5, Commander Foot to Sir John Tarleton (extracts), private, 6 July 1874.
2. ADM 127/42, Rear-Admiral Cumming to Admiralty (confidential), 19 May 1875.
3. ADM 127/41, Captain Brine to Rear-Admiral Cumming, number 31, 1 June 1874.

4. Ibid., Rear-Admiral Cumming to Admiralty, number 213, 1 July 1874.

5. FO 84/1398, pp. 83–8, Elton to Prideaux (acting consul), number 16, 18 March 1874; and pp. 121–42, 2 April 1874.

6. ADM 127/42, Prideaux to Derby (confidential), number 99, 24 November 1874: enclosure number 1, Holmwood to Prideaux, 17 November 1874. Holmwood was attempting to extrapolate from a small sample to arrive at the year's total. His figures were undoubtedly too high.

7. ADM 127/41, Commander Foot to Rear-Admiral Cumming, number 7, 14 February 1874.

8. FO 84/1404, pp. 63–4, memo, W. H. Wylde, 3 August 1874; and minute, Derby.

9. Creswell, pp. 188–9.

10. ADM 127/41, Commander Hope to Captain Malcolm, 16 October 1873, Rear-Admiral Cumming to Admiralty, number 369, 23 November 1873, and Commander Tuke to Rear-Admiral Cumming, 19 November 1874; and ADM 196/17, p. 117, service record, Marcus McCausland; and ADM 196/18, p. 265, service record, Percy Hockin; and Creswell, pp. 188–9. For an account of the incident see *The Times*, 3 November 1873, p. 5-c.

11. ADM 127/41, Lieutenant Walters to Captain Ward, 27 May 1873, Captain Ward to Admiralty, 2 June 1873, Political Resident, Aden to Secretary to the Government, Bombay, number 155/619, 3 June 1873, Admiralty to Vice-Admiral Shadwell, 9 July 1873, Captain Ward to Vice-Admiral Shadwell, number 18, 17 October 1873; and FO 84/1443, pp. 280–1, Admiralty (R. Hall) to Foreign Office, 28 February 1874, and pp. 337–9, Admiralty (V. Lushington) to Rear-Admiral Cumming, 27 March 1874.

12. FO 83/2362, Law Officers (J. Coleridge, G. Jessel, J. Deane) to Granville, 23 July 1873.

13. FO 84/1443, pp. 284–6, memo, W. H. Wylde, 4 March 1874.

14. Ibid., p. 378, Treasury (James Cole) to Admiralty, 13 April 1874 (print).

15. ADM 1/6244, memos, V. Lushington, 22 May and 19 October 1877.

16. Ibid., memos, V. Lushington and Dacres, 28 August 1872.

17. ADM 1/6284, Admiralty to Treasury, January 1873.

18. Ibid., Treasury to Admiralty, 31 January 1873.

19. ADM 127/41, Captain Malcolm to Kirk, 20 May 1873.

20. Ibid., Lieutenant Blaxland to Captain Malcolm, 25 June 1873; and Captain Malcolm to Rear-Admiral Cumming, reply to number 12372/73.

21. FO 84/1403, pp. 39–41, Rear-Admiral Cumming to Admiralty, 24 December 1873; and p. 9, Foreign Office (draft) to Admiralty, 7 February 1874; and ADM 127/41, Kirk to Rear-Admiral Cumming, number 326, 28 June 1873; and Court of Inquiry to Rear-Admiral Cumming, 26 July 1873.

22. FO 84/1375, p. 150, Boarding Instructions, enclosure in Rear-Admiral Cumming to Kirk, 13 July 1873.

23. FO 84/1375, pp. 59–63 and ADM 127/41, Kirk to Granville, number 80, 22 July 1873.

24. ADM 127/41, Captain Malcolm to Rear-Admiral Cumming, number 135, 31 December 1873.

25. ADM 127/42, Prideaux to Derby, number 99, 24 November 1874 and enclosures, Holmwood to Prideaux.

26. FO 84/1400, pp. 102–7, and ADM 127/41, Kirk to Lister, 19 September 1874.

27. FO 84/1419, pp. 84–96, and ADM 127/41, Rear-Admiral Cumming to Admiralty, number 344, 5 December 1874.

28. FO 84/1416, p. 115b, minute, W. H. Wylde, undated.

29. FO 84/1400, pp. 108–9, memo, W. H. Wylde, 13 October 1874.

30. ADM 127/41, Captain Malcolm to Rear-Admiral Cumming, 2 January 1874.

31. HCA 37/61, in folder 11042, Kirk to Rothery, private, 9 January 1874.

32. FO 84/1426, pp. 293–4, memo, W. H. Wylde, 8 August 1874.

33. FO 84/1409, pp. 1–5, Admiralty (V. Lushington) to Foreign Office, immediate, 18 November 1873.

34. Ibid., pp. 46–52, 16 January 1874.

35. Ibid., pp. 79–80, Admiralty (R. Hall) to Foreign Office, pressing, 11 June 1874.

36. FO 83/2362, Law Officers (H. James, W. Harcourt, J. Deane) to Granville, 8 December 1873 and 7 January 1874.

37. FO 84/1409, pp. 91–2, memo, W. H. Wylde, 23 August 1874; and FO 83/2362, Law Officers to Derby, 19 August 1874.

38. FO 84/1409, minute on Wylde memo of 23 August 1874.

39. Ibid., pp. 94–5, Foreign Office (draft) to Admiralty, 7 September 1874.

40. ADD 44165, ff. 121–6, Granville to Gladstone, private, 11 February 1867.

41. FO 84/1416, pp. 5–10, Captain Sulivan to Prideaux, 2 March 1875.

42. FO 84/1426, pp. 338–9, Foreign Office memo, unsigned, 29 January 1875. See also ADM 1/6351, Foreign Office to Admiralty, 8 April 1875, in which Derby admits that 'in the uncertainty which . . . exists at present as to the interpretation which the treaty can bear, (he) is not in a position to state positively what instructions . . . should be issued.'

43. See PP, Reports from Committees, 3, 1873, IX, 'Report from the Select Committee on Cape of Good Hope & Zanzibar Mail Contracts', 23 July 1873, iii–ix; and *The Times*, 19 July 1873, p. 6-f, and leading article, p. 9 e-i. See also Parry, Charles, 'The General Post Office's Zanzibar Shipping Contracts, 1860–1914, *The Mariner's Mirror*, 68, 1982, pp. 57–67.

44. *The Times*, 19 November 1873, p. 4-f.

45. Sulivan, p. 108.

46. Sulivan Papers, log, HMS *London*; and ADM 127/2, Admiralty (R. Hall) to Rear-Admiral Cumming, 17 June 1874.

47. ADM 127/2, Elton to Secretary to the Government of India, 15 December 1874.

48. Sulivan Papers, log, HMS *London*; and ADM 127/2, Captain Sulivan to Rear-Admiral Cumming, number 4, 11 January 1875.

49. Creswell, p. 143 and p. 146.

50. ADM 127/2, Rear-Admiral Macdonald to Admiralty, 31 July 1875.

51. Sulivan Papers and ADM 127/41, Prideaux to Rear-Admiral Cumming, number 55, 22 January 1875; and FO 84/1415, pp. 120–36, Prideaux to Foreign Office, number 21, 23 January 1875.

52. Sulivan Papers and ADM 127/41, Captain Sulivan to Rear-Admiral Cumming, number 10, 25 January 1875; and ADM 127/41, Commander Tuke to Captain Sulivan 16 January 1875.

53. ADM 53/10557, log HMS *Rifleman*, 18 January 1875; and Sulivan Papers and ADM 127/41, Captain Sulivan to Rear-Admiral Cumming, *op. cit.*; and ADM 127/42, Lieutenant Gray to Captain Sulivan, 11 June 1875.

54. FO 84/1415, pp. 120–36, Prideaux to Foreign Office, number 21, 23 January 1875; and ADM 127/41, Prideaux to Rear-Admiral Cumming, number 55, 22 January 1875.

55. FO 84/1419, pp. 18–19, memo, W. H. Wylde, 12 March 1875; and FO 84/1415, p. 136, minute on Prideaux number 21. There is an interesting account of the action at Mombasa from a local point of view; Ali Hinawy, Mbarak, *Al-Akida and Fort Jesus, Mombasa* (London, 1950). One of the items included in the booklet is a sample of poetry from Sheikh Suud bin Said al-Maamiry. The Swahili poet had returned to Mombasa with the ships and recorded his view of the attack. As the poet put it:

Akanena Ad'meri	The Admiral considered what
Sasa ni lipi shauri	was the best advice to give in
La kusema Zinjibari	Zanzibar about what should
Ambalo limelekeya	be done.
Tatengeza manuwari	I will order gunboats there by
Itambae na bahari	sea; he has chosen to rebel
Uwovo amekhitari	and must suffer for it.
Lazima kumtendeya	

In another passage, he describes how, 'Now, after a short while, we are concealed in an armoured battleship. The Palace of Kisra has been rent asunder.' See Ali Hinawy, p. 73 and p. 86.

56. FO 84/1417, pp. 463–7, Lieutenant Annesley to Captain Sulivan, 23 November 1875; and pp. 459–61, Kirk to Derby, number 171, 9 December 1875. There has been a brief biography written of Mathews. See Lyne, Robert, *An Apostle of Empire* (London, 1936).

57. FO 84/1344, pp. 404–5, Kirk to Foreign Office, number 77, 19 July 1871; and Foreign Office marginal notation, unsigned.

58. ADM 53/10498, log, HMS *Briton*, 5 August 1873; and FO 84/1375, pp. 230–1, Kirk to Foreign Office, number 97, 29 August 1873; and Le Cordeur, B. A., 'Natal, the Cape and the Indian Ocean, 1846–1880', *Journal of African History*, vii, 2 (1966) pp. 247–62.

59. 'Government Notice No. 177, 1873', published in *The Natal Mercury*, 2 September 1873.

60. *The Times*, 18 November 1872, p. 10-d, letter signed by W. C. Devereux.

61. Capel, W. Forbes, *Central African Mission Report* (London, 1871) pp. 346–66.

62. FO 84/1344, pp. 467–73, Kirk to Foreign Office, number 95, 22 September 1871; and FO 84/1357, pp. 341–2, Kirk to Captain Fraser, number 29, 13 January 1872. See also Coupland, pp. 178–81.

63. FO 83/2361, Law Officers (Robert Phillimore) to Lord Stanley, 31 May 1867.

64. FO 84/1400, pp. 353–7, Prideaux to Foreign Office, number 100, 23 November 1874.

65. Oliver, Roland, *The Missionary Factor in East Africa* (London, 1952, reprinted 1970) p. 16. Oliver suggests: 'The problem of freed slaves did much to attract missions to East Africa, and even more to interest the British government in missionary enterprise.'

66. FO 84/1357. pp. 88–94, Kirk to Foreign Office, number 11, 25 January 1872.

67. Fraser, H. A., Tozer, Bishop W. G., and Christie, James, *The East African Slave Trade and the Measures Proposed for its Extinction as Viewed by Residents in Zanzibar* (London, 1871), p. 26.

68. FO 84/1357, pp. 88–94, Kirk to Foreign Office, see above, n.66.

69. FO 84/1417, pp. 41–2, Price to Euan-Smith, 16 July 1875.

70. FO 84/1400, pp. 194–5, memo, W. H. Wylde, 19 November 1874.

71. FO 84/1415, pp. 22–9, Prideaux to Foreign Office, number 7, 2 January 1875.

72. ADM 127/42, Captain Sulivan to Rear-Admiral Cumming, 4 May 1875.

73. Sulivan Papers, 'Statement of Captain G. L. Sulivan in defence of his conduct when in command of HMS *London* and toward the chaplain of that ship,' 'Correspondence between the Lords of the Admiralty and Captain G. L. Sulivan, R.N.,' 'Copy of correspondence between the Admiralty and Rear Admiral Macdonald,' Sulivan's notes and marginal notations on above, and 'Memorial of George Lydiard Sulivan to Her Most Gracious and Excellent Majesty the Queen'; and Hansard, 3rd series, vol. CCXXX, 11 July 1876, ff. 1314–28 and 1332.

74. *Newcastle Daily Chronicle*, 20 April 1876. (Several press clippings are found in the Sulivan Papers).

75. The *Daily Telegraph*, 13 July 1876.

76. The *United Services Gazette*, 15 July 1876.

77. The *Scotsman*, 13 July 1876.

78. *Punch*, 22 July 1876.

79. *The Times*, 13 July 1876.

80. ADM 196/13, p. 284, service record, George Lydiard Sulivan; and Sulivan Papers, Sulivan to Secretary of Admiralty, private, undated draft, and Summary of Service, G. L. Sulivan.

81. See HCA 35/82, HCA 35/83 and HCA 35/84.

82. FO 84/1457, pp. 168–71, and ADM 127/42, Captain Sulivan to Rear-Admiral Macdonald, 17 November 1875. Any discussion of developments in 1875 would not, of course, be complete without mentioning Barghash's visit to Britain. For examples of the press coverage see *The Times*, 10 June 1875, p. 10 c-d, and 22 June 1875, p. 5-d.

83. The replacement of George Sulivan by Thomas Sulivan has led to some confusion. Several authors have failed to recognise that there were two Captain Sulivans in command of the *London* and attribute the actions of both to George. See, for example, Lloyd, pp. 270 – 1. For the service records of the two Sulivans, see ADM 196/13, p. 237, service record, Thomas B. M. Sulivan; and ADM 196/13, p. 284, service record, George L. Sulivan.

84. Personal recollections, Colonel J. A. Sulivan.

85. ADM 127/42, Captain Ward to Rear-Admiral Macdonald, number 32, 30 June 1875.

86. FO 84/1453, pp. 323 – 4, Kirk to Derby, number 104, 9 June 1876.

87. Ibid., pp. 41 – 4, number 58, 5 April 1876.

88. Ibid., pp. 76 – 7, Captain Sulivan to Kirk, number 34, 21 April 1876.

89. Blake, Robert, *Disraeli* (London, 1966), pp. 559 and 562. See also Hardinge, Sir Arthur, *The Life of Henry Howard Molyneux Herbert, Fourth Earl of Carnarvon* (London, 1925) 3 vols., vol. II, pp. 84 – 9, and ADM 127/42, Foreign Office (Lister) to Admiralty, 30 April 1875.

90. FO 84/1457, pp. 329 – 30A, Lieutenant O'Neill to Captain Sulivan, 14 January 1876.

91. FO 84/1458, pp. 442 – 5, Lieutenant Creswell to Captain Sulivan, 12 October 1876 and Pauncefote's memo on same.

92. Frere to Gifford Palgrave, 31 August 1868, as quoted in Martineau, vol. II, p. 67.

93. ADD 44170, f. 193, Granville to Gladstone, 26 December 1875 and ff. 196 – 9, Granville to Gladstone, 20 January 1876.

94. Ibid., ff. 190 – 2, Granville to Gladstone, 22 December 1875 (emphasis Granville's).

95. Hutchinson, Edward, *The Fugitive Slave Circulars* (London, 1876), pp. 4 – 5.

96. Parliamentary Debates, 3rd Series, CCXXVII, 22 February 1876, 685 – 845, and 24 February 1876, 820 – 901.

97. Parliamentary Debates, 3rd Series, CCXXVIII, 4 April 1876, 1216 – 9. At about this time a new consolidation act was passed, see PP Bills, Public, 1876, VII (39 and 40 Vict.).

98. It should be noted that the Commission was concerned only with the fugitive slave question and not with broader questions of slave trade suppression. See for example, Sulivan Papers, Henry Howard (secretary of the Fugitive Slave Commission) to Captain Sulivan 7 March 1876.

99. P.P., Reports from Commissioners, 14, 1876, XXVIII, p. v and xiii – xiv, and p. 67, Q1690; and p. 8, Q243, 251, and 252. In addition to service on the fugitive slave commission, Rothery had just finished an effort to promulgate new boat service instructions dealing with the same sort of issues. See Clement Hill Papers, Mss. Afr. s. 16, Rothery to Hill, 7 May 1875, p. 19.

100. P.P., Reports from Commissioners, *op. cit.*, pp. xix – xxi.

101. Ibid., p. lv.

102. Sulivan Papers, Captain Sulivan's marginal notations and notes on inside covers of his copy of Reports from Commissioners, 1876, XXVIII.

103. FO 84/1488, pp. 23–4, Hunt to Derby, private, 27 January 1877.

104. Ibid., pp. 19–20, Hunt to Rear-Admiral Macdonald, confidential, 1 March 1876.

105. Ibid., p. 20, Rear-Admiral Macdonald to Hunt, private, 25 March 1876 (emphasis Macdonald's).

106. Ibid., p. 22, memo, Lord Derby, 27 January 1877.

107. ADM 127/43, report, H. C. Rothery, 14 June 1877, enclosure in Law to Lord Tenterden, confidential, 23 June 1877; and FO 84/1484, pp. 254–5, deposition, Diwan Mambo Sasa, 12 March 1877; and p. 258, Captain Sulivan to Kirk, 10 March 1877; and pp. 260–2, statement, Boatswain George Downer, 9 March 1877.

108. FO 84/1484, p. 251, minute, W. H. Wylde, 15 March 1877.

109. Ibid., pp. 256–7, Kirk to Captain Sulivan, number 98, 9 March 1877.

110. Ibid., pp. 252–3, memo, J. Pauncefote, 11 May 1877.

111. FO 84/1489, p. 98b, unsigned minute, W. H. Wylde, 6 February 1877.

112. ADM 127/42, Commander Foot to Rear-Admiral Macdonald, number 13, 20 July 1875; and J. Miles to Derby, number 446, 29 October 1875.

113. ADM 127/43, Lieutenant O'Neill to Captain Earle, 28 December 1878.

114. Ibid., Captain Earle to Rear-Admiral Corbett, number 13, 6 January 1879.

115. FO 84/1549, pp. 33–4, memo, J. Pauncefote, 25 February 1879; and notation, Lord Salisbury, 27 February 1879.

116. ADM 196/18, p. 122, service record, J. P. O'Neill.

117. ADM 196/19, p. 150, service record, Neville Legh.

118. ADM 196/17, p. 370, service record, Henry O'Neill; and ADM 196/18, p. 83, service record Lloyd Mathews; and Creswell, p. 153 and vii–ix. Creswell's view of O'Neill as the model for Haggard's character is open to question. It has been suggested that the basis for Captain Good was actually a combination of the traits of Jack Haggard and Sir Frederick Jackson. Personal discussion, D. H. Simpson.

119. FO 84/1521, p. 222b, minute, W. H. Wylde on Admiralty to Foreign Office, M165, 17 April 1878.

120. Ibid., pp. 236–7, memo, J. Pauncefote, 7 February 1879.

121. Ibid., notation, Lord Salisbury, 8 February 1879.

122. FO 84/1484, pp. 36–9, Lieutenant Creswell to Captain Sulivan, 13 December 1876; and Creswell, pp. 155–63; and ADM 127/42, Foreign Office (Pauncefote) to Admiralty, 9 February 1877.

123. FO 84/1484, pp. 34–5, memo, W. H. Wylde, 5 February 1877.

124. Creswell, p. 156.

125. ADM 127/42, Kirk to Derby, number 71, 8 January 1877.

126. FO 84/1514, p. 209, Kirk to Derby, number 43, 7 March 1878.

127. Creswell, pp. 146–50 and 167.

128. FO 84/1485, p. 5, Kirk to Derby, number 50, 2 April 1877; and Creswell, p. 149.

129. Smith, C. S. in Anderson-Moreshead, A. E. M., *The History of the Universities' Mission to Central Africa* (London, 1897) pp. 388 and 407.

130. ADM 127/2, Captain Sulivan to Rear-Admiral Macdonald, 30 March 1876.

131. Creswell, pp. 167–74.

132. FO 84/1485, pp. 295–6, Kirk to Derby, number 97, 20 June 1877; and FO 84/1489, pp. 404–10, Captain Sulivan to Rear-Admiral Macdonald, number 26, 3 April 1877.

133. FO 84/1454, pp. 135–6, Kirk to Derby, number 148, 18 September 1876.

134. FO 84/1453, pp. 152–4, Kirk to Derby, number 78, 28 April 1876.

135. Mackinnon Papers, Kirk to Mackinnon, 5 February 1877, vol. 87.

136. FO 84/1416, pp. 116–18, Kirk to Secretary to the Government, India, number 38, 9 April 1875.

137. FO 84/1484, pp. 167–71, Kirk to Derby, number 31, 28 February 1877.

138. Creswell, p. 178.

139. See Coupland, *op. cit.*

140. Creswell, pp. 178–9.

141. FO 83/2362, Law Officers (H. James, W. Harcourt, J. Deane) to Granville, 12 January 1874.

142. ADM 127/40, Kirk to Secretary to the Government, Bombay, number 202/54, 16 May 1869.

143. Ibid., notation, Captain Sulivan on above, 13 September 1869.

144. FO 84/1268, pp. 171–7, Captain Bedingfeld to Commodore Hillyar, 25 June 1866.

145. Creswell, pp. 183–4.

146. ADM 127/41, Rear-Admiral Cumming to Admiralty, 28 July 1873.

147. FO 84/1376, pp. 169–70, Kirk to Foreign Office, number 148, 8 December 1873.

148. ADM 127/41, Captain Wratislaw to Rear-Admiral Cumming, number 20, 1 July 1872.

149. FO 84/1403, pp. 67–8, memo, W. H. Wylde, 9 February 1874.

150. FO 84/1404, pp. 213–223, Admiralty (V. Lushington) to Foreign Office, 6 November 1874; and FO 84/1521, pp. 10–17, Admiralty (R. Hall) to Rear-Admiral Corbett, 4 January 1878; and ADM 127/42, Admiralty (R. Hall) to Rear-Admiral Macdonald, 3 December 1875.

151. FO 84/1453, pp. 19–23, Kirk to Derby, number 55, 3 April 1876.

152. ADM 127/41, Rear-Admiral Cumming to Admiralty, number 210, 1 July 1873.

153. Ibid., Admiralty (R. Hall) to Rear-Admiral Cumming, number C92, 7 March 1874.

154. Ibid., Admiralty to Rear-Admiral Cumming, number C248, 23 November 1874.

155. FO 84/1547, pp. 293–5, Kirk to Salisbury, number 61, 21 April 1879.

156. Admiralty, *The Navy List* (London, 1885) pp. 273–4.

157. Sulivan went on to command HMS *Duncan* but retired in July 1881. See ADM 196/13, service record, Thomas B. M. Sulivan.

158. Returns for captured dhows and released slaves during the 'Sulivan era' are drawn from HCA 35/82, HCA 35/83, HCA 35/84, HCA 35/85 and HCA 35/86.

6

The 'Dark Ages'

When Thomas Sulivan left the East African coast in 1878, the navy's influence and effectiveness in the region were at an all-time high. The addition to the treaty structure of the major concessions of 1873 had been enhanced by the greatly improved potential to enforce the document provided by the *London*. Whether supporting the now highly dependent sultan, dispatching boats to cruise for slavers, or serving as a visible symbol of British influence and policy, the stationary guard ship significantly increased naval potential. The period in which the two Captain Sulivans commanded the *London* represented a new 'high-water mark' for the navy. After this period, however, a series of difficulties began to undermine this position and the next five years were marked by a decline in both naval prestige and effectiveness. The reasons for the decline are manifold. Less inspired leadership was one factor. The age and strain on the *London* was another. The whole problem can also be seen against the broader backdrop of naval history since the malaise reflected off Zanzibar was also seen in other areas and stretched all the way back to the Admiralty. Furthermore, the strengthening of the naval aspects of the British presence on the coast had further alienated the ambitious consul, and Kirk embarked on an anti-naval campaign designed to enhance his own position at the expense of the navy. It did not take long for problems to arise. Thomas Sulivan was relieved as commander of the *London* by Captain Hamilton Earle. Earle had served on the coast in the *Persian* in 1860 but he lacked both the flair for the job and the insight that both the Sulivans had possessed. Soon after taking command, the new captain found himself engaged in a major row over the boarding of an American whaler in Zanzibar harbour. There was more than a little justification in the action, but it was the procedure, reflecting a lack of experience, which caused the difficulties. The episode began with a friendly drinking session with two seamen from the American barque *Laconia* and two liberty men from the *London*. After having enough to drink to lose some inhibitions, the Yankee whalers confided that their captain had bought a slave at Johanna and had then seized two other Africans and that all three men were presently on the ship. On their return to the *London*, the sailors dutifully reported what they had been told and Earle decided to send Lieutenant William Johnson to investigate the charges. When he reached the barque, Johnson found that the captain was in a hotel in Zanzibar. Leaving another officer on board, Johnson went ashore to find him. When he did, the captain told him he could search the ship as much as he liked because there were no slaves on her. Returning with the captain, Johnson had the crew mustered and found the three Africans in question. Deciding that they were in fact slaves, he took them back to the *London*. In the meantime, the captain of the barque hurried to the United States consul who demanded their return in an official complaint to Kirk. Kirk asked Earle to return the three which he did after receiving a receipt from an officer on the whaler.

The scene of the controversy then shifted to the United States consulate where the case was presented. The captain claimed that he hadn't actually purchased the first man but that he had been given to him by an American slave owner at Johanna who regarded him as incorrigible. He claimed the other two had come aboard voluntarily after being offered clothes and tobacco although he admitted covering them up with sails to keep them from being seen after they had been taken into the *Laconia*'s boat. In reviewing the case later, Rothery observed, 'I confess that it appears to me that there is not very much difference between the two accounts.' It was clear that the first man thought he had been sold and was given no choice in leaving whether any money had been paid or not. It was also questionable, as Rothery pointed out, how much persuasion could have been used with the other two since they had no common language with the men from the whaler. Nevertheless, it was the question of the original boarding that was really at issue since an 1862 treaty between the countries said 'the right of search shall not be exercised by a vessel of war of either contracting party within the limits of a settlement or port or within the territorial waters of the other party.' The Royal Navy felt that meant a British man-of-war shouldn't search an American vessel in an American port. The United States government insisted that the treaty meant no search in any port or settlement. The British government finally disavowed Earle's actions but largely on the question of judgement. The Foreign Office view was that since there was a United States consul in the port, Earle should have left the problem to the consul and not have intervened. A disgruntled Earle told the commander of the station, Rear-Admiral John Corbett, 'A naval officer has at times to decide at once if he has the right to search.' Arguing that he had to act decisively he suggested, 'he looks at his instructions and finds in one set certain limits, and in the other no limits, he has no time to plod through a treaty before acting.'[1] Despite the unusual circumstances, the *Laconia* incident was really unique only in that it involved the United States. The presence of slaves on board a vessel was insufficient in the intricacies of the law. Earle, like many of his contemporaries, fell foul of a lack of clear instructions and his quick decision was rejected after more leisurely legal analysis at home.

Nevertheless, naval activity continued to centre round the *London* much as it had done under the Sulivans. Other aspects of the anti-slavery campaign, however, altered as significant changes took place ashore in an attempt to check the growing overland traffic in slaves. Kirk had ceased deprecating the significance of reports such as the one Elton had produced, and there was no longer talk of working off the slaves by 1876. Instead, the consul began to claim that he had seen the dangers all along and that the treaty, while practically ending the seaborne trade, had the effect 'at the same time of calling into existence the Land Route I had foretold.'[2] Kirk might be forgiven his memory of his former advice as he worked to correct the situation with vigour. Aided by the preponderant British influence on the coast, he was able to wrest a new concession from Barghash in April of 1876. The proclamation issued by the sultan announced:

> We have determined to stop, and by this order do prohibit all conveyance of slaves by land under any conditions; and we have instructed our Governors on the coast to seize and imprison those found disobeying this order, and to confiscate their slaves.[3]

Kirk believed that the proclamation was the most important he had ever forwarded from Zanzibar.[4]

Proclaiming the end of the overland trade, however, was a far different thing from stopping it. In fact, rebellion on the coast was feared by the consul, sultan and naval authorities alike. There was not much concern over the reaction in places such as Pemba, Bagamoyo or Pangani because they were within a day's strike for a force from the *London* and with this proclamation, as with earlier agreements, the only enforcement available was the navy. The real threat was thought to be in Kilwa which was farther removed from the major naval force and which had the most to lose through the proclamation. The governor of Kilwa also feared a revolt and asked for more troops while telling the sultan that the proclamation could only be kept posted by an armed guard. As a result, Ward was sent in the *Thetis* to show the flag and intimidate any would-be revolutionaries.

In the meantime, Kirk, with 212 soldiers of the sultan, prepared to leave for Kilwa in the sultan's steamer with a letter from Barghash telling the governor to put himself in the consul's hands.[5] But the issue was decided before Kirk arrived; when Ward reached the port the alarmed governor told him that he had learned that an attack was being planned for 16 August when men from the surrounding districts would sack the custom house and the houses of British Indian residents, tear down the proclamation and pack the governor and his forces off in a dhow. The strength of the attackers was estimated at 200 to 300 men and, since the governor only had 30, his position was precarious. Ward told the governor that he 'had come here to protect the lives and property of the Banians (British Indians) which could only be done by quelling insurrection which I was prepared to do.' Ward arranged that a gun shot would serve as a signal for him to land a force to check any attack night or day. The captain felt sure he would not have to fulfil the pledge and that the simple intimidating presence of the man-of-war would dissuade anyone from trying rebellion. He was right, although a few nights after the deadline had passed some wedding merry makers sparked off an invasion by firing a series of celebration shots. The navy's response was efficient. 'I landed the Marines and small arms men. It was only to find when we reached the shore that the firing was occasioned by a wedding and not by war,' Ward reported. After the storming of the wedding party, calm returned and by 23 August, when Kirk arrived, the ferment was over.[6] The government applauded the quick support of the sultan and expressed a willingness to assist him in maintaining his authority as much as possible. Of course, the amount of that help was strictly dependent on the naval strength at hand. As Wylde put it, 'we should afford him all the moral and material support in our power so far as the presence and cooperation of our ships of war may enable us to do so.'[7]

The sultan, having cast the die with the British government, and now relying more heavily on British support, pursued his new policy with as much vigour as possible and on 26 April freed his own household slaves.[8] Of course the proclamation did not immediately stop the overland route any more than the treaty had completely stopped the transit of slaves by sea. The fact was plain on the coast and from penetration into the interior as well. On 19 December 1877, Elton, on an inland expedition, died of sunstroke. His last journals, however, clearly showed that slaving continued to thrive near Lake Nyasa. 'A very considerable number of slaves, obtained in the neighbourhood of the Nyasa, are brought down to the East Coast of Africa,' Elton had observed.[9]

A particular difficulty in enforcing the sultan's proclamation ashore was the diminutive proportions of the Zanzibari military force and the unreliability of the troops on hand. As a consequence, an attempt had already been made to create an effective force and Sulivan had offered naval assistance in the formation of the group. The men due to become officers and non-commissioned officers were drilled on the *London*, but the most important naval involvement was that Lloyd Mathews supervised the drill. Mathews volunteered to take over the force and Sulivan approved the plan.[10] Kirk had already noticed the young lieutenant and was much impressed with his abilities. In fact, when Holmwood had to leave Zanzibar for a year to recoup his health, Kirk tried to arrange for Mathews to be appointed vice-consul in his stead.[11] However, delays in discussions between the Admiralty and the Foreign Office undermined the plan. Replacements had arrived for officers on the *London* and Mathews was forced to accept the government transportation home provided, or take some sort of appointment immediately. Barghash asked Sulivan to allow Mathews to take over command of the troops and the captain quickly authorised the move. As a consequence, Mathews accepted the military post before the Foreign Office confirmed its offer of the vice-consular position.[12] If the Foreign Office would have preferred to have Mathews working for them directly, they were well enough pleased he was still at Zanzibar. Wylde believed that 'It would be very unfortunate if Lieut. Mathews were removed.'[13]

When Mathews' extension of duty expired, however, the Admiralty and the Foreign Office became involved in a petty round of squabbling. Mathews wished to remain at Zanzibar in command of the forces he had trained. The government wanted him to stay as well, but neither the Admiralty nor the Foreign Office were willing to pay the bill. The Admiralty advised the Foreign Office that Mathews' chance for promotion as well as future assignments in the navy would be jeopardised if he did not remain in naval service and suggested that if he were to stay at Zanzibar, the Foreign Office should undertake to look after his career. The Foreign Office responded by saying that they 'cannot undertake to provide for Lieut. Mathews in the future and . . . if their Lordships' rule is inflexible his employment at Zanzibar cannot be continued.'[14] The Admiralty remained inflexible and Mathews was told that his naval prospects would be jeopardised if he remained in the service of the sultan.[15] It was finally Mathews himself who broke the deadlock and put his future in jeopardy by retiring from the navy to accept command of the sultan's troops. The decision was a fortunate one for the sultan and in the end for Mathews himself. In July 1881, Barghash gave the lieutenant a title to fit his responsibilities by naming him a brigadier-general.[16]

Another leading naval officer was also taking shore duties in the late 1870s. In 1875, the Khedive of Egypt, at the prompting of Gordon, used a former navy officer in his service, H. F. McKillop, to attempt an ill-fated occupation of Zanzibari territory. An irate Kirk helped prompt the government to apply pressure on Egypt to withdraw the force.[17] The failure of the mission, however, did not deter the Khedive from taking navy officers into his service and a post as director of the anti-slave trade police in the Red Sea was offered to George Malcolm who had recently retired. Malcolm, recommended for the post by the Foreign Office, took the position hoping to use it as a platform to continue his efforts against the trade. Unfortunately, the directorship made him subordinate to Gordon, a colourful and unorthodox slave trade suppressor in his own right. Two personalities like Gordon and Malcolm seemed unlikely to work well together and sooner or later a clash could be expected. It came sooner rather than later and, in less than a year, Malcolm 'Pasha' resigned in anger over a conflict with Gordon.[18]

The list of officers working on the mainland in various capacities would not be complete without Verney Lovett Cameron. The explorer's first contact with East Africa came as senior lieutenant of the *Star*. Cameron was with the ship for three years and spent much of that time cruising for slave dhows. He cited his naval experiences and an associated hatred for the slave trade as one of the factors which caused him to go into the interior. Cameron actually began his expedition at the same time as the Frere mission and promptly went down with fever. Some of his old messmates, however, took him on board the *Briton* where he recovered straight away. While his expedition was preparing to embark, Cameron commuted to Zanzibar from the mainland in a dhow which on one occasion was boarded by boat crews from the *Daphne* checking for slave trade violations. Cameron finally won recognition as the first European to traverse Africa from east to west. On the way, he confirmed the continuing activities of the slavers in the interior and used a book describing his journey as propaganda against the traders. 'Africa is bleeding her lifeblood at every pore,' he suggested. On a pessimistic note, he warned:

> The slave-trade is spreading in the interior and will continue to do so until it is either put down with a strong hand or dies a natural death from the total destruction of the population. At present events are tending toward depopulation.[19]

As the decade of the 1870s drew to a close, at least one question seemed to have been largely answered and that was the problem that Sulivan had stressed five years before — the disposition of the freed slaves. The various mission stations became the main resettlement centres. A hopeful experiment was developed by Steere's Universities Mission group; it involved relocating the former slaves near their own country. The first mainland station of the society was established at Magila in 1875. In the following year, the Makua and Nyanja slaves who were at the station were sent into the interior in hopes of relocating them near their former homes. The freed slaves themselves refused to go further inland than Masasi, about a hundred miles inland from Lindi, so a settlement was established there. Masasi then provided a base for later thrusts into the interior.[20] Included among the encouraging developments which Steere was able to report was the partial reunion of one of the families broken by the trade. As a new batch of Africans liberated by the cruisers was delivered to the station, a young boy ran to the group having recognised his father. The man had been away hunting when the slavers swept through his village and stole his family. He moved to another region where he too was captured.[21] In the columns of *The Times* the plan was contrasted with the old system in which, 'to the native the restraints of apprenticeship are much the same as slavery.' It was suggested that 'a settlement of freed slaves, each married couple with their own house and plot of ground, will tell another story.'[22] In 1877, the Foreign Office began to require a quarterly return from Kirk showing where the freed slaves had been relocated.[23] His first report was instructive in showing the dominance of Zanzibar as the receiving point and the increasing importance of the mission stations. Of the 270 slaves accounted for in the report, 77 were sent to Natal and two to the Cape while 42 were given freedom papers and left to their own devices in Zanzibar. Most, however, were sent to the missions with 93 going to the Universities Mission station, 16 to the Church Mission centre, and 30 to the Roman Catholic mission.[24]

If the question of disposition of slaves seemed to have been answered by the beginning of the 1880s, however, a whole series of continuing difficulties intensified the discomfort of the Royal Navy as the new decade began. For example, the old problem of lack of instructions continued to be acute well into the 1880s. A commission was established in the summer of 1881 to revise the slave trade instructions which had been in force since 1869. The panel, chaired by Sir Robert Phillimore, included Vice-Admiral Corbett and Clement Hill. After over a year of study, the long-awaited new instructions were finally prepared and ready for distribution to the fleet late in 1882.[25] But the new guidance still left much to be desired in the minds of some navy commanders. When Captain Robert Boyle came to the station in command of the *Tourmaline* in 1883 his chief guide was Colomb's book which had been written ten years earlier and some four years before the treaty of 1873. While Boyle admitted that some details stemming from the altered habits of the slave traders dated the book, he still regarded it as the best available.[26]

In the early 1880s, the centre of the navy's activities was still the *London* with her boats. On 13 November 1880, Sub-Lieutenant Charles Smith was in charge of the boats when a dhow carrying 99 slaves was captured. A total of 86 of the people being transported for sale had been recently captured in the interior and shipped from Kilwa.[27] The indication of active slaving in the interior continued; a year later, Lieutenant Robert Travers made an even larger capture off Pemba. The dhow had been pursued and struck a rock while trying to avoid the boats. The crew hurriedly rescued the slaves from the sinking vessel and found that 137 had been packed aboard. On interviewing those rescued, the authorities found that all had recently been captured near Lake Nyasa and then marched to the coast in ten separate gangs.[28] These large captures were not, however, routine since the intensity of the *London*'s blockade made the dangers too great for the slavers. Much more common were small captures of the handful of slaves that minor traders tried to smuggle as far as the plantations on Pemba. The captain of the *London* confided to the secretary of the British and Foreign Anti-Slavery Society that the situation was very difficult. 'They come over also in the fishing canoes by ones and twos', he reported.[29] Many of the navy's captures were actually being made on land and the boat depot at Funzi was significant in this regard. Two captures in December 1880 help to illustrate the point. On 10 December, Henry Storey, second captain of quarterdeck men, was assigned to the boat depot. A native of the island told Storey that a small shipment of slaves had just been landed on nearby Kokota Island so he decided to investigate. Taking Enock Russell, a seedie also on duty at the depot, he crossed in the punt and walked inland. The two seamen found 15 slaves and a two-man guard, but when they approached both slaves and slavers fled. Nevertheless, Storey and Russell were able to round up 14 of the slaves as well as one of the guards. Virtually the same situation occurred a week later on 18 December when George Taylor, able-seaman, was in charge of the depot. He was informed that a shipment of slaves had been landed nearby so he took Samuel Massey, able-seaman, and Amesi, seedie, in the dinghy and went after them. After landing near the spot where they had been told the slaves were put ashore, the seamen walked inland for over a mile where they surprised two Arabs guarding the slaves. The guards fled into the bush when they saw the sailors approaching and Taylor followed them only to be stabbed by one of the escaping Arabs. Not badly wounded, Taylor took the nine female slaves back in the small dinghy while the other two seamen took the nine men overland to the depot. On the way, they found three more slaves and, after the pinnace reached the depot, search parties recovered yet another five to bring the total number of slaves taken to 25.[30]

Such actions, in the boats and ashore, seemed to augur well for the success of the anti-slavery campaign. The blockade from the *London* looked as though it were strangling the trade. In the meantime, the sultan's forces under Mathews were meeting with successes on the mainland and, encouraged by this progress, the British government decided to honour Saiyid Barghash for his role in the apparent demise of the trade. On 14 September 1883, the sultan was invested with the insignia of the Order of St Michael and St George in a gala ceremony at Zanzibar. Rear-Admiral Hewett attended the festivities in the flagship, *Euryalus*, accompanied by the *Tourmaline*, *Ranger* and *Osprey*. The four men-of-war joined the ships already in the harbour including the *London*, *Briton*, *Dragon* and *Harrier*. All the ships were dressed rainbow fashion and Kirk, now Sir John, was inspired to report the fleet as 'the strongest and most numerous force ever seen here.'[31] It appeared to be a festive climax to the anti-slave trade campaign. The appearance, was, however, deceptive.

During the early 1880s, the Royal Navy was faced with several problems, the old question of measuring prizes being one of the most troublesome. The tendency of the Treasury to adjust prize tonnage claims and the resulting ill-will in the fleet as well as in the Admiralty has already been discussed but it should be noted that the question was a continuing one. Reviewers in the Treasury expected the strangely shaped dhows to conform to European standards and when the measurements failed to fall within the normal ratio, the tonnage of the vessel was revalued downward to bring it into line. The view expressed as early as 1866 that the 'dimension has doubtless been incorrectly taken,' was frequently repeated through the next fifteen years.[32] The result was hostility in the fleet and matters concerning measurement became a major part of the 'passed down' information when new ships joined the station. For example, when Commander Tucker brought the *Columbine* to the coast in 1872, he was told of some of the Treasury's idiosyncracies by the officers of the *Wolverine* who had in their turn been briefed by colleagues from the *Nymphe*.[33] Nor was the discussion confined to the officers. A seaman named James Woods served on the *London* in the early 1880s and recounted some of his experiences in a book written under the pen name Lionel Yexley. Some of his recollections are highly coloured and a few are simply incorrect but there is enough truth in the book to make it a useful indicator of the thinking of the seamen on the station at the time. 'Who it was that finally passed prizes before they appeared in the *London Gazette* as due to the captor I cannot say, but I do know that they had generally shrunk in size from say 50 tons to 30,' he wrote. The result was that seamen began to adopt a strategy of their own against the Treasury. This was especially true when petty officers were sent out in charge of the boats 'without any too great consideration for conventionalities.' According to Woods, a favourite technique was

> . . . after capture we would take a sheepshank in the lead line which would add to her length, girth, etc., in accordance with the size of the sheepshank, but as the same sheepshank was used for all measurements it generally resulted in such an extraordinary shaped vessel that some modifications in the dimensions had to be made.

The result, as he explained, was that after official reduction it would 'still leave us a bit to windward.'[34]

Shady measurements were not, however, limited to the boats cruising under petty officers and two captures by the *London* in 1880 brought the whole matter to a head. The captures, made by boats under Lieutenant W. L. Johnson and Sub-Lieutenant Pieter Vander Byl, brought a storm of criticism from the consul and the Treasury. One dhow taken at night and reported to have a large poop over the main deck was challenged and the measuring officers admitted a mistake. What was incredible was the size of the error they admitted. As Rothery put it the captors

> . . . who had at first claimed the tonnage of the vessel as 176 tons were afterwards ready to admit that her total tonnage was only 15.01 tons, or less than the tonnage of the imaginary poop so carefully described in the first certificate.

He went on to suggest that such a revelation might have prompted caution on the part of measuring officers but that on the contrary a more recent *London* capture had shrunk from 27 tons to 17.08 tons after Kirk ordered a survey. 'How such startling discrepancies between the certificates given by the captors and the actual dimensions of the vessels can have arisen, it is difficult to understand,' Rothery concluded.[35] The Admiralty was incensed. Captain Earle received a stern message from the Lords Commissioners 'expressing their sense of the discredit which such mismeasurements bring upon the Naval Service.' Vander Byl received a severe reprimand 'for his culpable carelessness and neglect of duty' in the measurement of the second dhow. Johnson had already been similarly reprimanded over the first capture.[36] The affair cast a shadow over the squadron and damaged the credibility of the officers on the station. If Woods is to be believed, however, it did not put an end to the sailors' attempts to even the score when they measured dhows in the future.

Earle left the ship under a cloud, retiring the next year. His successor, Captain Charles Brownrigg, was destined to have an even more tragic tour on the *London*.[37] Woods gives a picture of Brownrigg as a man who, if not a by-the-book captain, was at least a popular one with his crew. The bearded Brownrigg established himself on board with his wife and young daughter and had no hesitation, according to Woods, in helping coxwains juggle their figures to bring dhow measurements into line with design possibilities. His good humour prompted some of his men to take liberties with the new captain. Brownrigg believed that he should set an example and as a consequence went out cruising in the boats himself. Before his first foray to Pemba, some of the sailors thought it would be great good fun to coach Bin Juma, a local chief, on an 'appropriate' welcoming speech for the captain's arrival. Thus when Brownrigg landed on Pemba he was met by the local dignitaries and greeted by Bin Juma with a torrent of curse words that only a sailor could have taught him. Without batting an eye, Brownrigg met the profanity with a genial bow and congratulated the chief on his remarkable fluency in English.[38]

Diplomacy was not, however, of help when Brownrigg again took out a boat in early December 1881. The captain was in the steam pinnace, *Wave*, off Pemba searching for dhows when he approached a dhow flying the French flag. Brownrigg had always been careful on questions involving French colours and he approached the dhow, not to board, but to confirm her nationality. Since he had no intention of boarding the dhow, the captain did not arm his men and warned them not to board without his specific authorisation. Then, taking the tiller himself, he came alongside. The captain was alone with his steward in the stern, separated from the crew by a canopy and by a rain awning that had been rolled up and hung over the main boom. The coxswain started aft over the canopy when he saw eight to ten men crouching in the back of the dhow armed with rifles. He shouted to Brownrigg and hurled his boat-hook just as the men stood up and fired a volley into the boat. The coxswain jumped on the first of the assailants and both fell overboard. In the meantime, a wave of Arabs swarmed into the pinnace. The first volley killed one sailor and mortally wounded another; two men were less severely hurt. As over 15 Arabs boarded forward, the unarmed seamen remaining were forced overboard.

The only ones left on board were the captain and his steward. The steward, who was slightly wounded, escaped by pretending to be dead. Brownrigg, however, boldly attacked the boarders single-handed. He had a rifle and shot one of the Arabs but, as he attempted to reload, several others managed to climb aft where they struck down on him with their long swords. Taking his rifle and using it as a club, Brownrigg knocked two of his assailants overboard only to have their places filled by other boarders. A sword cut on the forehead partially blinded the captain but the thought of abandoning his vessel apparently never occurred to him. When one of the swordsmen cut Brownrigg across the hands so that he could not hold the rifle, he tried to leap onto the attackers and fight them by hand but it was hopeless — he was shot and killed. In the meantime, William Venniry, the leading stoker, was trying to assist ordinary seaman Thomas Bishop who was seriously wounded in the first volley. Wounded himself, Venniry managed to hoist Bishop onto the dinghy astern of the pinnace where he could support himself. The Arabs, however, pulled the dinghy to the pinnace and hacked the wounded man to death. Seamen Alfred Yates and William Colliston managed to swim to shore with another badly wounded crewman, Samuel Massey. The seamen in the water were fortunate in that the Arabs started cutting at the pinnace with their swords instead of trying to attack the men overboard. Apparently, one of the boarders hit the safety valve on the boiler with his sword and the valve lifted with a tremendous rush of steam. The dhowmen, knowing nothing about steam boats, were frightened back to the dhow and they then made off leaving the pinnace. Venniry, who had been in the water for the whole time, swam back to the boat, got up steam, and went in to pick up the men ashore.

The pinnace crew went off to find Lieutenant Henry Target who was in charge of the boats off Pemba. On hearing what had happened, Target returned to the scene where the dhow was found abandoned. Searching the nearby area, the seamen found several of the crewmen but could not locate the *nakoda*. In the meantime, the whole region had been electrified by the news, and the sultan's forces, under Mathews, were dispatched to Pemba in the *Star*. Mathews' men were efficient and quickly located the *nakoda* who was badly wounded in an escape attempt. The dhow captain, after the amputation of both legs, confessed the attack to Mathews before dying.

The navy's losses included Richard Monkley, stoker; Bishop; and John Aers, the ship's writer who had gone on the cruise in an effort to regain his health. Four men were also wounded. Of course the most shocking loss was Brownrigg, the only captain to be killed in the anti-slavery campaign on the East Coast. The loss was hard felt and as Woods recalled, 'At Pemba reprisals were the order of the day, and every Arab that we came in touch with for months after had to bear his share of the burden of retaliation.'[39] The repercussions rippled all the way to London where public attention was briefly focused on the East Coast again. A leading article in *The Times* praised Brownrigg's personal courage but deprecated the lack of precaution which had led to his death. The paper suggested:

> Captain Brownrigg died, not only as an Englishman, but as the bravest of Englishmen. It is to be regretted that precautions were not taken whereby we might have been spared the loss of so gallant an officer.

On the following day, the paper carried a long and detailed account of boat cruising activities. The *Illustrated London News* included a pictorial feature on the squadron as a result of the increased interest in the actions off East Africa.[40] On the coast itself, however, the death of Brownrigg, following on the heels of the earlier measurement scandal, further undermined morale.

Another significant morale problem was the condition of the *London*. The ship had been an old one when Sulivan brought her to the station but, refitted and repaired, the *London* proved well-suited to the stationary duties at Zanzibar. When Creswell joined the ship some years later, he was still impressed with the vessel's appearance and comfort. It was a far different impression that Woods received when he reported aboard as a young seaman in 1881. 'Her upper gear had long since gone — rotted away by the tropical heat, and only her lower masts were standing, the rigging of which was not safe enough for anyone to attempt to use it,' he reported. The climate had also taken its toll of the hull and Woods asserted that:

> Her sides were so rotten that at places a knife could be pushed into them right up to the hilt, the successive coats of paint with which they were covered being the only thing that prevented great holes showing through.

He described the ship as being infested with vermin ranging from bats to rats and cockroaches. The men amused themselves by running cockroach derbies he said.[41] The conditions were reflected in the health of the crew. In March 1881, Kirk reported that 'In H.M.S. *London* the sick list has of late seldom been under sixty while there have often been as many as seventy and even more unfit for duty at one time.'[42] In the spring of 1883, the Admiralty advised the Foreign Office that attention had 'been again called to the sickness amongst the crew of HMS *London* at Zanzibar during the year of 1882.'[43]

As the *London* declined, several experiments were attempted to upgrade the squadron. One of these brought two schooners, the *Harrier* and the *Undine*, to the station under the command of lieutenants. The idea of sending pure sailing ships to cruise against the dhows in an era when steam had become the norm, was an incongruous notion, largely the brainchild of the station commander. Some cruiser captains, when solicited for their opinions on the scheme, counselled against the schooners but their advice was rejected. Captain Percy Luxmore, who had taken over the *London*, was one of the sceptics but Vice-Admiral Gore-Jones, after seeking opinions, chided the captain for having questioned the vessels without having seen them. Luxmore suggested that 'they are ill adapted for the purpose.' Gore-Jones disdainfully replied, 'I consider such a remark as extremely ill judgement (sic) on the part of a "senior officer" whose duty will be to obtain experience of these vessels and not to condemn them while yet untried.'[44] It was the old case that sometimes permeates through military operations, 'don't tell me what you think, tell me what I want to hear.' The admiral would have been well-advised to listen to the captain since the schooners were indeed ill-adapted for the service. At one point, the current was so strong that the commander of the *Harrier* reported he could not even reach Zanzibar on the grounds that she was working too heavily and that her timbers were opening in several places.[45] In the end, the schooners were withdrawn, and while they had managed to make several captures none had been of a dhow underway. The ships were effective only in pouncing on dhows at anchor, and a steam vessel could have done that job even better.

The navy was not the only organisation on the coast having difficulties during this period. A series of complaints against the Frere Town settlement near Mombasa threatened the stability of the region not to mention the value of the mission as a repository for slaves freed by the cruisers. The initial complaints accused the lay superintendent, William Streeter, with having beaten slaves near the mission to extort confessions and with having imprisoned an Arab subject of the sultan without authority or justification. Streeter had already been in trouble with Kirk over his handling of fugitive slaves and his explanation about the present charges reflected astounding self-righteousness. 'I did not hear the case or judge him but saw at once he was in the wrong and ordered him to be shut up,' he said. In another account of the same incident, he explained 'I heard a few words only and knowing the man to be guilty had him shut up.' The more he explained his actions, the worse his actions seemed to be. Streeter had found some food supplies missing and believed they had been taken by slaves from a nearby plantation. He then cheerfully admitted having flogged the slaves until they confessed to the crime. When an Arab owner came to the mission station trying to recover one of his slaves on Sunday, Streeter had him clapped in gaol and proclaimed that he couldn't have turned the man over to the sultan's governor because it was Sunday and Sunday had to be 'strictly kept'. There seemed to be more than a little truth to the governor's agitated complaint to the sultan 'But oh, my Master, this missionary of Mombasa is the source of the whole trouble and intrigue; his head must be unsettled.' Barghash complained to Kirk with a stern warning that something must be done. Then in a private note, the sultan explained to the consul that he shouldn't be vexed by the tone of the letter but that he thought something had better be done 'while as yet nothing serious has occurred, than afterwards when there may be cause for regret.' Kirk's immediate response was to dispatch Holmwood to Mombasa for an investigation and to solicit naval assistance in the task. The naval participation took the form of Commander Mather Byles and his ship, the *Seagull*.[46]

The irascible Commander Byles was well-suited for the task after having already established a reputation for concern for liberated Africans and a notable tendency to be unimpressed with local civilian authorities. In 1880, he had been the senior officer on the Aden and Red Sea division when he had received eight fugitive slaves on board the *Seagull*. Despite the fact that several of the slaves had had to swim to the ship, the consul at Aden wanted them to be brought to the consulate for interrogation and reminded Byles that the rights of the owners would have to be taken into consideration. Byles began his reply in formal and moderate terms by suggesting, 'I have the honour to inform you that I do not agree with you.' He then went on to assure the startled consul that he viewed the rights of the owners as totally irrelevant and would not surrender the slaves under any circumstances. He proclaimed:

> I received these slaves on the ground of humanity, and under these circumstances could never suffer the poor emaciated creatures to return to a state of slavery, brutal treatment, and semi-starvation, which is a disgrace to . . . humanity.

The finality of the statement took even the Foreign Office offguard in reviewing the case. Pauncefort suggested that the Admiralty might be invited to recommend to the commander that he 'treat such cases in future in concert with the consul.' In the end, support of the station commander and the Admiralty made even that mild rebuke impossible. Nor was Byles content. A runaway from Zanzibar was entered as a seedie on the *Seagull* and when the ship returned to the port, the owner demanded his return. Kirk turned to Brownrigg who ordered Byles to surrender the man but the commander flatly refused to obey the direct order. Byles's view was that when the man went on the books of his ship as a seaman he was permanently freed. The Foreign Office accepted the argument and Byles was again upheld.[47] The commander was plainly a man of his own mind and not one likely to accept any holier-than-thou arguments from a missionary under investigation.

When the *Seagull* arrived at Mombasa with Holmwood, a flood of petitions and complaints met the investigators. As directed by Kirk, Holmwood persuaded Streeter to sign an apology in an effort to avoid prosecution. In the meantime, he accepted the petition of members of the mission to hear complaints against their supervisors and when the former slaves told their stories both Holmwood and Byles were shocked. A sadistic pattern of discipline had been imposed at the station. Several women complained that they had been publicly flogged, some by Streeter himself. One young married woman described how she had been tied to a tree to receive 25 lashes for a minor offence. A man came forward who clearly bore the marks of the 60 lashes which had been meted out to him. 'Anything approaching this in the way of severity I had never before witnessed,' a horrified Holmwood reported. As the former slaves told their stories, Streeter tried to stop the testimony. An irate Byles, however, shouted down the missionary and prohibited any further attempts to intimidate the witnesses. After the hearing, Byles continued the investigation by inspecting the prison at the station and found appalling conditions. 'I endeavoured to obtain information on the prison rules, but could not, as there were none,' he observed. Holmwood's report was an angry one but Byles's account was venemous. He said:

> Since I have been on the East Indies Station, I have been the means of freeing several fugitive slaves on account of the ill-treatment of their masters, but none of them had been beaten as severely as the two men I saw at the mission.

Byles was especially angered by the treatment of the women at the station. He insisted:

> It would scarcely be believed in England that at the present date there could exist a Mission station . . . where these young Christian women would be tied hands and body to a tree and so brutally flogged, or that there could be found Englishmen who would countenance such a thing.

His conclusions were sweeping. Nothing short of the complete removal of all the present white officials would suffice in Byles's estimation. The present staff would have to be replaced by 'those who can carry the Gospel into all parts of the world without bringing disgrace on the name of England.'[48]

The Foreign Office agreed with Byles's report in all recommendations and wrote to the Society calling for the removal of Streeter and all his staff. 'The state of things disclosed in the correspondence and more especially in the report made by Captain Byles,' would allow nothing less.[49] The governing committee of the Church Missionary Society were 'compelled to express their disapproval of some of the methods adopted,' and initiated reforms through new staff.[50] Unfortunately, however, the credibility of the dedicated missionaries in the region had been dealt a serious blow at home and on the coast by the incredible activities of Streeter. On 7 July 1881, a most astonishing episode in the anti-slavery campaign occurred — astonishing in that a Royal Navy captain felt obliged to rescue a slave from the missionaries. Accepting a plea from one of the brutalised mission residents, Byles and the *Seagull* departed from Mombasa with another freed slave on board — but this one had been rescued from the missionary station at Mombasa.[51]

Byles had clearly emerged as one of the navy's forceful men-on-the-spot on the strength of his pursuit of his ideals against consuls, missionaries and senior officers alike. He retained the *Seagull* until mid-1883. He later commanded the *Tourmaline* as a captain and after going on the retired pay list was made a rear-admiral in 1897. He held the rank until his death in 1917.[52]

Events, however, seemed to be moving away from the era of the colourful naval officer exercising discretionary powers with wide-ranging freedom of action. Avenues for governmental control had been expanding for several years. By 1875, for example, the mail steamers were operating regularly to Zanzibar with the British India Steam Navigation Company running its line from Aden to Zanzibar while the Union Steam Ship Company operated from Zanzibar to the Cape via Mozambique.[53] By the beginning of 1880, the telegraph provided yet another link. The immediacy of telegraphic communication tended to restrict the man-on-the-spot role of both consul and captain since major questions could be referred to London even when rapid decision making was necessary. Moreover, Kirk launched a campaign to increase the consular establishment at the expense of the naval presence. A major factor in this move by Kirk was the ill-will which had grown between the consul and the naval establishment. The repeated friction between captain and consul which had continued since the Crawford-Rigby affair, re-appearing frequently through Kirk's tenure, and the consul's increasing tendency to see the navy as a rival on the coast, finally came to a head. This new situation had the worst repercussions of all the consular-naval confrontations. Kirk confided his plan to Mackinnon as early as August of 1882 when he wrote, 'I am preparing a scheme for slave trade suppression based on a reduction of naval force, which is so costly, and an increase of political stations or consulates on the coast.' The end result of the plan in the consul's view would be to 'dispense with the navy as a branch of slave trade suppression.'[54] In November of 1882, Kirk officially proposed the plan in which 'our navy can be superseded by other agencies working on shore.' In a masterful bit of figure juggling, Kirk reasoned that the outlay on ships and bounties came to approximately £67,000 per annum, all of which would be saved if the ships were removed from the coast. As a consequence, he argued, his consular staff could be voted an increase of £13,000 per year and the country would still save £54,000 per year. The added funds would be used to employ consular agents inland and they would be able to replace the naval offshore force.[55]

The Admiralty informed the Foreign Office that estimates for the operation of the *London* were £17,000 per year while bounties were running at £9,700. Even that amount would not necessarily be total savings if the *London* were withdrawn. Nevertheless, the Foreign Office continued to visualise inflated savings.[56] In addition, as has been seen, the station's prestige was at a low ebb and the *London*'s deteriorating condition was forcing some sort of immediate action. Moreover, the whole situation must be seen within the broader context of naval history since Kirk's attack on the squadron came at a time which has been described as the 'Dark Ages of the Admiralty'. The earlier development period in which attempts were made to incorporate technological changes growing out of the shortcomings seen in the Crimean War gave way to a lethargy which undermined naval effectiveness on a global scale. Preston, for example, argues that the navy's role had become almost exclusively one of 'an Imperial gendarmerie' and suggests that growing neglect within the Admiralty, stimulated perhaps partially by Lushington's retirement, weakened both numbers and effectiveness of the fleet. Rodger claims that never before in its history had the navy 'attracted so little serious attention' and explains the malaise as an unfortunate outgrowth of a long period of peace and unquestioned superiority.[57] The forceful naval response to the Kirk initiative would have been to cite the significance of the naval campaign and the particular benefits of the guard ship in pressing for a new stationary vessel to replace the *London*. However, the general lethargy and retrenchment which marked the period made such a response unlikely. The capitulation came in July of 1883 when Vice-Admiral Hewett was told that the Admiralty had 'concurred in this proposal which will involve the discontinuance of the Stationary Ship at Zanzibar, and the present system of boat cruising for the suppression of the slave trade.'[58]

It should be observed that the idea of increasing the consular establishment ashore was not new nor had it originated with Kirk. Commodore Heath had advised such action before the slave trade committee in 1871 but had tied the plan to continued naval supervision.[59] The key difference in interpretation was that the naval presence would be maintained. For Kirk, a primary goal seems to have been to see that that presence would be reduced. In fairness to the consul, it might be argued that Kirk was simply reacting pragmatically to the changed situation on the coast. With a parsimonious Treasury, he could have felt it financially impossible to maintain both the naval establishment and the increased consular staff which would be needed to counter increasingly significant German moves in the interior. However, while these thoughts may have influenced Kirk, on balance personal pique seems to be the more significant motivating factor. The best evidence for this interpretation is that Kirk had been privately putting forward an anti-navy and pro-consular approach for some five years. While his campaign reached its climax during the early 1880s, the inspiration predated the German incursion and the particular circumstances of that period. In 1879, he privately confided to William Mackinnon that what should be done was to replace the men-of-war with vessels 'under the Consulate'. According to the consul, vessels under his personal control, and not that of the senior naval officer, would see 'the work ten times better done'.[60] It was on this score that Kirk made a serious mistake. What was required was a dual approach with officials in the interior attacking the inland trade and ultimately all slave trading at its source while the navy concentrated on strangling the remaining traffic at sea. The navy had not stopped the trade alone without support ashore. Similarly, inland suppression without an effective offshore presence was to prove just as impossible.

To many observers, however, the dangers were not readily apparent. Despite the reduction in the naval role, several officers not only accepted the plan but also took the consular posts. When asked to comment on the plan, Foot, then captain of the *Ruby*, observed that the cost savings were inflated but welcomed the general approach. He observed:

> It is my belief no stamping out of the slave trade can be attained by any efforts on the littoral or the sea and the evil will not cease till attacked at its root, viz: the interior and Lake Districts of Africa.[61]

Dedicated to the suppression of the trade, Foot welcomed the opportunity to put his beliefs into action and on 1 October 1883, he was confirmed as the British consul in the districts adjacent to Lake Nyasa.[62] It was an ill-fated appointment; within a year, Foot died in the African interior.[63] Other officers, however, followed suit and by the end of 1883, Commander C. E. Gissing, and Lieutenants J. G. Haggard and C. S. Smith had been brought into the consular service.[64] Lieutenant James Knowles was also temporarily named acting-consul at Tamatave at about the same time.[65]

The demise of the *London* came in late March 1884. She was towed to Funzi, her fittings were sold and she was then broken up. Kirk was well-pleased with the success of his campaign. His consular staff had been increased and the senior naval officer had been removed as a potential rival in Zanzibar. In addition, initial returns seemed to prove that the consul had been right all along and that the need for naval suppression had ended. When the admiral sent two cruisers to avoid leaving a noticeable void in the *London*'s place, Kirk ungraciously questioned his motives and gleefully welcomed the cruisers' lack of success. 'The *Osprey* and *Decoy* were sent here by the admiral who thought the *London* being gone he would make a pot of money and every dhow carry slaves,' he wrote. The two ship blockade failed to capture any 'raw' slaves — slaves brought down from the interior — and Kirk felt vindicated.[66] The major period of naval work off Zanzibar seemed to have ended by the middle of 1884 — the appearance, however, was deceptive.[67]

Notes

1. ADM 127/43, Lieutenant Johnson to Captain Earle, 28 December 1878; Captain Earle to Rear-Admiral Corbett, number 186, 31 December 1878; Rear-Admiral Corbett to Admiralty, number 98, 30 January 1879; Rothery to Lords Commissioners of H.M. Treasury, number 3566/79, enclosure in Foreign Office to Admiralty, 14 June 1879; and FO 84/1515, pp. 358–64, memo, W. H. Wylde, 13 February 1879; and FO 84/1550, pp. 41–2, Admiralty (R. Hall) to Foreign Office, 10 July 1879; and FO 84/1547, p. 15, Kirk to Salisbury, number 6, 2 January 1879. See also Bennett, pp. 45–6.
2. FO 84/1453, pp. 101–10, Kirk to Foreign Office, number 72, 20 April 1876.
3. Ibid., p. 123, proclamation, Saiyid Barghash, 18 April 1876 (print).
4. Ibid., pp. 250–5, Kirk to Wylde, private, 6 May 1876.
5. Ibid., pp. 280–4, Kirk to Derby, number 98, 18 May 1876.
6. FO 84/1458, pp. 266–73, Captain Ward to Rear-Admiral Macdonald, number 49, 23 August 1876.
7. FO 84/1453, pp. 288–94, Kirk to Derby, number 100, 1 June 1876; and minute, Wylde, on above.
8. Ibid., pp. 149–50, number 77, 26 April 1876.
9. FO 84/1514, pp. 68–9, Kirk to Derby, number 21, 30 January 1878; and pp. 98–101, notes, F. Elton. Elton's papers are preserved in the Public Record Office in FO 84/1514. His journal was also published in a version edited by H. B. Cotterill in 1879 and extracts formed the basis for *Elton and the East African Slave Trade* (London, 1952).

10. FO 84/1490, pp. 269–72, Captain Sulivan to Rear-Admiral Corbett, 21 August 1877.

11. FO 84/1486, pp. 214–18, Kirk to Derby, number 162, 14 November 1877.

12. FO 84/1514, pp. 257–9, Kirk to Derby, number 54, 5 April 1878.

13. FO 84/1515, p. 37, unsigned minute, W. H. Wylde, undated, on Kirk to Salisbury, number 104. See also FO 84/1522, pp. 174–5, Admiralty (R. Hall) to Foreign Office, C, 23 August 1878.

14. FO 84/1549, pp. 5–6, Foreign Office (draft) to Admiralty, 7 February 1879.

15. Ibid., p. 159, Admiralty (R. Hall) to Foreign Office, 11 July 1879.

16. PRO 30 29/369, p. 310, Kirk to Granville (print) number 99, 27 July 1881.

17. For details of the invasion see Turton, E. R., 'Kirk and the Egyptian Invasion of East Africa in 1875', in *Journal of African History*, XI, 3 (1970) pp. 355–70; and Coupland, pp. 271–99.

18. FO 84/1520, p. 82, Foreign Office (draft) to Admiralty, 30 July 1878.

19. Cameron, Verney Lovett, *Across Africa* (London, 1877) 2 vols., Vol. I, pp. 1–4, 8–9, 209 and 277. For a good brief account of Cameron's expedition see Hooker, James R., 'Verney Lovett Cameron: A Sailor in Central Africa', in Rotberg, Robert (ed.), *Africa and Its Explorers, Motives, Methods, and Impact* (Oxford, 1970). The subject of slavery and the slave trade also appeared in several of Cameron's fictional adventure stories for children such as *Harry Raymond* and *In Savage Africa*.

20. Oliver, pp. 38–9, and Lambourn, R., 'Zanzibar to Masasi in 1876, the Founding of Masasi Mission', *Tanganyika Notes and Records*, 31 July 1951.

21. Central African Mission Occasional Paper; number VI, letter, Bishop Steere, 27 July 1876; and Anderson-Moreshead, pp. 113–14.

22. *The Times*, 5 October 1875, p. 5-f.

23. FO 84/1483, pp. 96–7, Foreign Office (draft) to Kirk, number 46, 19 July 1876.

24. FO 84/1486, p. 75, return of slaves, enclosure in Kirk to Derby, number 132, 14 September 1877.

25. Clement Hill Papers, Mss. Afr. s. 16, Granville to Hill, 18 June 1881, p. 27; and 30 September 1882, p. 29; and FO 317/3, Minutes of the Commission.

26. ADM 127/44, Captain Boyle to Rear-Admiral Hewett, number 34, 8 June 1883.

27. FO 84/1575, pp. 247–8, Kirk to Granville, number 135, 13 November 1880.

28. FO 84/1601, pp. 68–9, Miles to Granville, number 134, 15 November 1881.

29. Mss. Brit. Emp. S22. G3, Captain Luxmore to the Secretary, British and Foreign Anti-Slavery Society, 11 July 1882.

30. FO 84/1605, pp. 166–9 and 176–8, Captain Brownrigg to Rear-Admiral Gore-Jones, number 64, 23 December 1880; and number 68, 28 December 1880.

31. ADM 50/298, journal, Rear-Admiral Hewett, quarter ending 30

September 1883; and ADM 127/44, Kirk to Granville, number 150, 15 September 1883.

32. HCA 35/81, pp. 235–6, George Dickins to Rothery, 22 March 1866.

33. ADM 127/41, Commander Tucker to Rear-Admiral Cumming, 15 June 1872.

34. Yexley, Lionel (pseudonym for Woods, James), *The Inner Life of the Navy* (London, 1908) pp. 81–2 and 89. Hereafter cited as Yexley.

35. FO 84/1578, pp. 47–8, Lieutenant Johnson to Captain Earle, 20 February 1880; and ADM 127/43, report H. C. Rothery (extract) 21 July 1880.

36. ADM 127/43, Admiralty (R. Hall) to Rear-Admiral Gore-Jones, number 25, 17 January 1881.

37. Brownrigg took command of the *London* in June 1880 and relieved Earle, not Sulivan as suggested in Lloyd, p. 171. See ADM 196/13, p. 303, service record, Hamilton Earle; and ADM 196/14, p. 664, service record, Charles Brownrigg.

38. Yexley, pp. 82–4 and 95.

39. ADM 127/43, Commander Goodridge to Rear-Admiral Gore-Jones, number 168, 7 December 1881; and ADM 127/44, Rear-Admiral Gore-Jones to Admiralty, number 200, 17 January 1882; and Yexley, pp. 84–9; and FO 84/1620, pp. 26–7, notes, 8 February 1882 on Miles, number 5, 5 January 1882.

40. *The Times*, 4 January 1882, p. 9 e-f and p. 11 b-c; and 5 January 1882, p. 3 a-c; and *Illustrated London News*, 17 December 1881.

41. Yexley, pp. 71–2.

42. FO 84/1599, p. 189, Kirk to Granville, number 42, 9 March 1881.

43. FO 84/1694, pp. 334–4, Admiralty (G. Gwyn) to Foreign Office, number M852, 18 April 1883.

44. ADM 127/44, Captain Luxmore to Vice-Admiral Gore-Jones, number 59a, 29 April 1882; and Vice-Admiral Gore-Jones to Captain Luxmore, 30 May 1882.

45. ADM 50/298, journal, Rear-Admiral Hewett, 4–30 June 1882. It is not surprising that the schooners found the monsoon difficult. One young lieutenant described the south-west monsoon by suggesting it 'generally announces its approach by the heavens being clouded over with dark greasy-looking clouds accompanied by thunder and lightning, the ship flying through the water at a rate of eleven miles an hour, and only a single topsail set.' See Symes, Ltd., 'A Cruise in the *Frolic*', *United Services Magazine*, 1877, part I, p. 232.

46. FO 84/1600, pp. 33–9 and 39–40, Streeter to Kirk, 18 June 1881 and Streeter to Governor of Mombasa, 13 June 1881, and pp. 63–4, Barghash to Kirk, 24 July 1881; and ADM 127/43, Streeter to Kirk, 18 June 1881, Mohammed ibn Suleiman to Barghash, and Kirk to Granville, number 85, 1 July 1881; and *Church Missionary Society Intelligencer*, January 1881, pp. 48–9.

47. FO 84/1604, pp. 27–8 and 33–4, J. Pauncefote to Dilke, private, 24 January 1881, and memo, J. Pauncefote, 29 January 1881; and FO 84/1605, pp. 88–95, Commander Byles to James Zohrab, 30 November 1880; and ADM 127/44, Lister to Miles, 10 March 1882.

48. ADM 127/43, Holmwood to Kirk (two dispatches) 7 July 1881, and Commander Byles to Captain Brownrigg, 12 July 1881.

49. PRO 30 29/264, tab 2, pp. 47–8, Lister to C.M.S. (Wigram) (conf. print), 27 October 1881.

50. *Church Missionary Society Intelligencer*, December 1881, pp. 753–4.

51. ADM 127/43, Holmwood to Kirk, 7 July 1881. The Streeter incident has been treated in detail due to its impact on the question of disposition of freed Africans and because of the role played by Byles in the investigation. It should not be taken as a general indictment of missionary activity on the coast which continued to offer the best placement for the liberated slaves. It should also be noted that naval officers, including Brownrigg, had made routine visits to Frere Town. Their letters, published in the *Intelligencer*, indicate that they failed to realise the problems developing at the station prior to the detailed investigation by Byles and Holmwood. See, for example, the *Intelligencer*, March 1880, pp. 167–9 and June 1881, p. 375, and Stock, vol. III, p. 90. Only extracts of Brownrigg's letter were published, but the original clearly shows where the captain's real interests lay. Feeling obliged to inspect the station, Brownrigg quickly tired of seeing classrooms and hearing recitations of verses. He persuaded Streeter to give his charges a holiday so that a sports day could be held. The captain was most impressed with the former slaves' ability at cricket and happily joined in their game. The most astute observation about the condition of the Frere Town settlement which the captain was able to give was that, on the cricket pitch, they 'show good form'. See CMS Archives, A5/0, Brownrigg to CMS, 4 April 1881. See also G/Y/A5/1/22, Hutchinson to Barghash, 16 November 1881.

52. ADM 196/14, p. 998, service record, Mather Byles.

53. FO 84/1452, pp. 183–7, Kirk to Foreign Office, number 37, 1 March 1876. The role of the private shipping lines continued to be of interest, since there was a hope within the government that they would serve as an anti-slavery device by stimulating legitimate commerce. While the Union Line's ships were at times erratic, the British India Steam Navigation Company service was steady and reliable. It is impossible to quantify the impact the lines may have had on the slave trade but their importance as communication links is undeniable. The key figure in the British India company, and in the later Imperial British East Africa Company, was William Mackinnon. His activities in the region have been considered in detail; see Galbraith, John, *Mackinnon and East Africa 1878–1895* (Cambridge, 1972). In connexion with the shipping line, see especially pp. 30–42.

54. Mackinnon Papers, vol. 91, Kirk to Mackinnon, 10 August 1882.

55. FO 84/1694, pp. 229–33, 'Memorandum respecting the change of policy in suppression of slave trade in Zanzibar, printed for use of the Foreign Office' (C. Hill in consultation with Kirk), confidential, 13 November 1882.

56. FO 84/1625, pp. 112–14, minute, T. V. Lister, Admiralty (G. Gwyn) to Foreign Office, number M1363, 11 July 1882, and minute, T. V. Lister on same; and FO 84/1694, 266–74, Admiralty (E. Swainson) to Foreign Office, number MO488, 20 December 1882.

57. Preston, Anthony, 'The End of the Victorian Navy' in *The*

Mariner's Mirror, Vol. 60, 1974, pp. 363–81; and Rodger, N. A. M., 'The Dark Ages of the Admiralty, 1869–85' (Part II, Change and Decay, 1874–86), in *The Mariner's Mirror*, Vol. 62, 1976, pp. 33–46. Preston dates the 'Dark Ages' from 1873–83 while Rodger prefers the slightly later span of 1874–86. Whichever is taken the demise of the *London* clearly comes at the peak of the period of neglect.

58. ADM 127/44, Admiralty (G. Gwyn) to Vice-Admiral Hewett, number M1702, 27 July 1883.

59. Select Committee, 1871, p. 53, Q690 and Q701.

60. Mackinnon Papers, vol. 89, Kirk to Mackinnon, 11 November 1879.

61. FO 84/1694, pp. 278–83, Captain Foot to Lord Northbrook, 6 December 1882.

62. ADM 127/44, Lister to Foot, number 16, 1 October 1883.

63. FO 84/1690, p. 11, Captain Woodward to Admiralty, telegram, 2 October 1884.

64. ADM 127/44, Lister to Kirk, number 151, 9 October 1883.

65. The appointment of Knowles does not result from the Kirk initiative. The lieutenant was pressed into the position by his captain when the consul, Thomas Pakenham, died and French activity required some sort of permanent British presence. See JOH/6, Commander Charles Johnstone to Granville, 26 June 1883.

66. FO 84/1688, p. 2, private letter, Kirk, 2 June 1884.

67. Professor Lloyd cites 1883 as the best choice for the end of the Arab slave trade. The choice is an unfortunate one. Lloyd's reasons for the date are twofold. First he points to the last use of naval vessels under sail in that year. He is referring to the withdrawal of the *Harrier* and *Undine* which, as has already been noted, were unsuccessful experiments. The trade had been combated by vessels with steam power since Oldfield's era and the removal of the two schooners hardly stands as the end of an era. The second point cited by Lloyd is the removal of the *London* which is certainly of importance although the *London* was not struck from the lists until 1884. Lloyd admits that captures were made on the station later and says that *Penguin* captured 15 dhows in 1888. The implication is that the total was unique, but in fact several ships were making numerous captures including six with ten or more during the last half of the decade. The most unfortunate result of choosing to end a study in 1883 is that it prompts the historian to ignore the resurgence of the trade after the withdrawal of the *London*.

7

The Consuls Fail

The first warnings of a revival in the slave trade did not take long to come. On 13 December 1884, Commander Charles Anson of the *Dragon* confirmed to Hewett that with the *London* gone the slavers were coming out into the open again. The *Philomel*, on the cruising ground off Ras al Hadd, made two captures. One of the dhows had 51 slaves and the other was packed with 154 slaves bound for the northern market. Anson warned of 'false rumours' that were being circulated all along the coast that the British were giving up their active suppression of the trade. 'They point to the fact that the visible sign of English interference at Zanzibar, HMS *London*, has been dismantled and broken up,' he explained.[1] The navy was not the only source of warnings. Lieutenant-Colonel S. B. Miles, the political agent and consul at Muscat, had already warned that northern Arabs had formed the impression that the British antagonism to the slave trade had changed. Trouble in the Sudan was one cause but the first was 'the break up of H.M. Ship *London* at Zanzibar and the removal of the Naval establishment for the suppression of the trade.'[2] One month later, an even more concerned Miles was pointing to landings of slaves and warning that, 'unless some repressive measures be adopted and a certain amount of vigilance displayed by the cruisers the Arabs will become emboldened and the following year will see a complete resuscitation of the traffic.'[3] On the home front, concern was also growing. One source closely monitoring the situation was *The Times*, which had not been pleased with the withdrawal of the *London* in the first place. Even before the ship was removed, the paper suggested, 'without the *London* and its launches neither the convention with the Sultan nor the skill of Sir John Kirk himself could prevent a scandalous revival of the export trade.'[4] When the revival of the trade began to become apparent, the view was seconded in the letter columns where it was suggested that 'the present outbreak of slavery is caused to a great extent by the withdrawal of Her Majesty's Ship *London*.'[5] By October of 1884, even Kirk was forced to shift his ground. Trying hard to play down the 'alleged revival' of the trade, the consul had to admit to the Foreign Office that 'there is no doubt the sale of HMS *London* and the withdrawal of our ships to the Red Sea at the time of the disasters in the Sudan gave our credit a serious shock.'[6] By the beginning of 1885, the argument was shifting to the establishment of a new depot ship at Zanzibar to stem the revival of the slave trade. 'The experiment of HMS *London* has proved that a single vessel with steam launches stationed at the port of export, Zanzibar, is a more efficient check on the slave trade than the endeavour to intercept slave dhows at sea,' insisted Miles.[7]

In November 1884, the consul-general at Bushiri joined the chorus by reporting a marked increase in the slave trade.[8] A drought had hit Zanzibar and Kirk tried to explain the revival of the trade on that basis. 'Under such circumstances it will be very difficult to stop the slaves from being sold or pawned,' he contended.[9] At the end of the year, the navy was back where it had been fifteen years before with cruisers trying to check a growing traffic in slaves with deployed boats. Lieutenant Francis Valentine of the *Osprey*, for example, was cruising in the cutter near Pemba and he sent the gig under Quartermaster Herbert Holyoake to cruise off nearby Mescale Island. Holyoake spotted a dhow which, as he approached, made sail and tried to escape. The gig crew fired shots ahead of the dhow and the sail was lowered again. On boarding, the crew found 169 slaves crammed into the dhow, six of them dying. The dhow was kept as a depot for the cruising boats in an effort to re-establish some sort of semi-permanent facility off Pemba. The old antics of the slavers were, however, reinforced all the time. Shortly after the major capture, the *Osprey* herself approached a dhow and two canoes one evening. A cry was heard in the water and a lifeboat was lowered to recover a young boy in the water. When the boy had been picked up, the ship fired at the vessel ahead and after boarding, the crewmen learned that when the dhowmen saw the ship's lights, they threw seven slaves overboard.[10] Early in 1885, Captain R. Woodward of the *Turquoise* expressed the naval view from the coast, informing Hewett, 'there is no doubt that the slave traffic is greatly increasing.'[11]

There was also an increase in the degree of difficulty for the naval suppressors with the passing of the *London*. The stationary ship had been located at the source of the seaborne trade and had sufficient boats to blockade the surrounding area adequately. The cruisers were less well situated and their increased mobility was of questionable value. Moreover the boats of the cruisers were not so well designed for the task as the larger boats of the *London* and, of course, any time boats were deployed there were associated dangers and difficulties for the crews. Some of the problems of boat cruising had been underlined in the early 1880s and even when the *London*'s boats were on patrol, rough and questionable tactics were sometimes employed. Woods gives a useful picture of boat cruising suggesting that the boat would usually tow a dinghy or canvas punt and when a dow was to be boarded, two men would go in to inspect it while the others covered them from the boat. If problems arose or dhowmen refused to part with their weapons, Woods recalled that fisticuffs were frequently the order of the day. As has been seen, the level of violence sometimes escalated even further. Woods offered what was probably the best possible summary of the sailors' view when he suggested, 'No doubt our actions were often arbitrary and illegal, but ten men in a sailing boat 100 miles from anywhere could not afford to take risks.'[12] Despite such problems, however, small boat cruising had been re-established as the daily routine with the revival of the trade at the end of 1884.

Another question which was somewhat unsettled was that of the disposition of liberated Africans, the Streeter episode having tended to discredit the mission stations. A survey of Kirk's location of former slaves, from late 1877 until mid-1885, shows that of the approximately 1,300 slaves he relocated, most were released to individuals in Zanzibar. Almost 42 per cent of all the slaves were dealt with in this way while the second most popular receiving point was the Universities Mission which took 35 per cent of the total. Only one former slave was sent to another colony, Natal, and 86 went to the French mission at Zanzibar while a handful were given freedom papers and released in Zanzibar. The Church Missionary Society's station near Mombasa was charged with 198 slaves but none were delivered there between late 1879 and March of 1885.[13] Streeter's actions had checked assignment to the station even before the full level of his activities had been discovered. Frere Town was, however, seeing a revival. W. S. Price, who had founded the station relying in part for catechists on 'Bombay Africans' who had been freed by the cruisers and taken to India, returned in December 1881. He was able to put the mission back on a firm footing before turning it over to a new lay superintendent, H. W. Lane. The improved situation at Frere Town was confirmed in March 1885 when 169 freed slaves were located at the station.[14]

One of the best indications of the general state of slave trade suppression following the demise of the *London* is the return of captures made on the station. During a five-year period, beginning in 1880, ships in the squadron captured 126 dhows while liberating over 1,200 slaves. Closer analysis reveals that there are really two sets of statistics during the period. For the first three years, the dominant factor in the totals was still the *London* with 65 captures and over 400 slaves taken. There is a void in the returns for the period immediately following the removal of the *London* but then a sudden burst of activity clearly reflects the renewed vigour of the slave trade. The stationary ship seemed to have served as a stopper in the Zanzibar bottle and when that stopper was removed, the flow began all over again. In the eighteen months or so following the removal of the *London*, captures soared with 59 dhows taken and almost 650 slaves liberated. In other words, nearly half the total captures and over half of the slaves taken during the five-year span were from the year or so following the removal of the *London*. During late 1884 and 1885, individual cruisers again appear repeatedly in the lists of captures led by Commander H. W. Dowding's *Osprey* with 13 dhows taken and 266 slaves freed. Anson's *Dragon* made eleven captures with 81 slaves and Commander John Ranier's *Kingfisher* made seven captures with 54 slaves. Woodward's *Turquoise* also added five dhows captured and the *Philomel* under Commander Henry Lang freed 205 would-be slaves.[15] The point was clear; there had been a resurgence of the slave trade and agitation had already begun for a 'New *London*'.

Events in East Africa had, however, undergone radical changes in the mid-1880s and political developments began to overshadow questions of slave trade suppression. It is likely, in fact, that instability on the coast stemming from the German incursion helped to stimulate the revival of the trade. There is no doubt that the assertion of Carl Peters' claims in East Africa by Germany upset the balance that had hitherto existed in the region. While it is beyond the scope of this study to trace the rise of German influence or the ensuing scramble for territorial acquisitions, it can generally be said that broad strategic questions such as Egypt made Britain ill-disposed to quarrel with Germany over colonial questions and the previously anti-colonial German Chancellor, Bismarck, decided to use the Peters' claims in Zanzibari dominions as a new trump card in his game of *realpolitik*. Settlement with Germany was deemed more important than maintenance of the British 'unofficial empire' in East Africa and eventually Barghash was abandoned to his fate while Britain tried to salvage what could be saved in the region during the rapid partition of East Africa.[16]

It is important to note that there are naval issues inextricably bound up in the whole question of the scramble. In the first place, a general decline in British naval strength can be put forward as one of the important factors in prompting the sudden surge of Imperial acquisition throughout Africa. For example, in assessing causes for the scramble, Sanderson cites the British naval hegemony as the 'indispensable foundation of the British unofficial empire,' and thus one of the principal stabilising factors prior to the burst of Imperial activity. Thus the decline in British naval preponderance represented a de-stabilising factor encouraging adventurism on the part of potential European competitors. As has already been stressed, the era of the late 1870s and early 1880s was a particularly difficult one for the navy. Capitulation over the *London* was only one facet of a general malaise which saw British naval superiority under challenge from both France and Germany by the mid-1880s.[17] Symptomatic of the growing naval strength of the European powers was the German use of Rear-Admiral Knorr in the *Bismarck* to finalise Barghash's acquiescence in Peters' profiteering within his dominions.[18] With German ships cruising off Zanzibar, the whole role of the Royal Navy in the region changed.

It should not be thought, however, that the changed political circumstances eliminated the anti-slave trade role which the navy had to play. In fact, the continuation of anti-slavery patrols provided a useful excuse for maintaining warships in the region. The earlier dual purpose of the squadron in stopping slave shipments while keeping an eye on the French was modified only in that the object of surveillance was now the German fleet. If the naval requirement to support the sultan had changed after the abandonment of Barghash, other basic British policy objectives remained and the navy continued to be the best visible symbol of the British stake on the coast. It can be argued that the political role was now the dominant one and that the slave trade campaign was reduced to a peripheral concern. It is true that the relative importance of political as opposed to slave trade questions had been modified in the mind of the government. Nevertheless, slave trade was still a useful rallying cry for humanitarians at home and the concern over the revival of the slavers continued to grow. Furthermore, as will be seen, the naval officers still had a man-on-the-spot influence to assert and in many cases their personal hostility to the trade assured that an aggressive policy would be maintained despite the changed ground-rules of a more and more Europeanised East African coast.

In the first instance, prosecution of the slavers was, however, lessened in the wake of the scramble. Official German acceptance of the Peters treaties came in February of 1885 and was quickly followed by the additional acquisition of Witu. Since the regions were in what had generally been accepted as Zanzibari territory, a Delimitation Commission was sent to determine the extent of the sultan's holdings. The situation distracted naval attention as ships were diverted to transport and assist the British commission member, Herbert Kitchener.[19] In the midst of these political manoeuvres, however, continuing reports of increased slave trade activities continued to intensify the debate over the form of the naval response and there was increasing support for a new stationary depot ship at Zanzibar despite the changing political background of East Africa. Ashley's letter in *The Times* pointing to increases in the slave traffic and blaming the increase on the withdrawal of the *London* had sparked off new discussion and doubts over the vice-consular approach within the Foreign Office.[20] Soon confirmation was coming from more official sources as even Kirk was forced to admit a revival of the trade. The increases he had tried to minimise a year before were admitted since, 'the evidence in each case discloses a serious renewal of the slave trade.' Not only that, Kirk also admitted that his consular establishment was not making inroads against the traffic. Blaming distractions by the Germans, he acknowledged 'we were thus compelled to leave the suppression of the slave trade to our naval force.'[21] Kirk's grand design had seen Gissing assigned to Mombasa, Haggard to Lamu and Smith to Kilwa. Probably the biggest problem for the coastal consuls was that their power was largely ephemeral. While naval authority to detain and search dhows as well as to confiscate slaves was clearly established by treaty, no such power had ever been given to the new consuls. As a consequence, they were left with no option but to try to cajole the sultan's local authorities into taking action. Not surprisingly, their efforts produced sparse results.[22] In the meantime, authorities in the northern Arab dominions were expressing concern about the revival of the trade in their areas. Lieutenant-Colonel E. C. Ross, political resident in the Persian Gulf, reported that 'the system of stationing a special vessel at Zanzibar, provided with steam launches, proved a success, and certainly whilst that system was in force the number of slavers reaching Oman greatly diminished.'[23] By the end of 1885, Miles informed the government that 'the East African slave trade has revived and is now again in full swing . . . the bulk of the slaves are exported from Zanzibar.'[24]

For its part, the Admiralty was quick to observe the failure of the consular system. By late 1884, Northbrook had already observed that 'the change from H.M. cruisers to the . . . vice consuls, for the prevention of the slave trade does not appear to have proved successful as yet.'[25] As the lack of success persisted, the Admiralty continued to emphasise that the changes at Zanzibar were the result of Foreign Office initiatives, not naval ones. 'The *London* has been put out of service . . . in accordance with Foreign Office letters,' Northbrook insisted at the beginning of 1885. He returned to the theme a month later, suggesting, 'the *London* . . . was removed from the East Coast of Africa at the pressing request of the Foreign Office.'[26] Soon, the navy on the coast was forced to attempt to revive the system which had centred around the *London*. Two of the *London*'s cruising boats had been left in Kirk's charge. Late in 1885 they were taken back under naval control by Captain Rodney Lloyd of the *Briton*. The two launches, *Olga* and *Helena* were refitted and sent back to their old cruising ground off Pemba.[27] Specific complaints were being lodged against the ineffectiveness of Kirk's consular system ashore by senior naval officers. Rear-Admiral Sir Frederick Richards, who had taken command of the station, advised the Admiralty that 'the consular service which was . . . to have put an effectual check upon the export slave trade and render the presence of the *London* at Zanzibar unnecessary, appears to have broken down altogether.'[28] The Treasury voiced the same complaint with Rothery noting that 'unfortunately Sir John Kirk's expectations, that the traffic had been materially crippled, were not fulfilled.'[29] The Treasury was a continuing source of complaint since the whole consular scheme had been partially justified as a major cost-saving programme. With the revival of the trade and the concomitant rise in bounties, expenditures were actually increasing instead. In

February of 1886, the Treasury advised the Foreign Office that based on their predictions, £2,000 had been placed on the estimates for tonnage and slave bounties but that now a supplementary estimate would be required. A total of £4,123 had already been paid out and it was Rothery's guess that almost another £2,000 would be needed by the end of the year. The Treasury note then chided the Foreign Office on the fact that the costs of new vice-consuls and the subsidy allocated to the British India Steam Navigation Company had been justified on the grounds that the slave trade and its resulting bounty payments would be reduced. 'This expectation does not, however, appear to be likely to be realized,' it was noted.[30] Nor was the problem going to end quickly. At the end of 1888, Richard Incledon, who replaced Rothery, observed that increases in the slave trade had again caused expenditures over the estimate to the amount of some £1,600.[31]

By the beginning of 1886, even Kirk himself admitted more of the facts. The Kilwa consulate had already been closed down and the shortcomings of the whole approach were obvious. 'My Vice Consuls having failed me I must do their work myself,' he complained.[32] Of course the failure of the consular system was an unfortunate sidelight for Kirk who was observing his whole design for East Africa crumble in the German intrusion. After having worked for years to establish a viable sultanate dependent on British assistance and control, Kirk could only preside over the dissolution of the system as the Delimitation Commission aided the governments in parcelling out the Zanzibari dominions. In July of 1886, Kirk left Zanzibar ostensibly on a year's leave, but with his grand design for the region in shambles, he did not return.

The navy's task, however, remained as the agitation over the resurgence of the slave trade continued. The call for additional navy support was still a priority for Miles, now political resident in the Persian Gulf and consul-general for Fars, who wrote the epitaph for Kirk's consular system:

> It is to the efforts of the officers of Her Majesty's navy that the suppression of the trade from 1874 to 1884 is almost exclusively due, and it is entirely on their efforts that Government will have to depend in future. The inefficacy of the consular or land system, which was introduced in 1884 when the consular staff at Zanzibar was increased by four or five new consuls, and which was intended to supersede naval operations, has

led to a complete revival of the slave trade, and the scheme as then organized may now be regarded as a failure.[33]

The same was being said on a variety of sides. Mathews, who had been involved in the land attack on the trade since leaving the *London*, urged the restoration of the old system. 'Since the *London* was broken up the slave trade has increased. A ship such as the *London* or a large frigate should be sent out . . . to work as a depot at Pemba,' he suggested.[34] In Parliament, the Under-Secretary for Foreign Affairs admitted that it would have to be considered 'whether it would be judicious again to have a stationary ship . . . from which swift vessels could go out to intercept the departure of the dhows from the mainland.'[35] Two leading figures among the younger generation of British officials in East Africa echoed the outcry. According to Frederick Lugard, the withdrawal of the *London* 'was interpreted by the slave traders as an indication of the wane of our interest in the suppression, and was immediately followed by a marked recrudescence of the slave-trade.' Lugard explained that 'in place of the *London* the three Vice-Consulates on the coast, and the Consulate on Nyassa, were established . . . It was, however, an abortive and ill-matured plan.'[36] Gerald Portal recommended, 'in the first place I would advocate the re-establishment without delay of a stationary guard-ship somewhat of the nature of the old *London*.'[36] Portal's views were based at least partially on recommendations of Rear-Admiral Sir Edmund Fremantle, station commander as the decade ended. Sir Edmund told Portal, 'I have always considered it specially unfortunate that the *London* was removed,' and suggested a 'New *London*' to take her place.[38] It should be noted that Fremantle and the other advocates of the return of the depot ship were not arguing that naval suppression was something which would stop the trade by itself. Instead they were returning to the sort of approach Heath had suggested years before with a two-fold attack; the naval and consular authorities should assist and complement one another. The situation was put into perspective by O'Neill who reviewed the possible avenues of slave trade suppression which were open and warned, 'It is of course, manifestly wrong to pit any one of these forces against the other, as it is by a union of them all that the slave trade will best be combatted.'[39] Kirk, influenced by personal self-confidence and ambition and agitated by the continuing friction between himself and the navy, lost sight of the usefulness of the naval establishment in such a cooperative role. The ill-fated consular system, largely excluding a naval presence, had been a significant and unfortunate outgrowth of the long history of rifts between consul and captains on the East Coast.

Notes

1. FO 84/1731, pp. 146–9, Brigadier-General J. Blaire to Secretary to the Government, Bombay, number 1/209, 4 November 1884; and ADM 127/44, Commander Anson to Rear-Admiral Hewett, 13 December 1884.

2. FO 84/1689, p. 50, Miles to Political Resident in Persian Gulf, number 144, 12 May 1884.

3. ADM 127/44, Miles to Political Resident in Persian Gulf, 9 June 1884.

4. *The Times*, 21 January 1882, p. 11 a-b.

5. Ibid., 20 January 1885, letter submitted by Cecil Ashley, p. 10 c-d.

6. ADM 127/44, Kirk to Granville, number 142, 25 October 1884.

7. ADM 127/45, Miles to Political Agent, Muscat, number 28, 18 January 1885.

8. ADM 127/44, Consul-General, Bushiri, to Foreign Office, telegram, 28 November 1884.

9. Ibid., Kirk to Granville, number 137, 24 October 1884.

10. FO 84/1732, pp. 186–91, Commander Dowding to Vice-Admiral Hewett, number 42, 7 December 1884.

11. ADM 127/44, Captain Woodward to Vice-Admiral Hewett, number 3, 16 January 1885.

12. Yexley, p. 77.

13. FO 84/1741, p. 248A, enclosure in Rothery to Treasury, 20 August 1885.

14. *Church Missionary Society Intelligencer*, February 1882, p. 116, May 1882, p. 300, and September 1882, p. 572; and Stock, Eugene, *The History of the Church Missionary Society* (London, 1899) Three Vols, vol. III, pp. 83–93; and FO 84/1741, Rothery to Treasury, 20 August 1885. For additional information on the revival of Frere Town including an account of reception of liberated Africans brought in by the *Osprey*, see the *Intelligencer*, January 1884, pp. 23–32 and March 1885, pp. 158–67.

15. Compilations of totals for captured dhows and released slaves are drawn from High Court of Admiralty documents, HCA 35/86, HCA 35/87, and HCA 35/88.

16. See, for example, Robinson, R. and Gallagher, J., with Denny, A., *Africa and the Victorians*, (London, 1961), pp. 189–209; Sanderson, pp. 22–66, Flint, J., 'The Wider Background to Partition and Colonial Occupation', deKiewet Hemphill, Marie, 'The British Sphere, 1884–94', and Freeman-Greenville, G. S. P., 'The German Sphere, 1884–98', in Oliver and Mathew, pp. 352–453; and Coupland, pp. 319–436. Carl Peters founded the Gesellschaft fur Deutsche Kolonisation in 1884.

17. Sanderson, G. N., 'The European Partition of Africa: Coincidence or Conjuncture', in *The Journal of Imperial and Commonwealth History*, III,

1 October 1974, pp. 1–54; Preston, *op. cit.*; Rodger, *op. cit.*; and Marder, pp. 119–39.

18. See, for example, Coupland, pp. 437–44.

19. Discussion of the Delimitation Commission and the Anglo-German agreement of 1886 can be found in Coupland, pp. 448–78 and Flint, in Oliver and Mathew, pp. 372–6. A brief account from the standpoint of the British Commissioner is in Magnus, Philip, *Kitchener, Portrait of an Imperialist* (London, 1958) pp. 69–70.

20. FO 84/1732, p. 186, minute, C. Hill, 20 January 1885. See also fn. 5, p. 190.

21. FO 84/1728, pp. 73–6, Kirk to Salisbury, number 250, 22 September 1885.

22. Gray, Sir John, 'The British Vice-Consulate at Kilwa Kivinji, 1884–1885', *Tanganyika Notes and Records*, number 51, December 1958, pp. 174–93.

23. ADM 127/45, Ross to Secretary to the Government, India, number 19, 23 January 1885.

24. Ibid., Miles to Ross, number 321, 24 November 1885, forwarded with concurrence in Ross to Secretary to the Government, India, number 174, 5 December 1885.

25. ADM 1/6726, Minute, Northbrook, on Admiralty to C in C, 6 December 1884, no. L2785.

26. ADM 1/6764, minutes, Northbrook, 13 January 1885 and 6 February 1885.

27. ADM 127/36, Captain Lloyd to Rear-Admiral Richards, number 12, 13 February 1886.

28. FO 84/1792, pp. 46–55, Rear-Admiral Richards to Admiralty, number 308, 30 August 1885.

29. FO 84/1781, pp. 111–11B, letter, Rothery (extracts), 4 February 1886.

30. Ibid., pp. 109–10, Treasury (M. Johnson) to Foreign Office, number 2261/86, 9 February 1886.

31. HCA 35/88, pp. 332–3, Incledon to Hunt, number 12, 479, 5 November 1888, and pp. 348–9, Incledon to Treasury, number 12, 490, 30 November 1888.

32. FO 84/1772, pp. 132–4, Kirk to Sir P. Anderson, private, 22 January 1886.

33. FO 84/1857, p. 115, Miles to Secretary to the Government, India, number 150, 18 October 1886.

34. FO 84/1981, pp. 206–12, Mathews to Portal, 22 October 1889.

35. Parliamentary Debates, 3rd Series, CCCXXXIV, 26 March 1889, 916–25, Sir J. Fergusson.

36. Lugard, F. D., *The Rise of our East African Empire* (London, 1893) 2 Vols., Vol. 1, pp. 61–3.

37. FO 84/1981, pp. 176–91, Portal to Salisbury, number 363, 29 October 1889.

38. ADM 127/38 and FO 84/1981, pp. 198–204, Rear-Admiral Fremantle to Portal, number 83, 18 October 1889.

39. O'Neill, H. E., *The Mozambique and Nyassa Slave Trade* (London, 1885), p. 15.

8

The End of the Trade

While the debate over establishing a 'New *London*' continued to rage, in the first instance, neither renewed slave trading nor the German incursion provoked an increase in naval strength off the coast. As a result, the navy was put back into a position reminiscent of the one which had existed in the late 1860s. It is true that the treaty structure had been improved since then, but the means of enforcing anti-slave trade provisions had reverted to cruising men-of-war. Without the guard ship at Zanzibar, the cruisers were once again forced to concentrate on the islands of Zanzibar and Pemba and soon reports were sounding much as they had done in the days before the 'spider's web'. In June 1886, for example, a pinnace and whaler were working in tandem when they attempted to board a dhow. The dhow crew ran their vessel aground on a reef and escaped leaving the slaves to their fate. The pinnace could not go into the shallow water so the whaler and the pinnace's punt were sent in to rescue the people trapped on board. Women and children from among the passengers and slaves were transferred back to the larger boat but when the seamen returned to the dhow, the whaler became water-logged and was forced to the beach with the male slaves. Four navy men were left on the dhow which suddenly broke in half. In trying to swim ashore, one of them was drowned.[1] Almost exactly the same situation developed a month later but with happier results. Richard Hammett, a quartermaster who had learned boat cruising on the *London* and who was due to retire within a year, was sent cruising off Pemba in a whaler. He closed on a dhow which the crew ran straight into a reef. Darkness had already fallen, but Hammett still managed to come alongside and save the 22 slaves found on board.[2] For the slaves, the story was much the same as well. Captain George King-Hall recalled the case of a boy taken by the *Garnet* in 1888. The young liberated African could remember nothing of his home. His earliest recollections were of the long march from the interior where he was looked after by a slave woman who had a baby of her own. His first vivid memory was of an Arab slave driver telling the woman that she was not strong enough to have a baby, taking it from her, and dashing its brains out. When the woman grabbed the slaver's sleeve in an effort to stop him, he snarled that she wouldn't be able to reach the coast herself and killed her with his sword.[3] For the seamen, too, who were forced to return to the old pattern of cruising in the small boats of the cruisers, many old complaints reappeared. Lieutenant Gordon Fraser described the discomfort of the heat for the men of the *Kingfisher*. With the thermometer hanging between 97 and 102 degrees day and night, the ship had 46 sick and the lieutenant reported 'no sleep and general prostration'. One dazed sailor actually committed suicide in the steaming conditions. Another was 'in his hammock with fever, was seized with heatstroke, fell out and was picked up dead.' According to Fraser, 'the upper deck all day was under water, the men who could move about being employed in throwing water over those who were suffering from heatstroke.'[4]

As naval pressure on the trade increased, the level of violence again intensified. In May 1887, a pinnace from the *Turquoise* was cruising under Lieutenant Frederick Fegen. As Fegen called on a dhow to lower its sail, the dhowmen suddenly turned their vessel and attacked the pinnace. Running straight at the navy boat, the dhow rammed in an attempt to capsize her. Just before the dhow struck the cutter, the Arabs fired a volley into the boat. In the collision, the rigging of the vessels became tangled, and Fegen, cutlass in hand, led the pinnace crew forward to engage the dhowmen in hand-to-hand fighting. In the ensuing melee nine crewmen of the dhow were killed but their compatriots managed to disengage their lines and try to flee. The pinnace pursued and a running battle followed with shots being fired on both sides. Finally a seaman hit the helmsman of the dhow, and as the helm swung free the dhow broached to and capsized in shallow water. Fegen quickly anchored as close to the dhow as he could and sent the unwounded members of his crew to save as many of the slaves as possible. They eventually managed to rescue 53 from the wreckage although many others were drowned in the fray. In the conflict, Fegen and four British sailors were wounded. They managed to land the slaves, limp into the old depot at Funzi, and send for help. News of the battle finally reached Lieutenant T. H. M. Jerram, of the *Reindeer*, who was cruising in the *Helena*. He hurried to the wounded with medical supplies but Fegen and his crew had been forced to make do without medicine for over a week by the time he arrived. One of the seamen, Benjamin Stone, died after the amputation of a leg. All three of the other seamen were invalided. Fegen and his crew were all promoted for their parts in the action,[5] but the attack by the dhow was an indication of further escalation to come.

In the meantime, other seamen were using information channels to good avail. William Cassidy, quartermaster, was in charge of the *Reindeer*'s gig off Pemba where he tried to re-establish the contact with the native population and boat crews from free traders which had proved a valuable source of information during the *London* era. The intelligence was translated into the capture of a habitual slaver on 13 December 1887.[6] Similarly, Lloyd sent his steam cutter to try to collect information and the crew were told of a dhow being loaded nearby. At high water, the captain took the *Briton* to the spot and captured the dhow as well as clearing a nearby slave barracoon.[7] King-Hall fastened on to an idea which was gaining acceptance among some navy men — using a dhow for cruising in an effort to blend in with local shipping.[8]

Resistance to naval action brought new casualties late in 1887 as the *Garnet* chased a dhow which was run behind a reef. Presuming that the dhow had been run aground, the ship dispatched the whaler under Lieutenant William Stewart to burn it if it had not been sunk. As the whaler came abreast of the spot where the dhow was thought to be, slavers opened fire on the boat killing Stewart and wounding three of his crew. The ship responded by shelling the shore but was unable to pursue the slavers.[9] Later, in 1888, another engagement brought more casualties. The *Griffon*'s steam cutter under Lieutenant Myles Cooper was sent to cruise off Pemba. The cutter approached a dhow which opened fire as soon as the boat came into range. Cooper and two seamen were wounded by the volley, and the lieutenant ordered Corporal John Bray to take over and try to capture the dhow. Bray and the four uninjured seamen, including one seedie, kept up fire on the dhow during a running battle of about half an hour. The dhowmen then turned toward shore and ran aground. The cutter followed and also went aground with the seamen continuing to fire at the dhow. The dhowmen managed to escape but the sailors were then able to get their boat off, attach a line to the dhow, and tow the slaver and its cargo of 74 slaves free. As the crew pulled the dhow off, however, Cooper began to worsen from his wounds and fearing for the lieutenant's life, Bray put a two-man prize crew on the dhow and immediately returned to the ship with the wounded. But the cutter was too late. As the boat pulled alongside the *Griffon*, Cooper died.[10]

The level of the revival of the trade and the navy's counter measures is reflected in returns for the period. From the beginning of 1886 to the beginning of 1890, the cruisers had already approximately equalled the combined totals for captures in the previous five years. Captures numbered 117 with over 1,000 slaves liberated. Individual ship totals during the period include Commander H. B. Lang's *Reindeer* with 14 captures, Lloyd's *Briton* with 12, *Kingfisher* under Commander R. B. Needham and the *Griffon* commanded by Commander J. G. Blaxland with 11 each, and Woodward's *Turquoise* and Captain Albert Jenkin's *Garnet* with 10 apiece. Totals for slaves released included the *Reindeer*'s 152 and King-Hall's *Penguin*, a new ship with an old name, with 104.[11] The statistics seemed to serve as additional fuel for the arguments for a revival of the *London* and the permanent naval presence at Zanzibar.

Events were, however, progressing rapidly and in a few years outstripped the whole concept of peripheral European presence as reflected in a depot ship in the harbour of Zanzibar. A politically motivated naval blockade at the end of the decade finally strangled the trade and when the blockade was lifted there was no major revival of the traffic in slaves, as a British protectorate was established over Zanzibar and the very institution of slavery began to die as a result.

In March of 1888 Saiyid Barghash, shattered by the rape of his dominions, died in his palace and was succeeded by his brother Saiyid Khalifa. Shortly thereafter, in August of 1888, the region which had passed under German control exploded into revolt largely under the leadership of Abushiri ibn Salim ibn Abushiri al-Harthi, a Swahili plantation owner from Pangani, against the rule of the German East African Company.[12] As a result, the German government suggested a joint Anglo-German naval blockade of the coast ostensibly as an anti-slavery device but in reality to provide an arms embargo. Several observers, including the departed Kirk, warned against the move. Kirk feared that by associating with Germany, Britain would lose its credibility and might even 'be expelled from our part of the coast.'[13] Salisbury was under no illusion about the purpose of the proposed blockade and advised the new consul at Zanzibar, C. B. Euan-Smith, who had taken over in 1887 after a brief caretaker period under Holmwood, that 'the real object is probably to provide a demonstration which shall persuade German public opinion that something is being done.' Salisbury was ready enough to commit ships to the operation, however, being prompted by a general lack of trust of the Germans. 'My disposition is to think that any naval measures Germany may wish to take, however innocent in name, will not be safe unless they are shared and controlled by at least an equal English force,' he candidly explained.[14] Salisbury initially tried to dissuade Germany from the blockade arguing that it could do no good and might do real harm by further irritating the people in the German sphere. He conceded though that if Germany proceeded, British ships would also be committed in the name of slave trade suppression.[15] The situation was reminiscent of 1860 when fears of French activity had complemented the initial commitment of ships to the East Coast. The anti-slave trade argument helped to make the House of Commons more willing to pay the bill for a deployment of ships which could then play a useful political role in the region. If Salisbury had no illusions about the reasons for the blockade, Bismarck was even more pragmatic. The Chancellor informed the Reichstag after the blockade had begun that he had never seen it as a measure to kill slavery but rather as a proof that Germany and Britain were united in regard to the African coast. 'If the blockade ceases without creating the impression of a breach of unity between England and Germany, I shall have nothing to say against it,' he explained.[16]

If the impression of solidarity had any basis, it did not carry over to mutual trust among the parties. Fremantle, who was charged with putting the blockade into operation, was told that he was to press for the exclusive employment of British ships on the coast of the British sphere because the government was suspicious of the abilities of the German commanders and feared that their lack of discretion could cause the revolt to spread north. 'Press for this not as part of your instructions from home but on ground of convenience and local responsibilities', he was advised.[17] Fremantle was receiving additional secret guidance which included reference to slave trade matters. The misuse of the French flag had continued to plague the cruisers. The blockade finally presented an opportunity to attack the abuse as all vessels could be stopped under blockade conditions. In instructions marked 'very strictly confidential' the admiral was told how to proceed on the matter. It would be safer, he was advised, that for vessels under the French flag 'the ground on which they are stopped should be that of breaking the blockade or carrying munitions of war. If proved to be slavers, slaves would of course be released.'[18] As the instructions were put into effect, the situation created problems for Euan-Smith. The consul reported that:

> The French consul has exhibited an extraordinary sensitive-ness with regard to the right of search of vessels carrying the French flag. I have done my very utmost to induce the English Admiral to humour this feeling as far as possible.[19]

As the blockade developed, Fremantle had no difficulty in ensuring that British ships patrolled off the coast of the British sphere. In fact, a shortage of German vessels forced one British cruiser to operate along the coast of German held territory. The arrangements for the blockade against slave trading and carrying munitions were promulgated in the admiral's general orders on 29 November 1888. There were four major cruising areas including station one from Ras Gomany to Kipini and including Lamu, station two running from Ras Gomany to Kuruitu and station three continuing to the Umba River. Station four, within the German sphere, included the coastline between the Rovuma River and Kiswere.[20]

Fremantle approached the blockade with thoroughness and if the government remained doubtful about the practicalities, the admiral had every intention of making the blockade an effective one. One of the most important facets of his organisational approach was the employment of a cruiser in a 'new *London* role'. The old goal of a central depot in Zanzibar harbour, reinforced by a number of coastal cruisers had finally been restored. As Fremantle described the approach in his memoirs:

> The *Agamemnon* remained at Zanzibar, chiefly, as she was not suitable for cruising, but her boats were made use of, and she was a valuable depot and repair ship, while it was useful to have her captain, Captain Cardale, senior officer at Zanzibar in my absence.[21]

The admiral also continually prodded his ships into more intense prosecution of the blockade. In December, he advised the fleet that ship's boats were not being used enough and that the blockade would be more effective if boats were deployed into the major ports. In that way, any vessel approaching any of the main harbours could be boarded. He cited Lamu in station one, Malindi in station two, Mombasa in station three, and Lindi in station four as places where special vigilance was required.[22] Fremantle insisted that the ships themselves were to be underway every day during daylight hours and to visit every part of the coast in their station at least once every 24 hours. Dhows were permitted to have a few rifles or muskets and Arabs were allowed to retain ornamental sidearms but any weapons beyond those exemptions were to be confiscated. All vessels under any flag were designated as liable to search and of course slaves were to be taken and slavers condemned.[23] Individual captains also tried to stimulate aggressive prosecution by their crews. King-Hall established his own personal bounty system. 'I have given the cutter's crew £5, as I told them I would to the first boat catching over 25 slaves, and £10 over 60; now I intend giving a rupee for each slave caught.'[24]

With seven men-of-war including the flagship *Boadicea, Agamemnon, Algerine, Garnet, Griffon, Penguin* and *Reindeer*, Sir Edmund hoped to put a final stop to the slave trade during the blockade. It was of critical importance that the admiral was serious about the slave trade aspect of the operation and while the governments were using the anti-slavery terminology largely as rhetoric, the navy was putting the rhetoric into practice. The admiral announced his intention of maintaining six cruising boats at Pemba at all times as an additional check against the slavers. 'It would be too ludicrous a result of the slave blockade if the numbers safely landed on that island were to be . . . increased,' he insisted.[25] There was a clear and familiar difference in emphasis between the naval and civil authorities with the navy insisting on maintaining slave trade suppression while the consul stressed political considerations and showing the flag. Euan-Smith described the situation by reporting:

I have spoken on this subject to the Senior Naval Officer . . . who though always most kind and courteous has informed me that this consideration must if necessary be made subordinate to his duty of suppressing the slave trade. I venture to think the former consideration more important.[26]

It did not take long for the ships and boats to begin achieving results. The German cruisers also began to take slavers, finding at first that the dhowmen did not even try to avoid their ships. The British vessels on the station, which had been the scourge of the slavers for so long, were painted white. Their German counterparts were painted black and the slavers seemed to think that their only fears were from the white ships. The German corvette *Carola* captured a dhow off Pangani with 80 slaves on board when the *nakoda* serenely sailed close by her not thinking he had anything to fear from the strangely painted vessel.[27] Eventually the heat forced the Germans to shift to white themselves.[28] The whole question of slave trade suppression was new to the Germans and Fremantle observed that 'the Germans when they capture any slaves do not know what to do with them.' He also ventured the guess that their solutions would not be particularly good ones. 'I very much fear their condition is not much improved even if they are not sold into slavery a second time,' he suggested.[29] The Germans did seem to be trying, however. Despite the long-standing complaints about lack of instructions, at least the Royal Navy had a prize manual and a set of slave trade regulations. In January, the Germans approached Salisbury to obtain copies because their cruisers were 'without any experience as to how to proceed.'[30] There was, however, some friction on the station between the British and German seamen. A typical view was King-Hall's that 'the Germans are carrying matters with a very high hand.'[31] He accused his German counterparts of recklessness suggesting 'German vessels go along the coast pitching shells into the villages.'[32] Mathews, who was working overtime in an effort to pacify the coast, admitted, 'I am getting terribly tired of the Germans, even the consular people annoy one.' Frayed nerves may have been a factor in Mathews' condemnation, 'They have no law or justice. Germans must always be right and they are without exception the biggest liars I have ever come across. A German never tells the truth except by mistake.'[33] The main factor in preventing such friction from threatening the whole blockade was the fact that the two admirals worked well together and suppressed the smoulderings among their subordinates. Fremantle could cite several situations in which Admiral Dienhard went out of his way to oblige the British admiral and the general operation of the two fleets was smooth.[34]

In the meantime, Fremantle's ships were slowly strangling the slave trade through the blockade. As many as 12 boats were at times cruising off Pemba[35] and statistics showed that in the month of December alone, 408 vessels had been boarded by the British ships. Of these vessels 12 per cent were under the French flag.[36] The leading vessel in numbers boarded was the *Penguin* which inspected 96 vessels during the month. Her log is instructive as to the intensity of the blockade. On one Sunday in December, the ship herself closed on and boarded two dhows before 9.00 a.m. After a break for church services she inspected another dhow during the morning and boarded two others before 2.30 p.m.[37] At one time the *Penguin* was using not only all her boats but also a captured dhow for cruising.[38] By the end of January, Fremantle was convinced that the trade had been stopped. 'I believe absolutely no slaves are run now,' he insisted as boardings, exclusive of those off Pemba, had increased to 637 during the month without a single slave being found.[39] One month later, the admiral reported 'I am informed that notwithstanding the extremely high price of slaves on the island (Pemba) the Arabs are afraid to take the risk.'[40] The intensity of the naval force had never been approached in the region before and the results were surprisingly effective. On 10 April 1889, Fremantle counselled that 'trying and monotonous' as the blockade was it should not be relaxed in view of the results it was achieving. The numbers of dhows boarded, taken from partial returns, showed 1,360. Of that number 684 had been boarded by the ships or by boats on detached service, 562 had been inspected at the entrance to Zanzibar harbour, and 114 had been inspected by the boats cruising off Pemba. The slavers were unwilling to attempt to run the close blockade and Fremantle was able to report, 'the net result has been the taking away of one gun from a passenger which I have ordered to be restored to him.'[41]

As the blockade continued, however, an underlying theme harkened back to previous experiences in the anti-slave trade patrol. As has been discussed, broad scope for independent action put the consul as well as navy officers in the role of man-on-the-spot in East Africa. When conflicting personalities and overlapping jurisdiction brought the civil and naval authorities into confrontation, rifts such as that between Rigby and Crawford developed. Playfair and Kirk had both fallen into conflict with naval officers with unfortunate results in the latter case. All the previous consular-naval rows, however, appeared amicable beside the crowning confrontation between Fremantle and Euan-Smith. The conflict produced a breach between the two British officials during a period of delicate international manoeuvres concerning the whole region. While the goal from the early 1880s had been toward greater control from Whitehall, the two men-on-the-spot still had considerable influence and power. It has been suggested that Euan-Smith, after the long era of Kirk and the shorter caretaker period under Holmwood, had been hand picked by Salisbury to curb the influence of the consul by serving as a 'yes man' for the Prime Minister's policies.[42] A consul appointed in this way would be deprived of some of the flexibility which his predecessors had enjoyed. But if there was a move to restrict the powers of consuls and captains, no one had told Fremantle. The admiral, by asserting his own authority, alienated the consul and trouble began.

Fremantle had been charged with responsibility for the execution of the blockade and he saw the issue as being a naval one under his exclusive control. He made the point less than diplomatically when Euan-Smith asked for information concerning details of the naval operations. 'For obvious reasons I am not at liberty to give you for general information "all the detailed regulations" to which you refer in your letter,' he informed the consul, explaining that the admirals were to carry out the blockade and that was being done. However, if Admiral Dienhard, his German counterpart, did not object, Fremantle advised the consul that he would forward him a copy of their agreement confidentially.[43] What Fremantle had done was to inform Euan-Smith that his chain of command ran to the Admiralty in London and not the consulate in Zanzibar. The tone, however, had the result which should have been expected, and the incensed consul responded that he had 'observed with surprise the calculated intention to "snub" me as if I had asked for information I had no right to ask for.'[44] The initial argument subsided but it was soon followed by another. Only about a month after the first row, the two were at it again over a letter which the German consul had addressed directly to the admiral. Apparently believing the admiral to be the real representative of British power in Zanzibar, the German consul wrote to him directly rather than going through Euan-Smith as called for by protocol. At least that was the interpretation the consul put on the situation when Fremantle called on him at his home and showed him the letter. The admiral, thinking the contents would be of interest to the consul, showed him the correspondence and the angered Euan-Smith immediately sat down to express his displeasure in a letter to the German consul. It was then Fremantle's turn to be annoyed as he explained to Euan-Smith that the letter had been addressed to him personally and that he had betrayed a confidence of sorts by showing it to the consul in the first place. On that basis, he argued, Euan-Smith ought not to make any comment on it at all, much less send a letter about the matter. At that point, the discussion declined into a shouting match with the consul claiming the right to make any use of the letter he saw fit. In response, Fremantle countered with the avowed intention of avoiding future social contact with Euan-Smith.[45]

After tempers had cooled, both men attempted to make amends with Fremantle writing to the consul, 'I mean to do my best to forget what I have felt and written and I hope you will do the same.'[46] Euan-Smith replied by citing ill-health which had in fact plagued him. On a note, probably written by his wife, the consul penned his own postscript hoping for a fresh start after a long letter which had said in part, 'I regret and express my regret should I have, as you say, ever treated you with a want of consideration. I shall be on my guard against this for the future.'[47] Euan-Smith had also confided to Mackinnon, 'I do not like to complain, but for weeks past I have been feeling seriously unwell; and I have had and am still subjected to, the most distressing sensations in my head, which I cannot throw off.'[48] With the attempted reconciliation, it looked as if an amicable relationship had been restored. Within a month, however, the height of the quarrel began over the question of consular passes for arms shipped to the coast. The cause of the disagreement was gun-powder being shipped to Mombasa under a pass given by Euan-Smith. The *Boadicea* had twice passed powder shipments on the strength of the consular pass and on both occasions, the admiral had asked the consul for advance notice of such shipments in the future. To enforce the request, he finally issued orders that no more munitions would be passed on consular authority without prior approval.[49] The third shipment of powder was found by the *Algerine* which turned the shipment back. Euan-Smith exploded in fury, claiming that the action had humiliated him and destroyed his credibility and authority. He wrote an ill-considered letter to Fremantle demanding the name and rank of the officer on the *Algerine* who had refused to honour the pass and, in an attempt to assert authority over the admiral, wrote, 'If your Excellency has issued such orders, I hereby have the honour to demand that they be at once cancelled.'[50] It was a clear challenge to Fremantle's authority and he met it bluntly but tried to calm the consul in a private letter enclosed with the official one. Euan-Smith refused to read the private letter.[51] The next day he sent back an official letter in which he accused Fremantle of having 'made use of your high office to strike a secret blow at my lawful authority and to lower the dignity of my office.'[52] By this time, the relations between the two men had degenerated to such an extent that they would not even speak to one another and were dealing through an intermediary, the flag captain, Captain Asheton Curzon-Howe. In the end, Euan-Smith withdrew his demands and agreed to issue no more passes for arms except on men-of-war and always to notify the senior officer at Zanzibar.[53] But the relations between the two were never completely repaired. It is true that they returned to speaking terms and Fremantle eventually reported home that they had become quite friendly. He could not, however, conceal his real feelings and his references to his new cordiality with the consul seem more an attempt to convince himself than to describe the true state of affairs. In reference to maintaining a large naval presence in harbour, Fremantle wrote in June 1890, 'It is Euan-Smith who gets them (the Foreign Office) into these messes, and I marvel greatly that they have such confidence in him. I have *none*, though he has considerable talents, and we are very good friends.'[54]

The blockade of the northern or British sphere continued to concentrate primarily against the slave trade since there was no real hostility on that coast. The action on the German coast, however, intensified as Abushiri continued to hold sway. In April 1889, partly in reprisal for continued shelling of the coastline by the German ships, Abushiri's force attacked a German mission station 15 miles inland from Dar-es-Salaam. In the ensuing conflict, three missionaries were killed and three others were taken captive. Eventually the surviving missionaries were ransomed but the action signalled the start of a major German initiative against the rebels.[55] The thrust was led by Lieutenant Hermann von Wissmann who had been sent out to command a force of Sudanese troops under German officers. Wissmann attacked Abushiri's stockaded camp near Bagamoyo on 8 May 1889, aided by some 200 sailors from the German fleet, and succeeded in routing approximately 600 defenders.[56] By the next month, heavy shelling of Saadani preceded an attack there and before the end of the year, Abushiri had been caught and hanged.[57]

The success of the German force coupled with financial problems surrounding the expense of the blockade made Bismarck begin efforts to call off the operation in late August. By this time, Gerald Portal was acting in Euan-Smith's stead at Zanzibar. In confirming Portal in the post, Salisbury admitted that the acting-consul had many problems to contend with. 'The task you have kindly undertaken in Zanzibar will not be an easy one. You have to govern an imbecile sultan and make him like the operation,' he suggested.[58] Portal also had to handle problems associated with the blockade and by 1 June was ready enough to see it called off. In a private letter to the Prime Minister's secretary seeking some sort of subsistence allowance, he confided that the navy was eating him out of house and home. Charged with officially entertaining the various naval dignitaries, poor Portal reported, 'The Queen's birthday alone cost me quite half a month's pay.' He explained:

> At the present moment there are 10 men of war in the harbour — five English, of which one flagship, one huge iron-clad, two Italian, one German and one French. All these expect to be entertained, and then they go away and others come.[59]

Meanwhile the groundwork was being laid for the end of the blockade, but as Portal was advised in a secret telegram, Bismarck wanted to finish it with a flourish.[60] The flourish took the form of a wide-reaching new agreement between Portal and the sultan which was signed on 30 September. The sultan granted to the British and German navies the permanent right to search any of his subject's vessels within the territorial waters of Zanzibar. More important was the agreement that all persons entering Zanzibari dominions after 1 November 1889 were to be free and all children born in the dominions after 1 January 1890 were born free.[61] With the signing of the new agreement, the Anglo-German naval blockade was lifted on 1 October 1889.[62] A total of eleven British ships had been involved in the operation and Fremantle was congratulated on all sides for the way he had conducted their activities. With Euan-Smith temporarily away, Portal heaped lavish praise on the admiral. 'I must ask you to accept also my best congratulations on the management, arrangement and termination of the whole very difficult business,' he wrote. There was a striking contrast with the prior correspondence between Fremantle and Euan-Smith. Portal cited 'the benefit of your presence and cordial assistance during the time that we have worked together in this most thorny spot.'[63] Another vote of confidence came from Francis de Winton of the Imperial British East Africa Company, formed to develop the British sphere. De Winton advised Fremantle that the 'charitable construction' would be to blame the problems with Euan-Smith on the consul's illness which 'has produced a morbid sensitiveness and great irritability sufficient to cloud his judgement and warp his mind.'[64]

By the end of 1890, the final act in the slave trade campaign was being played out. In February Khalifa died and was succeeded by his brother Saiyid Ali. Fremantle deployed ships in various regions to guard against any possible civil unrest but the accession was greeted calmly.[65] There soon followed one of three death blows to the slave trade. The new sultan agreed to promulgate a decree which prohibited persons from leaving slaves to any but members of their immediate family, prohibited the sale or purchase of any slave, and allowed slaves to buy their freedom at a fixed rate. In addition, he agreed to decree the total abolition of slavery with the granting of general emancipation at a future date.[66] A second development in 1890 was the publication of the conclusions of the Brussels conference where Lord Vivian and Kirk were serving as British delegates. The findings called on European powers newly established in the African interior to take 'protective or repressive action' against the slavers.[67] The third and most significant development of the year came on 1 July with a new Anglo-German treaty on East Africa. Terms included extension of the boundaries previously established for the two countries' holdings, cession of the German strip by the sultan and the cession of Witu to Britain. The most important agreement was the exchange of British sovereignty over the North Sea island of Heligoland for the establishment of a British protectorate over Zanzibar itself.[68] With the British protectorate, the end of the Zanzibar slave trade was effectively assured since public opinion would not tolerate even vestigial slave trading in an area controlled by Britain.[69]

With the treaty there was, however, an additional naval action to be conducted. After the treaty ceding Witu had been signed but before any change of administration had taken place, nine Germans were killed by troops of the sultan of Witu. Fremantle, now a vice-admiral, was put in charge of what was described as an 'exclusively punitive' expedition designed 'to satisfy German opinion which is much irritated by it.'[70] On 21 October 1890, Fremantle and his old antagonist Euan-Smith presented a joint ultimatum to Fumo Bukari, the sultan of Witu, giving him two days to surrender with the persons who had killed the Germans.[71] A declaration of martial law proclaimed by Fremantle also went into effect.[72] When the ultimatum expired, Fremantle organised the largest striking force to have ever entered the region and advanced on Witu. Sir Edmund had shown a concern for detail and thoroughness during the blockade and carried it over to the Witu intervention. He had also had experience with difficult actions for Naval Brigades both in New Zealand and the Ashanti war and wanted no debacles in East Africa.[73] Taking all the forces on hand, he drew men from all the ships then off the coast including *Boadicea, Turquoise, Conquest, Cossack, Brisk, Kingfisher, Pigeon* and *Redbreast*. The total finally reached 700 seamen and marines as well as some 150 Indian and native police provided by the Imperial British East Africa Company. The imposing force was headed by the admiral himself, along with three captains, 23 other naval officers, and three officers from the Imperial British East Africa Company.[74] Action began with boat expeditions to two nearby villages where atrocities had been reported. Fremantle hoped that the attacks would divert attention from the main advance. One boat detachment, comprised of men and boats from *Boadicea*, was led by Curzon-Howe while the second was drawn from the *Cossack* under McQuhae; both villages were burned without casualties among the boat crews. A base camp was established at Kipini under Commander R. A. Montgomerie who enclosed his men in a zariba. The camp was attacked during the night but the opposition was repelled; three sailors were wounded. As Fremantle recalled the incident, 'A more careless occupation of the post would have probably resulted in great loss . . . but Commander Montgomerie had had Soudan experience, and I knew I could rely on him.'[75]

Meanwhile, Fremantle had hoped to march the main force to Witu in a square but found that the terrain would not allow it. Instead, when confronted by Witu defenders, he deployed the Indian police on the extreme right, seamen in the centre and left, and marines on the right and centre. The line opened fire on the sultan's troops and after about an hour and a half of firing, the Witu contingent fell back toward the town. The British force made camp for the night and at daybreak resumed their advance to Witu. Reaching the town proved an anti-climax for, after the gate had been blown open, the town was found to be abandoned. The naval force responded by blowing up the palace and burning down the town.[76] The admiral was pleased with the result and, finding a large tusk of ivory among the spoil from the palace, sent it to Queen Victoria 'as a memorial of the "little war" in which Her Majesty's Naval forces have been engaged.'[77] He was especially pleased that he had reduced the sultanate without the loss of a single man. In fact, the only serious threat to the men's safety had been the heat. There were 27 cases of sunstroke on the march but all the men recovered.[78] Accolades for the attack were not unanimous and, as might have been expected, Euan-Smith led the critics. Before the action the consul urged a massive reaction suggesting 'it will require a very considerable armed expedition to deal adequately with the situation.' After the fact, however, he chided the admiral for having used an over-adequate force suggesting 'it should be understood that a *moderate* display of force . . . is really all that is required to deal with any situation that is likely to arise in these latitudes.'[79] The consul also criticised Fremantle for not having kept a larger reserve on his ships.[80] Despite this official criticism sent to London, Euan-Smith was ready enough to accept what he saw as the benefits of the attack. He informed Mackinnon that the Imperial British East Africa Company could feel secure as 'for a long time to come you need now have little apprehension as to the risk of there being any rising or unfavourable demonstration upon your coastline.' The reason was 'the facility and success with which the Witu expedition was pressed to a conclusion.'[81] A telling criticism, however, was Buxton's which came in a letter to *The Times*. No one could doubt Sir Edmund's zeal or his men's gallantry, he argued, 'but so far as it involved the destruction of many lives and houses at Vitu (sic) and the villages on the coast, there can be no pretence of justification.'[82] In addition, the attack did not prove to have been as crushing as it seemed. Open resistance had been broken but guerilla warfare continued in the region for several years.

Nevertheless, in a sense it was appropriate that such a large naval force provided a climax to the events of 1890 because the tempo of operations was not the same after that year. The concentration on slave trade suppression duties by the navy was more and more eclipsed by an even more purely political role. That transition had already begun. A case in point is the situation in 1889 with growing tension over delimitation of boundaries in the interior with Portugal. The Portuguese refused overtures to discuss their extravagant claims and Fremantle, with a large fleet, was actually on the verge of sailing to capture Mozambique and Quilimane when the intimidated Portuguese finally gave in.[83] Similarly, in 1896, the death of the sultan of Zanzibar sparked off a rebellion by one of the royal princes. The challenge was met by Rear-Admiral Sir Henry Rawson and his five ships in harbour.

The admiral gave the young prince an ultimatum to surrender but was met instead by a hostile display by some 2,000 rebel troops in the palace not to mention a flotilla of armed dhows clustered around the sultan's ship *Glasgow*. When the ultimatum expired, the ships opened fire with a 37-minute bombardment in which the usurper's palace, ship and several dhows were destroyed. The rebel forces suffered some 500 casualties yet the gunfire was so accurate that no town buildings were damaged. Within a matter of hours, the revolt had been quashed and the preferred sultan, totally dependent on British arms, had been installed.[84] While such political action was to continue well past 1890, with British control over Zanzibar established and the end of slavery already being prepared on paper, there was no real danger that the slave trade which had been stopped during the blockade would resume with the vigour which had marked the years after the withdrawal of the *London*. The political pressure associated with the Anglo-German treaty along with the naval activity during the blockade had combined to end the trade. The blockade checked the day-to-day slave-running of the dhowmen while the political groundwork was being laid for the permanent end to slavery.[85] As a consequence, if any date must be chosen for the effective end of the slave trade in East Africa and the naval response to that trade, 1890 is the best choice which can be made. It would be wrong, of course, to think that the change was total and that slave trading ended overnight. Far from it, as captures of isolated dhows carrying small slave cargoes continued to the end of the century and beyond. It would be too much to have expected the habits of generations to be completely changed by decree, and the naval presence continued even after the proclamation ending the legal status of slavery in Zanzibar in 1897. At the turn of the century, the Salisbury government was still receiving reports of fears of increases in the slave trade.[86] In 1904, the *Forte* and *Barracouta* were stationed off the East Coast of Africa and despatched their boats to board and inspect dhows for possible slave trade violations.[87] Even after the First World War, the navy was still involved in anti-slave trade operations and as late as 1922, the *Cornflower* captured a dhow with 29 slaves on board in the Red Sea.[88] By 1925, the government was even considering aerial observation against slave dhows as the commanding officer of the *Clematis* suggested that 'the use of aerial observation appears to present the best chance of capturing slave dhows.'[89] In mid-July of 1927 the Foreign Office advised the Admiralty: 'Sir Austen Chamberlain . . . has had under consideration the question of the slave traffic across the Red Sea from Africa to Arabia.'[90] In January of 1928, three ships, *Clematis, Waterhen* and *Vendetta*, boarded and examined 34 dhows for possible involvement in the slave trade.[91] Such residual activity against the slave trade was not, however, on a par with the persistent naval commitment of the late-nineteenth century. By 1890, the transformation was well under way. As one young boat officer noted, 'my letters and journal record that we played a good deal of tennis and cricket.'[92] That was a change from the old routine of seemingly endless weeks of boat cruising. The continuing day-to-day confrontation between the navy and the slavers which had continued since Oldfield's day had effectively ended by the time of the Witu incursion of 1890. The end of the Anglo-German naval blockade and the establishment of the Zanzibar protectorate represented the end of an era.

Notes

1. FO 84/1788, pp. 177–84, Captain Lloyd to Rear-Admiral Richards, number 55, 9 June 1886.
2. FO 84/1790, pp. 138–42, Captain Lloyd to Rear-Admiral Richards, number 68, 19 July 1886.
3. King-Hall, L. (ed.), *Sea Saga* (Being the Naval Dairies of Four Generations of the King-Hall Family), (London, 1935), p. 283.
4. FRR/4 and FRR/3, Journal and Remark Book, Lieutenant Gordon C. Fraser, HMS *Kingfisher*, 1888. The heat was a source of continuing concern to Fraser but he managed to keep his sense of humour. In the pages of his remark book he described the situation in a light hearted poem called 'The Tar's Ingenuity'. The lieutenant wrote:

The 'Tar' stood burning on the deck
and held his aching head,
Twas 10 am, he felt a wreck
and wished that he were dead.
He could not drink until the sun
Above the foreyard rose
— Now why that rule was first begun
sure goodness only knows —
But see! his eye is growing bright,
he looks exceeding wise,
The sentry flies with footsteps bright
and for the boatswain cries.
The boatswain comes, 'Oh Pipes,' says he,
'I think that yard is sprung,
We'll get it down on deck and see,
So get that yard unstrung.'

The boatswain cries 'hey cheerly hearts'
— As Avon's bard might say —
'Down with the foreyard, yare, she starts,
A'hold, heigh, lower away'
With creak and groan the great fore yard
Comes down on deck at last
Of course quite sound and strong and hard.
But neath the sun it's passed
Our tar flies quickly down below
Straight to the bell and trow.

5. FO 84/1853, pp. 26–9, Holmwood to Foreign Office, number 107, 5 July 1887; and FO 84/1867, pp. 210–16, Commander Lang to Commander Woodward, 12 June 1887; and pp. 205–9, Captain Woodward to Admiralty, 20 June 1887; and pp. 203–4, Admiralty (R. Rowley) to Foreign Office number L2058, 15 August 1887; and *The Times* 15 June 1887, p. 7–d; and 13 August 1887, p. 11–f; and JRM/4, Journal and Remark Book, Lieutenant T. H. M. Jerram, *HMS Reindeer*, 1884–1887 (entry for 9–10 June).

6. FO 84/1917, pp. 124–5, Commander Lang to Captain Jenkings, 19 December 1887.

7. FO 84/1784, pp. 22–6, Captain Lloyd to Rear-Admiral Richards, number 8, 13 February 1886.

8. FO 84/1907, pp. 217–18, Euan-Smith to Salisbury (forwarding King-Hall's suggestion) number 126, 4 June 1888.

9. FO 84/1864, pp. 85–90, Commander Bradford to Admiral HRH the Duke of Edinburgh, number 37, 2 May 1887.

10. FO 84/1910, pp. 61–5, Euan-Smith to Salisbury, number 310, 22 October 1888. For press report see *The Times*, 20 October 1888, p. 5–a.

11. Compilations of totals for captured dhows and released slaves are drawn from High Court of Admiralty documents, HCA 35/88 and Foreign Office documents, FO 84/1904, FO 84/1975, FO 84/1980 and FO 84/2059.

12. There is good account of the rebellion available. See Jackson, Robert, 'Resistance to the German Invasion of the Tanganyikan Coast, 1888–1891,' in Rotberg, Robert and Mazrui, Ali (eds), *Protest and Power in Black Africa* (Oxford, 1970), pp. 37–79.

13. Mss. Brit. Emp. S 22.G7, Kirk to Buxton, 5 November 1888.

14. FO 84/1912, p. 114, memo for telegram to Euan-Smith, Salisbury, 11 October 1888.

15. Ibid., pp. 128–9, Salisbury to Euan-Smith, draft of telegram, 15 October 1888. Another problem from Salisbury's point of view was that a rebellion in Haiti led to a blockade of northern ports of that island at about the same time. See for example ADM 1/6935, blockade correspondence, Haiti, 1 November 1888.

16. ADM 127/38, copy of speech by Bismarck to Reichstag, 26 January 1889, extract from *North German Gazette*, 27 January 1889.

17. Ibid., Foreign Office (J. Pauncefote) to Admiralty, secret, 5

November 1888; and Admiralty to Rear-Admiral Fremantle, number 33 (copy of telegram), 6 November 1888.

18. FO 84/1932, pp. 338–9, Admiralty (E. MacGregor) to Foreign Office, confidential, 19 November 1888; and Admiralty to Fremantle, number 37, very strictly confidential, 17 November 1888. MacGregor, the Admiralty clerk responsible for the blockade action, sent two telegrams to assure strict secrecy over plans for stopping French vessels. See ADM 1/6935, minute, MacGregor, 20 November 1888.

19. Salisbury Papers, A/79, Euan-Smith to Salisbury, 18 December 1888, pp. 87–96.

20. ADM 50/372, journal, Rear-Admiral Fremantle, 1 October to 31 December 1888. Fremantle's blockade memos also appear in FRE/137 and in ADM 1/6935. Italy also assigned a ship to the blockade but the Italian involvement was largely irrelevant from a naval point of view. For an analysis of Italian political activity in the region, see Hess, H. L., *Italian Colonialism in Somalia 1885–1941* (Chicago, 1966).

21. Fremantle. Sir E. R., *The Navy As I Have Known It* (London, 1904), p. 348. *Agamemnon* was a representative of the modern class of war ships designed without sails — the first assigned to the station. She was specially detached from the Mediterranean station for the blockade. See ADM 1/6935, Admiralty to Foreign Office, 16 October 1888.

22. ADM 127/38, blockade memo number four, Rear-Admiral Fremantle, 19 December 1888.

23. Ibid., General Orders relative to blockade, Rear-Admiral Fremantle, 29 November 1888.

24. King-Hall, p. 284.

25. FO 84/1935, pp. 129–40, Rear-Admiral Fremantle to Admiralty, number 285, 19 November 1888.

26. Salisbury Papers, A/79, Euan-Smith to Salisbury, 2 July 1888, pp. 39–42.

27. FO 84/1987, pp. 39–49, Rear-Admiral Fremantle to Admiralty, number 331, 18 December 1888.

28. *The Times*, 1 January 1889, p. 3–b.

29. FO 84/1989, pp. 97–106, Rear-Admiral Fremantle to Admiralty, number 22, 16 January 1889.

30. FO 84/1986, pp. 361–2, Foreign Office (E. Barrington) to Admiralty (Captain Lord Walker Kerr) private, 12 January 1889.

31. King-Hall, p. 285.

32. Mss. Brit. Emp. S22.G3, King-Hall to Allen, 30 February 1889.

33. Salisbury Papers, A/79, Mathews to Euan-Smith, 4 May 1889, pp. 160–164. Mathews' role at Zanzibar had become a key one. Euan-Smith cited his unique position and suggested 'he is universally looked up to and respected.' But even more important was that 'his influence has always been exerted whenever practical on the side of English interests.' See Salisbury Paper, A/79, Euan-Smith to Salisbury, 2 April 1888, pp. 17–18.

34. See for example, Fremantle, pp. 350–1.

35. FRE/139, Fremantle to Sir Vesey Hamilton, private, 25 September 1889.

36. FO 84/1989, pp. 97 – 106, Rear-Admiral Fremantle to Admiralty, number 22, 16 January 1889.

37. ADM 53/14948, log, HMS *Penguin*, 9 December 1888.

38. See, for example, ADM 53/14947, log, HMS *Penguin*, 23 April 1888.

39. FO 84/1976, pp. 449 – 52, Rear-Admiral Fremantle to Euan-Smith, number 14, 16 February 1889.

40. FO 84/1993, pp. 342 – 9, Rear-Admiral Fremantle to Admiralty, number 135, 3 April 1889. It has been suggested that the blockade was largely unsucessful in that it only diverted the slave and arms trades southward. Given the pattern of the slave trade and the reports of the naval observers, it seems unlikely that this is the case. The resurgence of the trade following the withdrawal of the *London* was based on Persian Gulf markets along with the never-really-closed clandestine trade to the Pemba plantations. Completely closing both these areas of demand supressed the trade. It is arguable that the diversion theory might be more substantial in regard to arms traffic. For the argument, see Beachey, R. W., 'The Arms Trade in East Africa in the Late Nineteenth Century,' *Journal of African History*, III, (1962), pp. 451 – 67.

41. FO 84/1994, pp. 291 – 4, Rear-Admiral Fremantle to Admiralty, number 148. 10 April 1889.

42. Galbraith, pp. 144 – 5. There had been another interesting change in personnel as the Foreign Office slave trade department had been replaced by an African department headed by Sir Percy Anderson. That change tended to produce a shift in attitude as well since Anderson differed in outlook from the Assistant Under-Secretary, Lister. See Louis, William 'Sir Percy Anderson's Grand African Strategy, 1883 – 1896', *The English Historical Review*, LXXXI, 1966, pp. 292 – 314. Louis suggests, 'Lister, in the anti-slave trade tradition saw foreign policy in terms of honesty and dishonesty, loyalty and disloyalty, and right and wrong . . . Anderson was no less scrupulous, but his was a more complex world, a world in which Britain was no longer free to bully other nations with impunity, even on the straightforward issue of suppression of the slave trade.'

43. FRE/137, Fremantle to Euan-Smith, 9 November 1888.

44. Ibid., Euan-Smith to Fremantle, private, 10 November 1888.

45. Ibid., Fremantle to Euan-Smith, private, 10 December 1888. It is interesting to note that Euan-Smith had difficulties with others in connexion with misuse of private correspondence. He was, for example, forced to try to make amends with Mackenzie of the Imperial British East Africa Company over charges that he had 'betrayed or abused your confidence with reference to your confidential letter of the 5 of December.' See the Mackinnon Papers, vol. 16, Euan-Smith to Mackenzie, 3 February 1891.

46. FRE/137, Fremantle to Euan-Smith, 12 December 1888.

47. Ibid., Euan-Smith to Fremantle, private, 19 December 1888.

48. Mackinnon Papers, vol. 13, Euan-Smith to Mackinnon, 1 January 1889.

49. ADM 127/38, Rear-Admiral Fremantle to Euan-Smith, 27 January and 29 January 1889.

50. Ibid., Euan-Smith to Rear-Admiral Fremantle, number 27, 26 January 1889.

51. FRE/137, Euan-Smith to Fremantle, private, 27 January 1889.

52. ADM 127/38, Euan-Smith to Rear-Admiral Fremantle, number 29, 27 January 1889.

53. Ibid, number 50, 4 February 1889.

54. FRE/139, Fremantle to Hamilton, private, 21 June 1890. Emphasis Fremantle's.

55. FO 84/1978, pp. 230–5, Captain Hawes to Salisbury, number 207, 29 April 1889; and FO 84/1984, p. 34, cypher from Euan-Smith, number 18, 16 January 1889.

56. FO 84/1978, pp. 334–9, Portal to Salisbury, number 224, confidential, 16 May 1889. There is an interesting translation of Wissmann's activities in 1886 and 1887; see von Wissmann, Hermann, *My second Journey through Equatorial Africa from the Congo to the Zambezi* (London, 1891).

57. FO 84/1979, pp. 117–23, Portal to Salisbury, number 251, 24 June 1889; and FO 84/1982, pp. 168–70, Euan-Smith to Salisbury, number 411, confidential, 23 December 1889.

58. Salisbury Papers, A/80, Salisbury to Portal, private, 4 April 1889, pp. 242–5.

59. Salisbury Papers, A/79, Portal to Eric (Barrington), 1 June 1889, pp. 177–8.

60. FO 84/1984, p. 291, Foreign Office (cypher telegram) to Portal, number 121, 22 August 1889.

61. ADM 127/38 and FO 84/1980, pp. 275–6, agreement between H.H. Saiyid Khalifa ibn Said and Gerald Portal, 30 September 1889.

62. ADM 127/38, Declaration of Conclusion of the Blockade, Fremantle and Dienhard, 29 September 1889. For press reports of the blockade see, *The Times*, 7 September 1888, p. 3-b, 13 November 1888, p. 5-c, 30 November 1888, p. 5-b, 8 January 1889, p. 5-a, and 2 October 1889, p. 5-f, etc.

63. FRE/137, Portal to Fremantle, private, 1 October 1889.

64. Ibid., de Winton to Fremantle, private, 21 October 1890.

65. FO 84/2059, pp. 271–81, Euan-Smith to Salisbury, number 59, 14 February 1890.

66. FO 84/2062, pp. 148–61, Euan-Smith to Salisbury, number 252, secret, 20 June 1890.

67. Correspondence relating to the Brussels Conference is found in FO 84/2010. For the text of the treaty see P.P. Accounts and Papers, 10, 1890, L, 'General Action, the Brussels Conference.' The provisions prompted a new revision of the naval slave trade instructions. See Clement Hill Papers, Mss, Afr. s. 16, Salisbury to Hill, 2 June 1891, p. 44. The best account of the conference and its impact is an unpublished thesis, Miers, Suzanne, *Great Britain and the Brussels Anti-Slave Trade Act of 1890*, London, 1969. A shorter published account by the same author is 'The Brussels Conference of 1889–90: The Place of the Slave Trade in the Politics of Great Britain and Germany', in Gifford, P. and Louis, W., (eds) *Britain and Germany in Africa* (Yale, 1967) pp. 83–118.

68. Copies of the Anglo-German agreement of 1890 are found in FO 84/2063 and FO 84/2085.

69. For an account of the protectorate and the general efficiency of British control during the last decade of the century, see Hollingsworth, L. W., *Zanzibar Under the Foreign Office 1890–1913* (London, 1953).

70. Salisbury Papers, A/80, Salisbury to Euan-Smith (copy of telegram) 12 October 1890, p. 259.

71. FO 84/2065, p. 236, Fremantle and Euan-Smith to Fumo Bukari, 21 October 1890.

72. Ibid., p. 245, Declaration of Martial Law, Vice-Admiral Fremantle, 20 October 1890.

73. Parry, Ann (ed.), *The Admirals Fremantle* (London, 1971) pp. 202 and 213.

74. FRE/137, Final Orders and Disposition for March on Vitu (sic), mimeograph, 25 October 1890, note on source of forces, and de Winton to Fremantle, private, 20 October 1890. Witu memoranda can also be found in JRM/11.

75. Fremantle, pp. 380–1.

76. FRE/137, Final Orders: and ADM 127/37, Vice-Admiral Fremantle to Admiralty, 1 November 1890.

77. FO 84/2096, pp. 314–15, Admiralty (E. MacGregor) to Foreign Office, number MO354, 11 December 1890.

78. FO 84/2094, pp. 25–6, Fremantle to Admiralty, number 78 (telegram), 31 October 1890; and Keyes, pp. 85–6.

79. FO 84/2066, pp. 21–2, Euan-Smith to Salisbury, number 434, secret, 2 November 1890; and FO 84/2070, pp. 267–8, number 265, cypher telegram, 2 October 1890.

80. Salisbury Papers, Euan-Smith to Salisbury, private, 3 November 1890, pp. 139–42.

81. Mackinnon Papers, vol. 16, Euan-Smith to Mackinnon, 3 January 1891.

82. *The Times*, 10 January 1891, p. 12-b. General press accounts of the action are found in *The Times*, 25 September 1890, p. 5-a and 30 October 1890, p. 3-a.

83. ADM 127/37, Admiralty to Vice-Admiral Fremantle (copies of telegrams) number 2, 9 January 1890 and number 3, 10 January 1890; and Parry, p. 234; and Axelson, Eric, *Portugal and the Scramble for Africa 1875–1891* (Johannesburg, 1967) pp. 201–31.

84. For an account of the action see, Preston, Anthony and Major, John, *Send a Gunboat! A Study of the Gunboat and its Role in British Policy, 1854–1904* (London, 1967) pp. 155–6, and Hollingsworth, pp. 119–30.

85. For a good account of this period, see Glyn-Jones, *op. cit.*

86. ADM 123/34, V. K. Kestell-Cornish to Sir A. Hardinge, number 80, 24 February 1900.

87. Ibid., Vice-Admiral A. W. Moore to Admiralty, number 2/161, 1 January 1904.

88. ADM 116/2474, Commander L. G. B. C. Campbell to C-in-C Mediterranean, 5 July 1922.

89. Ibid., Commander H. Woodward to C-in-C Mediterranean, number S.O./P/12, 20 April 1925.

90. Ibid., Foreign Office to Admiralty, number J 1441/55/1, 20 July 1927.

91. Ibid., Commander C. Coding to C-in-C Mediterranean, number P/7, 26 January 1928.

92. Keyes, p. 58.

9
Conclusions

Several significant points concerning the naval campaign against the East African slave trade have emerged from this study. One factor to be kept in mind, is the consistency of the motives of British policy makers. The three basic considerations of British policy in East Africa which generated commitment of cruisers to the coast in 1860, were still in effect when Fremantle took command of the station in the late 1880s. Protection of British strategic interests and concern for the sea lanes to India was still the dominant factor. One change was that the chief potential rival after 1885 was Germany whereas the traditional adversary in the region had been France. Nevertheless, a strong British presence, as reflected by naval forces, was maintained to counter the challenge of European rivals. A related consideration was trade which helped Britain to maintain its position in the region while also, hopefully, countering the slave trade. The concept of supporting trade initiatives as a way to maintain British influence without the difficulty and expense of direct government involvement could hardly be more clearly seen than in the activities of the Imperial British East Africa Company. It is interesting that the last major naval action during the period of this study, the Witu incursion, was made in conjunction with, and in support of, the Company.

The final consideration was the slave trade itself. In some instances, the humanitarian justification for anti-slavery activities was a convenient excuse for maintaining the ships needed to support the first two requirements. Despite a certain measure of cynicism, however, there was a heartfelt opposition to the trade both in London and within the naval squadron. For example, the

216

Anglo-German blockade was not principally motivated by concern over the slave trade. The humanitarian justifications for the action were simply a smokescreen to cover military intervention. Nevertheless, Fremantle attacked the trade with a sense of commitment which resulted in a strangling of the traffic. This individual hostility to the trade among naval officers was a consistent feature which provides a common link from Oldfield to Heath to the Sulivans to Fremantle.

The structure for advancing British policy in East Africa consisted of three main components. The first was a steadily expanding system of treaty provisions which ultimately made the slave trade completely illegal throughout the region. Working within the treaty framework were the consul and the senior naval officers on the coast. The consul was the government's representative permanently on the scene who attempted to advance British policy through diplomacy, influence or threats as the situation dictated. The most important of the three components, however, must certainly have been the navy. From the Moresby Treaty to the final anti-slavery blockade of the late 1880s, the only effective means of enforcing treaty provisions was the navy. The Moresby Treaty, the Hamerton Treaty and the treaty of 1873 would all have been so much waste paper had it not been for the cruisers charged with enforcing the documents. Of course, the consul's role in East Africa was a highly significant one, a fact emphasised by Coupland and other historians. It must be remembered, however, that the consul's position was a viable one only because of the British pre-eminence in the region and that position of strength rested firmly on the navy. Kirk did not succeed in negotiations with Barghash, where Frere had failed, because he was more able, persuasive or astute. He succeeded because the government decided to use force to bring the sultan to heel. There was, of course, only one form which that force could take — the navy. Significantly, too, in the aftermath of Barghash's acceptance of the treaty, only strong naval support such as Sulivan's Mombasa action, preserved the integrity of the sultan's East African dominions. When the German incursion upset the previously existing balance in the region, it was the navy which was used to restore confidence. Throughout the period of this study, the naval presence, ostensibly for anti-slavery purposes, was a constant reminder of British interests and British strength in East Africa. Kirk's attempt to reduce the naval role in the structure of British operations off East Africa was an unqualified failure which was greeted by a reduction in general stability and an increase in the slave trade. British activity in the region depended on a balance between basic elements and the navy was an indispensable element in the East African structure.

While the importance of the navy in the region is obvious, the historian must not be lulled into the easy error of viewing the naval force as an important, but faceless, entity providing background support but failing to influence policy directly. This view of the naval authorities, as cyphers, is taken by Coupland, Lloyd and a host of their followers. The view is an easy, but inaccurate one. Naval officers were forced into a position of policy making on the East Coast of Africa. Distance involved was a factor causing this situation. The cruising zone of the navy off the coast was immense and broad strategic considerations dictated that ship numbers for the squadron were always low. The primary emphasis of naval strategists during the second half of the nineteenth century was to counter potential European foes. The majority of ships, including newer and more efficient vessels, were assigned to home and Mediterranean waters where they could best be used in possible fleet actions in case of a European conflict. The various Imperial commitments were met with whatever ships were left over and the problem of shortage of vessels was one of the most consistent difficulties facing the navy on the East Coast. Only at the time of the Anglo-German blockade did the involvement of the German fleet produce a significant increase in vessels available for East African service. The station commander was always forced to enforce treaties, support the consul, and generally maintain British policy in the region with only a handful of ships at his disposal. The senior officer in his turn had to dispatch his boats to extend his cruising range. Distances made consultation virtually impossible and when quick decisions were required, they were taken by the navy officer who was the 'man-on-the-spot'. Even had ship numbers been greater and communication easier, the Admiralty was in no position to exercise close control over navy officers on the coast. Even a permanent secretary of the calibre of Lushington was forced to admit that London could not keep a tight rein on the far-flung captains. Lushington's support of Heath over questions arising from the spider's web was a clear admission that the initiative was with the captains and that the organisation of the Admiralty made continuation of loose control necessary. Wide discretion on the part of the naval officers also had a certain limited appeal within the Foreign Office. Successive governments declined to provide clearly stated instructions to naval officers and thus forced them into independent action. The dominant motivating factor in this regard seems to have been the belief that officers left to their own devices would pursue a more aggressive policy while leaving the government with an escape route since the actions were not specifically authorised. With Derby, aided and abetted by the senior slave trade department advisors, and more particularly with Salisbury, there seems to have been a feeling that inactivity on the question of instructions in Whitehall would produce a more forward policy on the coast of East Africa.

Clearly the navy officers were forced to accept considerable responsibility in East Africa and their decisions had a far-reaching impact on development of policy in the region. There can be no question that men like Oldfield, Heath, the Sulivans, Malcolm and Fremantle put the marks of their personalities not only on the anti-slave trade campaign, but also on the general thrust of British policy in the region. A related theme, shown repeatedly in this study, is that the wide range for independent action open to naval officers brought them into confrontation with the consul. Both were 'men-on-the-spot' with significant range for individual action. Wide discretionary powers were vested in both men and their spheres of operation overlapped providing room for friction and conflict. The friction frequently developed with the Rigby and Crawford conflict setting the tone for later hostilities such as those marking Kirk and Heath and between Fremantle and Euan-Smith. The results, as was the case in Kirk's 'dry-land-only' scheme, were sometimes unfortunate. The most significant single point to be made in this regard is that the naval officers were far more than cyphers and that they, like the consul, played an important role in shaping British policy in the region — a role for which historians have been slow to give proper credit and consideration. When Heath, on his own volition, shifted the emphasis of the slave trade campaign, he forced a major review of British policy in the region which ultimately led to the Frere mission. The goals of that mission were finally gained by naval threat and by the pressure exerted by Malcolm operating on his own authority in conjunction with Kirk. Sulivan did not turn to London for approval of his attack on Mombasa in support of the weakened sultan. Instead, he acted decisively and effectively and advanced British influence as a result. The government viewed anti-slave trade justifications for the Anglo-German blockade largely as rhetoric. But Fremantle pursued the anti-slavery campaign with sufficient vigour to strangle the trade. Clearly, any review of the development of British policy on the East Coast of Africa in the second half of the nineteenth century must take into account the role and contribution of senior naval officers serving in that region.

Of course, the political role of the navy was its dominant one during this period. As Preston has shown, the major task of the Victorian Navy was to act as an Imperial gendarmerie. But it should be remembered that the stated goal of the navy on the East Coast was to end the slave trade and, on the surface, the fleet failed to achieve that goal. From 1860 until 1890, the cruisers captured some 1,000 dhows, liberating approximately 12,000 slaves. The total is not insignificant, but when compared with the estimates for slaves transported during the period, it becomes clear that the total returns represent a small percentage of the number of slaves shipped or dhows carrying slaves. Nevertheless, it can be forcefully argued that the traffic would have been even greater without the pressure of the fleet and this interpretation is supported by the events following the withdrawal of the *London*. The increase in the slave trade in late 1884 and after, immediately following the removal of the most visible symbol of the navy's continuing presence, does demonstrate the inhibiting pressure which the navy exercised. The best analogy is to a loose stopper in a bottle which allows a slow trickle while preventing a steady flow. The *London* was that sort of stopper which inhibited slave shipments at Zanzibar while allowing cruising ships to operate further afield against the slavers. The fact does not, however, negate the obvious observation that the navy was unable to check the trade completely and was never even able to stop the majority of the slaves being shipped. The one exception was the massive naval blockade of 1888–9 which seems to have temporarily checked the trade in its entirety. But it is clear that the Admiralty could never have kept eleven ships off the East African coast and as a consequence the trade would have been expected to revive again without the restraints imposed by the major political developments of 1890.

This obvious conclusion, however, does not give full credit to the naval attack on the trade. As has been seen, slave trade objectives in East Africa were complementary to broader political and strategic questions. The squadron increased British prestige in the region and that prestige allowed political pressure to be brought on the question of slave trading. The navy was a potent political force and from the early years of Saiyid Said, the power of the navy convinced the sultan that cooperation with Britain was essential to the maintenance of his dominions. If the rationale broke down during the German incursion into the region, it was still a powerful factor in the development of policy within the sultanate. The fleet was influential as an ever-present reminder of British power and the reminder was at times less subtle than the presence of one or two cruisers. The best example of effective use of the navy in this context is the treaty of 1873. The treaty was signed because a British fleet had been dispatched to blockade the port of Zanzibar and strangle its commerce. It was not a move of great finesse but it was a successful example of power politics with the fleet serving as the tool for intimidation. Barghash was convinced at that time that his lot could only be cast with Britain and that the slave trade was ultimately doomed. The point was certainly entrenched in subsequent years. When his own authority was challenged in the aftermath of the treaty, the naval establishment was employed to maintain the integrity of his dominions. Sulivan's Mombasa campaign reasserted the sultan's authority on that key part of the coast but also stressed the dependence of the sultan and the fact that the naval presence was the underpinning of his authority. The forays against the *akida* at Mombasa, the city forts of the Somali coast, and the slave chieftains near Kilwa, combined to produce a blueprint for gunboat diplomacy. This political role of the navy was substantial and it had far-reaching impact on the slave trade campaign. Of course, the slave trade originated deep in the interior and the gunboats could only hold sway near the coastline. Thus the end of the slave trade could only be produced by a many-sided attack, a fact which Kirk ignored when he argued for the premature withdrawal of the squadron. In addition, the scramble for territorial acquisition clouded the whole slave trade question but undoubtedly speeded up the demise of the traffic. The German incursion produced the changed atmosphere which ultimately led to the establishment of the British protectorate at Zanzibar which in turn hastened the end of the slave trade. In the end, developments in the interior complemented the political pressures emanating from the new British protectorate to check the slavers permanently. The blockade had helped the cause by strangling the trade immediately before the protectorate came into effect. The significant point is that while the navy never stopped the majority of slaves being shipped, it played a vital role in the continuing series of political initiatives which finally ended the trade. While it is obvious that the navy did not, by itself, stop the slave trade, it is equally clear that the trade would not have been stopped without the persistent presence of the navy and the significance of its political role in the region.

The most important aspect of the navy's operations off East Africa was the political power exercised by the cruisers and the scope for using that power which was vested in individual commanders. With an Admiralty which was not organised to maintain close control over remote stations, with a commander-in-chief generally far from the centre of coastal activity, and with difficult problems of communication, the senior officers on the East Coast were forced to use the formidable power of their cruisers as they thought best. In general, they exercised their obligations with a professional efficiency which advanced British policy objectives. They maintained British strategic dominance but at the same time, a strong sense of personal commitment prompted them to apply constant pressure against the slave trade. Preston and Major have argued that the nineteenth century was an era of gunboat diplomacy with the Royal Navy serving as the main instrument of national policy. Their definition of gunboat diplomacy is 'the use of warships in peacetime to further a nation's diplomatic and political aims'.[1] Clearly the anti-slave trade campaign on the East Coast of Africa stands as a classic example of this use of naval power and is thus an important episode in nineteenth-century naval history. In the end, the navy proved an efficient, if strong-willed, instrument of policy which did, indeed, advance British national policy. Strategic dominance was maintained, trade initiatives were stimulated, and, in the end, the slave trade was ended. It was a significant contribution and when assessing the development of European involvement in East Africa, the list of men like Kirk, Frere, Mackinnon, and Euan-Smith is not complete unless it also encompasses men like Heath, Sulivan, and Fremantle, as well.

Note

1. Preston and Major, p. 3.

Bibliography

Books

Admiralty, by authority, *The Navy List* (London, published annually, 1860–1890 examined).
Ali Hinawy, Mbarak, *Al-Akida and Fort Jesus Mombasa* (London, 1950).
Alpers, Edward, *The East African Slave Trade* (Historical Association of Tanzania, 1967).
—— *Ivory and Slaves in East Central Africa* (London, 1975).
Anderson-Moreshead, A. E. M., *The History of the Universities' Mission to Central Africa* (London, 1897).
Anstey, Roger, *The Atlantic Slave Trade and British Abolition 1760–1810* (London, 1975).
Archibald, E. H. H., *The Fighting Ship in the Royal Navy* (London, 1984).
Asiegbu, U. J., *Slavery and the Politics of Liberation* (London, 1969).
Assad, Thomas, *Three Victorian Travellers, Burton, Blunt, Doughty* (London, 1964).
Axelson, Eric, *Portugal and the Scramble for Africa 1875–1891* (Johannesburg, 1967).

Baker, S. W., *The Albert Nyanza*, 2 vols. (London, 1867).
—— *Ismailia: a narrative of the expedition to Central Africa for the Suppression of the slave trade* (London, 1874).
Banaji, D. R., *Slavery in British India* (Bombay, 1933).
Barnard, Frederick, *A Three Year Cruise in the Mozambique Channel* (London, 1848, reprinted with introduction by D. H. Simpson, 1969).
Barnwell, P. J. and Toussaint, A., *A Short History of Mauritius* (London, 1949).
Bartlett, C. J., *Great Britain and Sea Power 1815–1853* (Oxford, 1963).
Baynham, Henry, *Before the Mast* (London, 1971).
—— *From the Lower Deck* (London, 1969).
Beachey, R. W., *The Slave Trade of Eastern Africa* (London, 1976).
—— *A Collection of Documents on the Slave Trade of Eastern Africa* (London, 1976).
Belgrave, Sir Charles, *The Pirate Coast* (London, 1966).
Bennett, Norman, *Studies in East African History* (Boston, Mass., 1969).
—— *Captain Storm in Tanganyika 1882–1885* (Dar-es-Salaam, 1960).
—— *Stanley's Despatches to the New York Herald* (Boston, Mass., 1970).
—— *A History of the Arab State of Zanzibar* (New York, 1978).
Bharati, Agehananda, *The Asians in East Africa* (Chicago, 1972).
Blaikie, William, *The Personal Life of David Livingstone* (London, 1880).
Blake, Robert, *Disraeli* (London, 1966).
Blake, W. H., *The Adventures of a Naval Chief Gunner* (Brisbane, 1905).
Boteler, Thomas, *Narrative of a Voyage of Discovery to Africa and Arabia Performed in His Majesty's Ships Leven and Barracouta* (London, 1835).

Bibliography

Bouniol, J., (ed.), *The White Fathers and their Missions* (London, 1929).
Bradley, John, *History of the Seychelles* (London, 1940).
Brady, Cyrus, *Commerce and Conquest in East Africa* (Salem, Mass., 1950).
Briggs, Sir John, *Naval Administration 1827–1892* (London, 1897).
Brodie, Fawn, *The Devil Drives* (London, 1967)
Brooks, George, *The Kru Mariner in the Nineteenth Century* (Newark, Delaware, 1972).
Brown, Robert, *The Story of Africa and its Explorers*, 4 vols., (London, 1892–1895).
Burrows, E. H., *Captain Owen of the African Survey 1774–1857* (Rotterdam, 1979).
Burton, Isabell, *The Life of Captain Sir Richard F. Burton*, 2 vols., (London, 1893).
Burton, Sir Richard, *Lake Regions of Africa* (London, 1860).
—— *Zanzibar: city, island and coast*, 2 vols., (London, 1872).
Buxton, T. Fowell, *The African Slave Trade and Its Remedy* (London, 1840, reprinted in 1967).

Cairns, H. A. C., *Prelude to Imperialism* (London, 1965).
Callender, Geoffrey, *The Naval Side of British History* (London, 1924).
Cameron, Verney L., *Across Africa* (London, 1877).
—— *In Savage Africa* (London, n.d.).
—— *Harry Raymond* (London, n.d.).
Capel, W. Forbes, *Central African Mission Report* (London, 1871).
Cecil, Lady Gwendolen, *Life of Robert Marquis of Salisbury*, 4 vols., (London, 1921–32).
Chaille-Long, Colonel C., *Central Africa: Naked Truths of Naked People* (London, 1876, reprinted in 1968).
Chaudhuri, K. N., *Trade and Civilisation in the Indian Ocean: An Economic History from the Rise of Islam to 1750* (Cambridge, 1985).
Chittick, Neville, *Kilwa: an Islamic Trading City on the East African Coast* (Nairobi, 1974).
Christlieb, Th. (tr. by W. Hastie), *Protestant Missions to the Heathen* (Edinburgh, 1882).
Clarence-Smith, Gervase, *The Third Portuguese Empire 1825–1975* (Manchester, 1985).
Clarke, P. H. C., *A Short History of Tanganyika* (London, 1935).
Collister, Peter, *Last Days of Slavery* (Dar-es-Salaam, 1961).
Colomb, Philip, *Slave Catching in the Indian Ocean* (London, 1873, reprinted in 1968).
—— *Naval Warfare* (London, 1891).
—— *Essays on Naval Defence* (London, 1896).
—— *Memoirs of Sir Astley Cooper Key* (London, 1898).
Cooper, Frederick, *Plantation Slavery on the East Coast of Africa* (Yale, 1977).
—— *From Slaves to Squatters: Plantation Labor and Agriculture in Zanzibar and Coastal Kenya, 1890–1925* (Yale, 1980).
Cooper, Joseph, *The Lost Continent, or Slavery and the Slave Trade in Africa* (London, 1875, reprinted in 1968).
Cotterill, H. B., *African Slave Traffic* (Edinburgh, 1875).
Coupland, Sir Reginald, *East Africa & Its Invaders* (Oxford, 1938).

224

—— *The Exploitation of East Africa 1856–1890* (London, 1939).
—— *Wilberforce* (Oxford, 1923).
—— *Kirk on the Zambezi* (London, 1928).
—— *The British Anti-Slavery Movement* (London, 1933).
—— *Livingstone's Last Journey* (London, 1945).
Crofton, Richard, *The Old Consulate at Zanzibar* (Oxford, 1935).
Creswell, Sir William, *Close to the Wind* (London, 1965).
Curtin, Philip, *The Atlantic Slave Trade: A Census* (Madison, Wisc., 1969).
—— *The Image of Africa* (Madison, 1964).

Davidson, B., *The African Slave Trade: Pre Colonial History 1450–1850* (Boston, 1961).
Davis, David, *The Problem of Slavery in Western Culture* (Ithaca, N.Y., 1969).
de Blij, Harm J., *Mombasa* (Northwestern University, 1968).
—— *Dar es Salaam* (Northwestern University, 1963).
Deane, H. Bargrave, *The Law of Blockade* (London, 1870).
de Kiewet Hemphill, M., see Oliver and Mathew.
Delf, George, *Asians in East Africa* (Oxford, 1963).
Devereux, W. C., *A Cruise in the Gorgon* (London, 1869, reprinted with introduction by D. H. Simpson, 1968).
Dow, George, *Slave Ships and Slaving* (Port Washington, N.Y., 1927, reprinted in 1969).
Dowdeswell, George, *The Merchant Shipping Acts (with an Explanation of the Law Relating to it)* (London, 1856).
Duffy, J. E., *Portuguese Africa* (Cambridge, Mass., 1959).

Eliot, Sir Charles, *The East African Protectorate* (London, 1905).
Elton, J. F., *Travels and Researches among the Lakes and Mountains of Eastern and Central Africa* (London, 1879).

Farrant, Leda, *Tippu Tip and the East African Slave Trade* (London, 1975).
Farwell, Byron, *The Man Who Presumed: A Biography of Henry M. Stanley* (New York, 1957).
Fisher, Allan and Herbert, *Slavery in Muslim Society* (London, 1970).
Fitzgerald, William, *Travels in the Coastlands of British East Africa and the Islands of Zanzibar and Pemba* (London, 1898).
Flint, John (ed.), *The Cambridge History of Africa, vol. 5: c1790–1870* Cambridge, 1976).
Fitzmaurice, Lord Edmund, *The Life of Lord Granville*, 2 vols., (London, 1905).
Foran, W. Robert, *African Odyssey — The Life of Verney Lovett Cameron* (London, 1937).
Forbes, Lieutenant, R.N., *African Blockade* (London, 1849, reprinted in '1969).
Ford, V. C. R., *The Trade of Lake Victoria* (Kampala, 1955).
Foskett, Reginald (ed.), *The Zambesi Journal of Dr. John Kirk 1858–63* 2 vols. (London, 1965).
Fraser, H. A., Tozer, Bishop W. G., and Christie, James, *The East African Slave Trade and the Measures Proposed for its Extinction as Viewed by Residents in Zanzibar* (London, 1871).

Freeman-Grenville, G. S. P., *The French at Kilwa Island* (Oxford, 1965).
—— *The East African Coast, Select Documents from the first to the earlier nine-teenth century* (Oxford, 1962).
—— See also Oliver and Mathew.
French-Sheldon, M., *Sultan to Sultan, Adventures among the Masai and Other Tribes of East Africa* (London, 1892).
Fremantle, Sir Edmund, *The Navy as I Have Known It* (London, 1904).
Frere, Sir Bartle, *Eastern Africa as a Field for Missionary Labour* (London, 1874).

Galbraith, John, *Mackinnon and East Africa 1878–1895* (London, 1972).
Gann, Lewis, *The End of the Slave Trade in British Central Africa* reprinted from *Rhodes-Livingstone Institute Journal* and bound as booklet (London, 1954.
Gann, L. and Duignan, P., *The Rulers of German Africa 1884–1914* (Stanford, 1977).
Gardener, Leslie, *The British Admiralty* (London, 1968).
Gifford, P. and Louis, W. R. (eds.), *Britain and Germany in Africa* (Yale, 1967).
Goldthorpe, J. E., *Outlines of East African Society* (Kampala, 1958).
Goodall, Norman, *History of the London Missionary Society 1895–1945* (Oxford, 1954).
Graham, Gerald S., *Great Britain in the Indian Ocean* (Oxford, 1967).
—— *The Politics of Naval Supremacy* (Cambridge, 1965).
—— *The Navy and South America 1807–1823* (London, 1962).
—— *The China Station: War and Diplomacy 1830–1860* (Oxford, 1978).
Grant J. A., *A Walk Across Africa* (Edinburgh, 1864).
Gray, Sir John, *History of Zanzibar* (London, 1962).
—— *The British in Mombasa 1824–1826* (London, 1957).
Gray, Richard, *A History of the Southern Sudan 1839–1889* (Oxford, 1961).
Gregory, J. W., *The Foundation of British East Africa* (London, 1901).
Gregory, Robert, *India and East Africa* (Oxford, 1971).
Grenville, J. A. S., *Lord Salisbury and Foreign Policy* (London, 1964).

Hailey, Lord, *An African Survey* (London, 1938, revised 1956).
Hall, Basil, *The Lieutenant and Commander* (London, 1866).
Hall, Richard, *Stanley An Adventurer Explored* (London, 1974).
Hamilton, Genesta, *Princes of Zinj* (London, 1957).
Hardinge, Sir Arthur, *The Life of Henry Howard Molyneux Herbert, Fourth Earl of Carnarvon*, 3 vols., (London, 1925).
Heanley, R. M., *A Memoir of Edward Steere* (London, 1888).
Heath, Sir Leopold, *Letters from the Black Sea during the Crimean War* (London, 1897).
Hertslet, Sir Edward, *The Map of Africa by Treaty*, 2 vols. (London, 1894).
Hess, R. L., *Italian Colonialism in Somalia 1895–1941* (Chicago, 1966).
Hindlip, Lord, *British East Africa: past, present and future* (London, 1905).
Hine, J. E., *Days Gone By* (London, 1924).
Hollingsworth, L. W., *Zanzibar Under the Foreign Office 1890–1913* (London, 1953).
—— *A Short History of the East Coast of Africa* (London, 1929).

Holman, Thomas *Life in the Royal Navy* (London, 1892).

Hooker, James, see Rotberg (ed.).

Hourani, George, *Arab Seafaring in the Indian Ocean in Ancient and Early Medieval Times* (Princeton, 1951).

Hoyle, B. S., *The Seaports of East Africa* (Nairobi, 1967).

Hurwitz, Edith, *Politics and the Public Conscience* (London, 1973).

Hutchison, Edward, *The Slave Trade of East Africa* (London, 1874).

—— *The Fugitive Slave Circulars* (London, 1876).

—— *The Victoria Nyanza, A Field for Missionary Enterprise* (London, 1876).

—— *The Lost Continent* (London, 1879).

Iliffe, J., *A Modern History of Tanganyika* (Cambridge, 1979).

Ingham, Kenneth, *A History of East Africa* (London, 1962).

Ingrams, W. H., *Zanzibar, its History and its People* (London, 1939).

Jackson, Sir Frederick, *Early Days in East Africa* (London, 1930).

Jackson Haight, Mabel, *European Powers and South-East Africa* (London, 1942, reprinted 1967).

Jackson, Robert see Rotberg and Mazrui.

Jakobsson, Stiv, *Am I Not a Man and a Brother?* (Uppsala, 1972).

Johnston, Sir Harry, *The Kilimanjaro Expedition* (London, 1886).

—— *History of a Slave* (London, 1889).

—— *British Central Africa* (London, 1897).

—— *The Uganda Protectorate*, 2 vols., (London, 1902).

—— *The Nile Quest* (London, 1903).

—— *A History of the colonization of Africa by alien races* (Cambridge, 1899).

—— *The Opening Up of Africa* (London, 1911).

—— *The Story of My Life* (Indianapolis, 1923).

Jones, Ray, *The Nineteenth-Century Foreign Office* (London, 1971).

Jones, Roger, *The Rescue of Emin Pasha* (London, 1972).

Kelly, J. B., *Britain and the Persian Gulf* (Oxford, 1968).

Kemp, Peter, *The British Sailor* (London, 1970).

Kennedy, A. L., *Salisbury* (London, 1953).

Kennedy, Paul, *The Rise and Fall of British Naval Mastery* (London, 1976).

Kimambo, I. N. and Temu, A. J. (eds.), *A History of Tanzania* (Nairobi, 1959).

King-Hall, L. (ed.), *Sea Saga* (London, 1935).

Kingsnorth, G. W., *Africa South of the Sahara* (Cambridge, 1962).

Kirkman, James, *Fort Jesus: A Portuguese Fortress on the East African Coast* (Oxford, 1974).

—— *Men and Monuments on the East African Coast* (London, 1964).

Klingberg, Frank, *The Anti-Slavery Movement in England* (Yale, 1926).

Krapf, Johann, *Travels, Researches and Missionary Labours during an Eighteen Years Residence in Eastern Africa* (Boston, Mass., 1860).

Laffin, John, *Jack Tar* (London, 1969).

Langer, W. L., *The Diplomacy of Imperialism* (New York, 1951).

Lewis, I. M., *The Modern History of Somaliland* (London, 1965).

Lewis, Michael, *The Navy in Transition 1814–1864* (London, 1965).

—— *The History of the British Navy* (London, 1959).

Livingstone, David, *Narrative of an Expedition to the Zambezi and its Tributaries* (London, 1865).

—— *Last Journals* (London, 1874).

Lloyd, Christopher, *The Navy and the Slave Trade* (London, 1949, reprinted 1968).

—— *The British Seaman* (London, 1968).

Loftus, Ernest, *Elton and the East African Coast Slave Trade*. (Pamphlet being largely an abridgement of portions of Elton's journals.)

Lovett, Richard, *The History of the London Missionary Society*, 2 vols., (London, 1899).

Low, Charles, *History of the Indian Navy* (London, 1877).

Lowe, C. J., *Salisbury and the Mediterranean* (London, 1965).

Lugard, Sir Frederick, *The Rise of our East African Empire* (London, 1893).

—— *The Dual Mandate in British Tropical Africa* (London, 1922).

Lyne, Robert, *An Apostle of Empire, being the Life of Sir Lloyd William Mathews, K.C.M.G.* (London, 1936).

—— *Zanzibar in Contemporary Times* (London, 1905).

MacLeod, Lyons, *Travels in Eastern Africa*, 2 vols., (London, 1860).

Magnus, Philip, *Kitchener, Portrait of an Imperialist* (London, 1958).

—— *Gladstone, A Biography* (London, 1954).

Maitland, Alexander, *Speke* (London, 1971).

Mangat, J. S., *A History of the Asians in East Africa* (Oxford, 1969).

Maples, Ellen, *The Life of Bishop Maples* (London, 1897).

Marder, Arthur J., *British Naval Policy 1880–1905* (London, 1941).

Markham, C. R., *History of the Abyssinian Expedition* (London, 1869).

Marsh, John, and Stirling, W. H., *The Story of Commander Allen Gardner, R.N.* (London, 1878).

Marsh, Z. A., and Kingsnorth, G. W., *An Introduction to the History of East Africa* (Cambridge, 1965).

Marston, Thomas, *Britain's Imperial Role in the Red Sea Area 1800–1878* (Hamden, Conn., 1961).

Martin, Esmond, *The History of Malindi* (Nairobi, 1973).

Martineau, J., *Life of Sir Bartle Frere*, 2 vols. (London, 1895).

Mathieson, W. L., *Great Britain and the Slave Trade 1839–1865* (London, 1929).

—— *British Slave Emancipation* (London, 1932).

May, W. E., *The Boats of Men of War* (Maritime Monographs and Reports, 1974).

Mbotela, James, *The Freeing of the Slaves in East Africa* (London, 1956).

McDermott, P. L., *British East Africa or I.B.E.A.* (London, 1895).

Middleton, Dorothy, *Baker of the Nile* (London, 1949).

Miers, Suzanne, and Koptyoff, Igor, *Slavery in Africa* (Wisconsin, 1977).

Mill, Hugh, *The Record of the Royal Geographical Society 1830–1930* (London, 1930).

Miller, Charles, *The Lunatic Express* (New York, 1971).

Munro, J. F., *Africa and the International Economy, 1800–1960* (London, 1976).

Moore, Sir Alan, *Sailing Ships of War, 1800–1860* (London, 1926).

Moorehead, Alan, *The White Nile* (London, 1960).
Moyse-Bartlett, *The Pirates of Trucial Oman* (London, 1966).
Mutibwa, P. M., *The Malagasy and the Europeans* (London, 1974).

Nabhany, Ahmed, *Sambo Ya Kiwandeo (The Ship of Lamu Island)* (Leiden, 1979).
New, Charles, *Life, Wanderings and Labours in Eastern Africa* (London, 1873).
Newitt, M. D. D., *Portuguese Settlement on the Zambezi* (London, 1973).
Newman, Henry, *Banani, the transition from slavery to freedom in Zanzibar and Pemba* (London, 1898).
Nicholls, C. S., *The Swahili Coast* (London, 1971).
Nwulia, Moses, *Britain and Slavery in East Africa* (Washington, D.C., 1975).

O'Connor, A. M., *An Economic Geography of East Africa* (London, 1971).
O'Neill, Henry, *The Mozambique and Nyassa Slave Trade* (London, 1885).
Oliver, Roland, *The Missionary Factor in East Africa* (London, 1952, reprinted in 1970).
—— *Sir Harry Johnston and the Scramble for Africa* (London, 1957).
Oliver, Roland and Mathew, Gervase (eds.), *History of East Africa* (Oxford, 1963).
Oliver, Roland and Sanderson, G. N., *The Cambridge History of Africa, vol. 6: c1870–1905* (Cambridge, 1985).
Ommanney, F. D., *Isle of Cloves* (London, 1955).
Owen, William F., *Narrative of Voyages to Explore the Shores of Africa, Arabia and Madagascar*, 2 vols., (London, 1833, reprinted in 1968).

Padfield, Peter, *Rule Britannia: The Victorian and Edwardian Navy* (London, 1985).
Parry, Ann (ed.), *The Admirals Fremantle* (London, 1971).
Pearce, F. B., *Zanzibar* (London, 1920).
Perham, Margery, *Lugard: the years of adventure*, 2 vols., (London, 1956 and 1960).
—— *The Diaries of Lord Lugard* (London, 1959).
Perham, M., and Simmons, J., *African Discovery* (London, 1957).
Pim, Sir Alan, *The Financial and Economic History of the African Tropical Territories* (Oxford, 1940).
Portal, Gerald, *The British Mission to Uganda in 1893* (London, 1894).
Preston, A. and Major, J., *Send a Gunboat! A Study of the Gunboat and its role in British policy, 1854–1904* (London, 1967).
Prins, A. H. J., *The Swahili-Speaking Peoples of Zanzibar and the East African Coast* (London, 1961).

Ramm, Agatha, *The Political Correspondence of Mr. Gladstone and Lord Granville 1876–1886* (Oxford, 1962).
Ranger, T. O., *Emerging Themes of African History* (London, 1968).
Ransford, Oliver, *The Slave Trade* (London, 1971).
Reynolds, Clark, *Command of the Sea* (New York, 1974).
Richards, Charles and Place, James (eds.), *East African Explorers* (London, 1967).
Rodger, N. A. M., *The Admiralty* (Lavenham, 1979).

Robinson, R. and Gallagher, J. with Denny, A., *Africa and the Victorians* (London, 1961).

Rotberg, Robert, *Joseph Thomson and the Exploration of East Africa* (London, 1971).

———— (ed.), *Africa and Its Explorers, Motives, Methods and Impact* (Oxford, 1970).

Rotberg, Robert and Mazrui, Ali (eds.), *Protest and Power in Black Africa* (Oxford, 1970).

Ruete, Emily, *Memoirs of an Arabian Princess* (New York, 1888).

Russell, C. E., *General Rigby, Zanzibar and the Slave Trade* (London, 1935).

Said-Ruete, Rudolph, *Said bin Sultan* (London, 1929).

Sainty, J. C., *Admiralty Officials 1660 – 1870* (London, 1975).

Salim, A. I., *The Swahili Speaking Peoples of Kenya's Coast 1895 – 1965* (Nairobi, 1973).

Sanderson, G. N., *England, Europe and the Upper Nile* (Edinburgh, 1965).

Schurman, Donald M., *The Education of a Navy* (London, 1965).

Shore, Hon. Henry, *The Flight of the Lapwing* (London, 1881).

Smith, C. S., see Anderson-Moreshead.

Speke, J. H., *What Led to the Discovery of the Source of the Nile* (Edinburgh, 1864).

———— *Journal of the Discovery of the Source of the Nile* (London, 1863).

Stanley, Sir Henry, *How I Found Livingstone in Central Africa* (London, 1872).

———— *In Darkest Africa*, 2 vols., (London, 1890).

———— *My Dark Companions and Their Strange Stories* (London, 1893).

———— *Through the Dark Continent*, 2 vols., (London, 1899).

———— *The Autobiography of Sir Henry Morton Stanley* (London, 1909).

Steere, Edward, *Central African Mission — Its Present State and Prospects* (London, 1873).

———— *Swahili Tales* (London, 1870).

———— *The Universities' Mission to Central Africa* (London, 1875).

Stevenson, James, *The Arabs in Central Africa and at Lake Nyassa* (Glasgow, 1888).

Stigand, C. H., *The Land of Zinj* . . . *an account of British East Africa* (London, 1913, reprinted 1966).

Stock, Eugene, *The History of the Church Missionary Society*, 3 vols., (London, 1899).

Sulivan, George, *Dhow Chasing in Zanzibar Waters* (London, 1873, reprinted with introduction by D. H. Simpson, 1967, and in 1968).

Swann, Alfred, *Fighting the Slave Hunters in Central Africa* (London, 1910, reprinted with introduction by Norman Bennett, 1969).

Taylor, A. J. P., *Germany's First Bid for Colonies 1884 – 1885* (London, 1938).

Temperley, Howard, *British Anti-Slavery 1833 – 1870* (London, 1972).

Temu, A. J., *British Protestant Missions* (London, 1972).

Thomson, Joseph, *To the Central African Lakes and Back*, 2 vols., (London, 1881).

—— *Through Masai Land* (London, 1885).

Toussaint, Auguste (tr. by June Guicharnaud), *History of the Indian Ocean* (London, 1961).

Townsend, Mary, *The Rise and Fall of Germany's Colonial Empire 1884–1918* (New York, 1930).

Trimingham, J. Spencer, *Islam in East Africa* (Oxford, 1964).

Trevelyan, G. M., *British History in the Nineteenth Century* (London, 1928).

Tucker, Alfred, *Eighteen Years in Uganda and East Africa* (London, 1908).

Uzoigwe, G. N., *Britain and the Conquest of Africa — the Age of Salisbury* (Ann Arbor, Mich., 1974).

Vesey Hamilton, Admiral Sir, *Naval Administration* (London, 1896).

Waller, Horace, *On Some African Entanglements* (London, 1891).

—— *Heligoland for Zanzibar, or One Island Full of Free Men for Two Full of Slaves* (London, 1893).

—— *Ivory, Apes and Peacocks* (London, 1891).

—— *Slaving and Slavery in our British Protectorates* (London, 1894).

Walvin, James, (ed.), *Slavery and British Society 1776–1846* (London, 1982).

Ward, W. E. F., *The Royal Navy and the Slavers* (New York, 1969).

Ward, W. E. F. and White, L. W., *East Africa, a century of change* (London, 1971).

White, Colin, *Victoria's Navy: The End of the Sailing Navy* (Havant, Hampshire, 1981).

Williams, Eric, *Capitalism and Slavery* (London, 1944).

Wilson, C. H., *History of the Universities' Mission to Central Africa* (London, 1936).

Wilson, J. Leighton, *The British Squadron on the Coast of Africa* (London, 1851).

Wissmann, Hermann, *My Second Journey Through Equatorial Africa from the Congo to the Zambezi* (London, 1891).

Worsfold, W. B., *Sir Bartle Frere*, (London, 1923).

Yexley, Lionel, pseudonym for Woods, James, *The Inner Life of the Navy* (London, 1908).

Ylvisaker, Marguerite, *Lamu in the Nineteenth Century* (Boston, Mass., 1979).

Younghusband, Ethel, *Glimpses of East Africa and Zanzibar* (London, 1910).

Articles

Anstey, Roger, T., 'Capitalism and Slavery: a Critique', *Economic History Review*, series 2, 21, 1968.

Ballard, G. A., 'British Sloops of 1875', *Mariner's Mirror*, 24, 1938.

Beachey, R. W., 'The Arms Trade in East Africa in the Late Nineteenth Century', *Journal of African History*, XI, 3, 1970. 'The East African

Ivory Trade in the Nineteenth Century', *Journal of African History*, VIII, 2, 1967.

Becker. A. (tr. by Davies, I.), 'The Capture and Death of the Rebel Leader Bushiri', *Tanganyika Notes and Records*, 60, March 1963.

Berg, F. J., 'The Swahili Community of Mombasa 1500–1900', *Journal of African History*, IX, I, 1968.

Brassey, Thomas, 'The Administration of the Navy 1880–1885', *Nineteenth Century*, October 1885.

Bridges, R. C., 'The R.G.S. and the African Exploration Fund, 1876–80', *The Geographical Journal*, 129, 1963.

Cameron, Verney, 'Slavery in Africa — The Disease and the Remedy', *National Review*, October 1888.

Colomb, Philip, 'Naval and Military Signals', *Journal of the Royal United Services Institute*, VII, 1864.

Etherington, Norman, 'Frederic Elton and the South African Factor in the Making of Britain's East African Empire', *The Journal of Imperial and Commonwealth History*, IX, 1981, No. 3.

Fremantle, Sir Edmund, 'Ironclads and Torpedo Flotillas', *Nineteenth Century*, October 1885.

Gann, Lewis, 'The End of the Slave Trade in British Central Africa', *Rhodes-Livingstone Institute Journal*, XXXV, March 1959. (See also under Books.)

Gavin, R. J., 'The Bartle Frere Mission to Zanzibar', *The Historical Journal*, V, 2, 1962.

Gillard, D. R., 'Salisbury's African Policy and the Heligoland Offer of 1890', *English Historical Review*, LXXV, 1960.

—— 'Salisbury's Heligoland Offer: The Case Against the Witu Thesis', *English Historical Review*, LXXX, 1965.

Gleig, G. R., 'The Church in the Army and the Navy', *Blackwood's Magazine*, March 1868.

Gray, Sir John, 'The British Vice-Consulate at Kilwa Kivinji, 1884–1885', *Tanganyika Notes and Records*, 51, 1958.

Harries, Lyndon, 'The Arabs and Swahili Culture', *Africa* (Journal of the International African Institute), XXXIV, 1964.

Hayman, Philip, 'My First Slaver — A Tale of the Zanzibar Coast', *United Services Magazine*, 1880.

Holmes, C. F., 'Zanzibar Influence at the Southern End of Lake Victoria: The Lake Route', *African Historical Studies*, IV, 3, 1971.

Lambourn, R., 'Zanzibar to Masasi in 1876, the Founding of Masasi Mission', *Tanganyika Notes and Records*, 31, 1951.

Louis, William, 'Sir Percy Anderson's Grand African Strategy,1883–1896', *English Historical Review*, LXXXI, 1966.

LeCordeur, B. A., 'Natal, the Cape and the Indian Ocean, 1846–1880', *Journal of African History*, VII, 2, 1966.

Martin, B. G., 'Notes on Some Members of the Learned Classes of Zanzibar and East Africa in the Nineteenth Century', *African Historical Studies*, IV, 3, 1971.

Murray, Sir O., 'The Admiralty', *Mariner's Mirror*, 23, 1937.

Oliver, Roland, 'Some Factors in the British Occupation of East Africa, 1884–1894', *Uganda Journal*, 15, 2, September 1951.

Parry, Charles, 'The General Post Office's Zanzibar Shipping Contracts, 1860–1914', *The Mariner's Mirror*, 68, 1982.

Preston, Anthony, 'The End of the Victorian Navy', *Mariner's Mirror*, 60, 1974.

Rodger, N. A. M., 'The Dark Ages of the Admiralty', *Mariner's Mirror*, 62, 1976.

Sanderson, G. N., 'The Anglo-German Agreement of 1890 and the Upper Nile', *English Historical Review*, LXXVIII, 1963.

—— 'The European Partition of Africa: Coincidence or Conjuncture', *Journal of Imperial and Commonwealth History*, III, 1974.

Symes, Lieutenant, 'A Cruise in the *Frolic*', *United Services Magazine*, 1877.

Turton, E. R., 'Kirk and the Egyptian Invasion of East Africa in 1875', *Journal of African History*, XI, 3, 1970.

Unpublished theses

Ekemode, G. O., *German Rule in North-East Tanzania, 1885–1914*, Ph.D., London, 1973.

Gavin, R. J., *Palmerston's Policy Towards East and West Africa, 1830–1865*, Ph.D., Cambridge, 1959.

Glyn-Jones, Eleanor, *Britain and the End of Slavery in East Africa*, B.Litt., Oxford, 1956.

Miers, Suzanne, *Great Britain and the Brussels Anti-Slave Trade Act of 1890*, Ph.D., London, 1969.

Sheriff, Abdul, *The Rise of a Commercial Empire: An Aspect of the Economic History of Zanzibar, 1770–1873*, Ph.D., London, 1971.

Spray, W. A., *Surveying and Charting the Indian Ocean: the British Contribution, 1750–1838*, Ph.D., London, 1966.

Government correspondence held in the Public Record Office

Foreign Office files

FO/84, Slave Trade. Entire series from 958 (1855) to 2276 (1892) examined, 125 volumes cited.

FO/83, General Correspondence: Great Britain and General. Consular Services: 180 and 388, Law Officers Reports; 2203, 2312, and 2356–62.

FO/54, Muscat. Volumes 5–24a. After 1867, this series incorporated into FO/84.

FO/317, Archives of Commissioners, Miscellaneous. Volume 3, minutes of the 1881 commission to revise the slave trade instructions.

FO/541, Confidential print, slave trade. Volumes 1–15, 19–41, 40–50.

Admiralty files

ADM/127, Station Records: East Indies: Correspondence. General 1–6; India, Ceylon and Burma, 12, 14–15; Persian Gulf, 25–7; Aden and the Red Sea 8, 11, 31–4, Islands in the Indian Ocean and the East Coast of Africa, 10, 35–45.

ADM/123, Station Records: Africa. Correspondence. General service, 1–11, Cape of Good Hope, 15–34; Naval Establishments, 47–50; Slave Trade, 170–85.

ADM/1, Admiralty and Secretariat, Papers. Series from 2269 to 6775 examined selectively.

ADM/8 List Books. Cape of Good Hope and East Indies Station, 125–69 (1845–1890).

ADM/50, Admiral's Journals. Sir F. W. Grey, 283; Sir H. Keppel, 284; James Hope, 285; Sir Baldwin Walker, 289; G. King, 290; Sir Leopold Heath, 293, Sir W. Hewett and Sir F. Richards, 297; W. Gore-Jones, 298; Sir F. Richards, 371; and Sir Edmund Fremantle, 372.

ADM/52, Master's Logs. Volume 3940 (Lieutenant Emery's journal).

ADM/53, Ship's Logs. *Agamemnon* (1887–90) 12325–7; *Algerine* (1868–71) 9862–4; *Ariel* (1856–59) 6286–89, (1860–63) 8063–67, (1864) 8079–80; *Boadicea* (1888–92) 12777–80; *Briton* (1871–76) 10497–500; *Daphne* (1871–74) 10372–74, (1875–78) 10902–905; *Dryad* (1867–71) 9912–15, (1871) 9946–7, (1874) 10803; *Forte* (1868–72) 9931–33; *Gorgon* (1859–63) 7795–7803; *Harrier* (1882–1885) 12, 136–38; *Lyra* (1857–62) 7039–46; *Nymphe* (1867–69) 9547–48, (1869–71) 9732–33; *Pantaloon* (1864–67) 8770–72; *Penguin* (1861–64) 1977–82, (1886–91) 14, 946–50; *Reindeer* (1884–91) 15349–54; *Rifleman* (1873–76) 10, 556–58; *Seagull* (1879–83) 11, 791–94; *Sidon* (1859–62) 7148–52; *Star* (1866–70) 9604–07; *Thetis* (1873–77) 10, 729–32; *Undine* (1882) 12, 129, (1883) 11, 861, (1883) 12, 008, (1884) 12, 167, (1884) 12, 168; *Wasp* (1860–61) 7025–27, (1863–68) 9049–52; *Wolverine* (1870–74) 10, 224–12, 327.

ADM/116, Admiralty and Secretariat, Cases. Volume 2474, Red Sea slave traffic, 1925–1929.

ADM/196, Records of Officers Services, Naval Cadets to Admirals. Volumes 13–20 (entry dates 1803–1881).

Other government files in Public Record Office

High Court of Admiralty

HCA 35, Slave Trade. Volumes 76–89.

HCA 36, Slave Trade, Additional Papers. Volumes 2–8.

HCA 37, Slave Trade, Treasury Papers. Volumes 25–101.

Treasury documents

T5, Outletters, Admiralty. Volumes 2–20.

T12, Outletters, Foreign Office. Volumes 2–19.

Colonial Office

CO 172, Mauritius, Reports of Protectors of Slaves (1833–1835). Volumes 32–36.
CO 167, Mauritius, Original Correspondence. Volumes 521–522.
CO 168, Mauritius, Offices and Individuals. Volumes 55–56.

Government correspondence held in the India Office Library

Reports from the Persian Gulf

Bushire, Slave Trade, R/15/1/168, 171, 177.
Muscat, R/15/3/A/4–7.

Political and secret department files

L/P&S/. Persian Gulf, 1869–74, 17–25; Aden, 1842–58, 26–36; Aden and Zanzibar, 1859–1860, 37; Zanzibar, 1861, 38; Aden, 1861–62, 39; Aden, Muscat, and Zanzibar, 1863–65, 40–42; Zanzibar, 1867–69, 47; (vols. 2–4) Zanzibar, 1875–83, 1.

Parliamentary Papers

Parliamentary Debates, 3rd Series

1860 (159) 202, 908, (160) 588.
1862 (166) 1360, 1744 (165) 1746.
1863 (170) 859.
1864 (175) 981, (176) 1613.
1865 (177) 846, (179) 431, 877, 1025.
1867–68 (190) 1687, (191) 1578, (192) 1130.
1870 (199) 119, (203) 1770.
1871 (207) 952, 1631.
1872 (210) 970, (212) 1608.
1874 (218) 929.
1876 (227) 230, 266, 398, 685, 820, 903, (228) 72, 1216, (229) 1117, 1976, (230) 6, 128, 236, 249, 734, 848, 869, 943, 1235, 1815, 1962.
1877 (232) 172, (233) 1670, (235) 88, 199, 1578.
1878 (237) 623.
1879 (243) 951, (248) 273, (249) 979.
1882 (268) 1711.
1883 (276) 838, (278) 1416.
1886 (302) 1766.
1887 (313) 497.

1888 (328) 569, (330) 1234, 1385, 1505, (331) 502, 1016, 1611, 1760, 1764.
1889 (333) 717, 1806, (334) 886, (336) 228, 1258 (338) 265, (339) 328, 550.
1890 (347) 716, 1545.
1891 (349) 128, 651.

Parliamentary Debates, 4th Series

1892 (1) 1225, (3) 586.

Other Parliamentary Papers

1859 XXVII, Accounts and Papers (13), XVI, Accounts and Papers (3).
1860 LXX, Accounts and Papers (32).
1861 XXXIX, Accounts and Papers (1), LXIV, Accounts and Papers (31).
1862 1, Bills Public (1), XXXV, Accounts and Papers (7), LXI, Accounts and Papers (33).
1863 XXXVII, Accounts and Papers (9), XXXIX, Accounts and Papers (11), LXX, Accounts and Papers (42), LXXI, Accounts and Papers (43).
1864 XXXVII, Accounts and Papers (6), XXXIX, Accounts and Papers (8), LXVI, Accounts and Papers (15), LXI (I), Accounts and Papers, 30 (I).
1865 XXXVI, Accounts and Papers (7), LVI, Accounts and Papers (27).
1866 XLVIII, Accounts and Papers (10), LXXV, Accounts and Papers (37).
1867 XLVII, Accounts and Papers (29), LXXIII, Accounts and Papers (35).
1867–68 XLVII, Accounts and Papers (8), LXIV, Accounts and Papers (25).
1868–69 V, Bills Public (5), LVI, Accounts and Papers (23).
1870 LXI, Accounts and Papers (21).
1871 XII, Reports from Committees (6), LXII, Accounts and Papers (26).
1872 LIV, Accounts and Papers (19), LXX, Accounts and Papers (35).
1873 V, Bills Public (5), LXI, Accounts and Papers (23), IX, Reports from Committees (3).
1874 LXII, Accounts and Papers (28).
1875 LXXI, Accounts and Papers (30.)
1876 VII, Bills Public (7), XXVIII, Reports from Commissions (14), LXX, Accounts and Papers (29), LXXXIV, Accounts and Papers (43).
1877 LXXVIII, Accounts and Papers (30).
1878 LXVII, Accounts and Papers (2).
1878–1879, VI, Bills Public (6), LXVI, Accounts and Papers (25).
1880 LXIX, Accounts and Papers (30), LXXVIII, Accounts and Papers (39).

1881 LXXXV, Accounts and Papers (29).

1882, LXV, Accounts and Papers (29).

1883 LXVI, Accounts and Papers (29).

1884 LXXV, Accounts and Papers (29).

1885 LXXIII, Accounts and Papers (29).

1886 XLII, Accounts and Papers (5), LXII, Accounts and Papers (25).

1887 LXXVIII, Accounts and Papers (30).

1888 VII, Bills Public (7), LXXIV, Accounts and Papers (10), XCIII, Accounts and Papers (29).

1889 VII, Bills Public (7), LXXII, Accounts and Papers (26), LVI, Accounts and Papers (10).

1890–1891 VIII, Bills Public (8), L, Accounts and Papers (10), LVII, Accounts and Papers (17).

1892 LXXIV, Accounts and Papers (27), XCV, Accounts and Papers (48).

1893–1894 LXXXV, Accounts and Papers (36).

1895 LXXI, Accounts and Papers (11).

Private papers held in public repositories

National Maritime Museum

These papers are those of naval officers who served on the East Coast of Africa at some stage of their careers.

Owen Papers, COO/3/C and COO/3A.

Doughty Papers, DTY/2.

Johnstone Papers, JOH/6.

Fraser Papers, FRR/3 and FRR/4.

Jerram Papers, JRM/4 and JRM/11.

Fremantle Papers, FRE/137, FRE/139 and FRE/142.

Public Record Office

Russell Papers, PRO 30/22. Correspondence, First Lord of the Admiralty, 24; Turkey, etc., 116.

Granville Papers, PRO 30/29. Correspondence, Cabinet, Admiralty, Foreign Office, etc., 54, 55, 137–40; Correspondence, Gladstone, 57–62, 123–9; Slave Trade, 258, 367–9; Africa (East), Zanzibar, 264.

Clarendon Papers, FO/361. Correspondence 1867–70, 1.

Tenterden Papers, FO/363. Correspondence, 1–5.

Carnarvon Papers, PRO 30/6. First Lord of the Admiralty 1874–78, 5; Mauritius, 1874–78, 37; Fugitive Slaves, etc., 1871, 71.

British Museum

Owen Papers, ADD 33837.

Gladstone Papers, ADD 44165–44180 (Granville), 44184–44186 (Halifax), 44271–44273 (Palmerston), 44609–44642 (Cabinet Papers), and various volumes with slave trade references: 44441, 44729, 44732, 44777 and 44793.
Ripon Papers, ADD 43617 (correspondence with Frere).

Papers held in various repositories at University of Oxford

Bodleian Library

Anti-Slavery Society Papers, Mss. Brit. Emp. S22.G.3–7.
Clarendon Papers, Ms. Clar. Dep. C. 510 (letters from Murchison).
Horace Waller Papers, Mss. Brit. Emp. S22.G.7–16 (correspondence concerning Universities Mission, etc.).
Monk Bretton Papers (Correspondence from Frere on East Africa).

Rhodes House Library

Clement Hill Papers Mss. Afr. s. 703 (1 volume on East Africa).
Portal Papers Mss. Afr. s. 103–14.

Christchurch Library

Salisbury Papers (Zanzibar correspondence plus files referred to from card index to individual correspondents including Frere, Kirk, Colomb, Mackinnon and Portal).

Other university holdings

School of Oriental and African Studies, London

Mackinnon Papers. Private Correspondence, Euan-Smith, 10–17; Sir H. H. Johnston, 77; Kirk, 86–103; Pelly, 175–81; Stanley, 217–21; Waller, 243–50; Wylde, 252.

Private collections

I was able to consult some useful works dealing with maritime law in the Supreme Court Library, Royal Courts of Justice, Admiralty section, at a time when the library was in the process of moving and organising its Admiralty section. When fully catalogued, it will be a useful source of Admiralty and Vice-Admiralty material.

Church Missionary Society Archives, 157 Waterloo Road, London, S.E.1.

East African Mission Correspondence, A5.
Correspondence with Consul at Zanzibar, G/Y/A5/1/22.

Private Papers Held by Heirs

Heath Family Records.
Sulivan Papers. These papers have been extremely useful in providing insight into George Sulivan's activities. In addition to the specifically East African material cited in this study, there is also important information concerning Sulivan's service on the West Coast of Africa. Excellent photographs are also included. The papers could easily provide the basis for a detailed study of Sulivan's career. The collection is held by Major D. L. S. Hodson, Good Easter, Essex.

Contemporary periodical literature

The Times. Issues from 1860–1890 surveyed.
The Church Missionary Society Intelligencer. Vol. XI, 1860 through vol. XV, 1890.
In addition, *Punch* and the *Illustrated London News* have been consulted at times when interest was concentrated on East African operations, i.e. 1872–1876, 1883–1885, 1888–1890.

Index

240